EVIL HARVEST

THE TRUE STORY OF CULT MURDER IN THE AMERICAN HEARTLAND

Rod Colvin

Addicus Books, Inc.
Omaha, Nebraska

An Addicus Nonfiction Book

ISBN# 1-886039-42-9

Cover design by Darcy Lijoodi
Cover photo © Pierre Arsenault / Masterfile

Library of Congress Cataloging-in-Publication Data

Colvin, Rod
    Evil Harvest : the true story of cult murder in the American heartland / Rod Colvin.
        p. cm.
     ISBN 1-886039-42-9 (alk. paper)
     1. Murder—Nebraska—Rulo—Case studies.
     2. Cults—Nebraska—Rulo-Case studies.
     3. Posse Comitatus (Group)
    I. Title.
HV6534.R85C65 1999   99-39530
364.15'23'09782282-dc21   CIP

Addicus Books, Inc.
P.O. Box 45327
Omaha, Nebraska 68145
Web site: http://www.AddicusBooks.com

*To the memory of
my brother, Randy*

AUTHOR'S NOTE

Years have passed since Rulo, Nebraska, made national news when members of a survivalist cult were arrested and were charged with murder. If the story shocked a national audience, it stunned the local folks. Brutal murder is not the kind of thing that is *supposed* to happen in small towns, where folks are friendly and everyone pretty much knows everyone else. But unfortunately we've learned in recent years that we live in a much different world. Tragedies can happen to any of us—whether we're from small towns or big cities. It happened in Rulo in 1985.

I first became interested in this story in 1986, when, as a reporter in Omaha, Nebraska, I covered portions of the seven-week trial for two of the defendants. As a journalist should, I listened to sometimes gruesome testimony with objectivity. However, after I began digging into the story behind the crime and interviewing former cult members and survivors of the deceased, I was struck by the shocking reality of what had transpired on the Rulo farm. To me, this was no longer just a news story with a list of names. It became a real story about real people.

In this book, I have attempted to tell that story—to

answer the question: how did these individuals get pulled into this cult? And, once they were there...what happened to make things go so terribly wrong? In order to recreate these events, I have conducted considerable research that has taken me across the states of Nebraska, Kansas, and Missouri. I have culled through more than two thousand pages of court transcripts, depositions, exhibits, personal letters, investigative reports, press accounts, video and audio tapes.

I interviewed several dozen individuals, including former members of the Rulo cult, friends and relatives of the cult members, area farmers, former members of the Posse Comitatus, cult experts, theologians, and law enforcement officers—local, state and federal. The identities of only a few peripheral characters have been altered. The names Janet Carter, Ted Stone, and Bob Kelley are fictitious, as are the names Elizabeth, Eric, Josh, Brian, and Heather.

I had only two interviews with Mike Ryan, the leader of the cult. After the first interview, Ryan wrote to me, saying he'd asked his god, Yahweh, about doing a second interview and that he'd been instructed by his god to say no. When I suggested that he ask again, he did, and I was granted a second interview. However, thereafter, Ryan's god instructed him not to speak with me. In a letter to me, Ryan said he felt that Yahweh would not like the outcome if he spoke with me again.

Finally, I would like to thank the many people who helped make this book possible. Many of you invited me into your homes and shared your personal stories. I wish to extend a special thanks to Terry Becker, former investigator for the Nebraska State Patrol; Rob Hendricks, former Brown County Sheriff, former FBI agent John Evans, and Cory McNabb, former Richardson County Sheriff. They provided much help as I shaped this story. I also wish to express my gratitude to family and friends whose support make this book possible. A special note to thanks to friends Susan, Rosalea, Betty, and Jack for their ongoing support and inspiration.

into your homes and shared your personal stories. I wish to extend a special thanks to Terry Becker, former investigator for the Nebraska State Patrol; Rob Hendricks, former Brown County Sheriff, former FBI agent, John Evans and Cory McNabb, former Richardson County Sheriff. They provided much help as I shaped this story. I also wish to express my gratitude to family and friends whose support make this book possible. A special note to thanks to friends Susan, Rosalea, Betty, and Jack for their ongoing support and inspiration.

The tissue of the Life to be
    We weave with colors all our own,

And in the field of Destiny
    We reap as we have sown

        —John Greenleaf Whittier

PROLOGUE

AUGUST 18, 1985

The soft pastel dawning of another seemingly peaceful summer day was at hand in rural Rulo, Nebraska. But outside Rulo—on a once productive farm which had for months been the centerpiece of unsettling and often menacing rumors—worst suspicions were about to be confirmed.

Promptly at six o'clock on that August morning, grim-faced men of the Federal Bureau of Investigation and the Nebraska State Patrol SWAT team, and lawmen from surrounding counties, began arriving at the eighty-acre farm. A trail of dust streamed behind the caravan of official vehicles rumbling down the gravel road to the farm. A hand-lettered sign—POSITIVELY NO TRESPASSING—VIOLATORS WILL BE PROSECUTED—was tacked to the padlocked gate. Officers cut the lock and moved with purpose onto the premises. Altogether, sixty law enforcement officers were involved in the action.

What had brought them to this once serene and unlikely destination in the timbered hills of southeast Nebraska was a tip from a reliable informant who claimed two bodies were buried in unmarked graves in one of the farm's pastures. And now, reports had surfaced of a torture-slaying.

Everyone in Rulo knew the farm was a paramilitary encampment and the home of a religious cult led by survivalist Mike Ryan; it was the talk of the town. Law enforcement officials had known it, too. A year earlier local officers had checked out the farm on complaints from neighboring farmers.

Often these neighbors had heard the sharp whine and crackle of gunfire from the woods; and young men attired in the greens and browns of camouflage clothing—guns slung over their shoulders—had been seen running across the fertile pastures, as if engaged in a sinister and deadly military game. This was not the stuff of rural Nebraska with its limitless blue horizons, endless acres of golden summer wheat, and friendly socials. Neighboring farmers had every right to feel alarm. It wasn't against the law to form a survivalist group, law enforcement officials had told them; neither was it against the law to own guns. But with the informant's tip, a concerted action had been initiated immediately.

Now investigators in navy blue jackets with F-B-I in tall yellow letters on their backs, along with officers from the state patrol and neighboring county sheriffs' departments, fanned out over the farm to make sure it was secure for investigation. Nebraska State Patrol Investigator Terry Becker stepped through the gate. As if in search of encouragement, he scanned the large open field that extended past the house and outbuildings. But Becker would soon learn what had transpired on the farm was to be, overall, a chilling memoir in madness.

Just beyond the rusty gate with its no-trespass warning, a yellow Jeep Wagoneer was parked on the gravel driveway. Written in the thick dust of the Jeep's rear window were the letters *YHVH*. In days to come, investigators would learn that the letters were the cult's name for God.

The living quarters were about a hundred yards beyond the entrance gate. The main house—or north house, as it came to be known—was once a mobile home. It spoke of a future gone awry and promises unfulfilled.

In what was an evident attempt to remodel the mobile home, a wooden frame had been built around it, set on cement blocks, and covered with black tar paper. Slats of lumber had been nailed across the tar paper to hold it in place. An east entrance to the house had been secured with a solid wooden door, painted white.

Thirty yards to the south was a second trailer—called south trailer—which was a shabby white with faded brown shutters at the windows. A wobbly wooden deck extended from the main entrance.

Between the trailers, two clotheslines were strung between rickety poles. The sagging lines held clothespins turned a splintered gray by the weather.

Adjacent to the south trailer, a small wire enclosure held a lonesome-looking, dirty white goat. The goat was the only sign that this might ever have been a farm. There were no chickens, no pigs, no other signs of life. The high-tech satellite dish that beamed cable television into the main house was an anomaly; it didn't fit the dilapidated surroundings.

Nearby, a meandering creek lined with trees divided the property. Then, another clump of trees, enticing and green in the early morning haze, interrupted the pasture before the land flowed upward to the property line. Not more than a quarter mile away was the mighty Missouri River with its verdant growth, fishing, and boating. Becker sighed and turned away. Today, he wearily reminded himself, held little promise.

Around ten thirty, Becker watched as a bulldozer was directed to the pasture where the grave sites had been pinpointed by former cult members. "We think the bodies are about five or six feet down," he heard one of the FBI men say. "Scrape off the topsoil. Then we'll go down about four feet with the backhoe."

The bulldozer moved in to clear a large area where the bodies were believed to be. That done, a backhoe arrived, its long mechanical arm scooping up bucket after bucket of reddish-brown loam, a mixture of clay, silt, and sand, then swiveling each time to allow the clods of dirt to roll out gently—like a child pouring sand from his hand.

Once the first four feet of clay had been removed, investigators began using metal probes. The probes were round steel rods, about four feet long, and were used to identify a difference in ground texture. Methodically the probes were moved by hand around the open trench, seeking the softness of the unmarked graves.

It was now late morning. Reporters from the cities of Lincoln and Omaha flocked to the southeastern corner of Nebraska, hoping to break the biggest crime story to hit the state for thirty years. Since 1957, in fact, when Charlie Starkweather gained notoriety as one of the nation's first high-profile mass murderers. Starkweather killed eleven Nebraskans in a forty-four-hour murder spree, terrorizing the state and stunning the nation. Today just might prove itself equally newsworthy.

Becker looked up at a helicopter hovering above the scene; a cameraman, from WOWT television news in Omaha, was shooting video from aloft as the grave diggers searched for the bodies.

Around noon, the diggers felt something give beneath their delicate probing. "I think we've got something here!" one of them shouted.

Other men joined in now, working like eager archaeologists, carefully shoveling dirt away by hand. Minutes later, a crude outline revealed itself.

"Yeah, it's a body!" a shoveler confirmed. "I can make out the head and feet."

The man need not have bothered with his announcement. The stench of decaying flesh rolled out, overwhelming the onlookers.

"Let's be careful," Becker cautioned. "Leave enough dirt around the body. We don't want to lose evidence." He mopped his brow with a white handkerchif from his hip pocket; the stench, combined with the midday heat, was catching up with everyone.

The body had been buried in a dark green sleeping bag and resembled nothing more than a large, dirt-encased cocoon. The diggers hoisted the body, sleeping bag and all, into a bright green body bag. The bag was zippered and carried to a waiting ambulance.

Another hour passed before a second body was unearthed

thirty feet from where the first one had been found. It, too, was zippered into a body bag and carried to the ambulance. The bodies were to be driven seventy miles north to Lincoln, Nebraska, where autopsies would be performed at Lincoln General Hospital.

Now, the investigators concentrated on the burial site. The location could not be seen from any land adjoining the farm. It was bottom land, hills to the south and trees to the north—the perfect cemetery. The rich soil that had once yielded row upon row of sweet corn was now overrun with weeds and wild clover. The clover's bulbous, purple blossoms were the only flowers ever to decorate the graves.

Becker swallowed hard and squinted into the sun as the ambulance thumped away over thick weeds. Today had held no promise, and sadly, his worst fears had been confirmed. He walked up to Cory McNabb, the county sheriff. "You know," he began tentatively, "a man can't help but wonder if this might never have happened if we had taken a closer look at this place a year ago."

How had Ryan convinced his followers to believe he was a divinely inspired prophet? How had his domination led these conservative folks from Middle America to unthinkable acts . . . in the name of God?

Becker just shook his head; words failed him. For now, all he could think about was how pathetic, even pitiful it was; and the irony, of course. He couldn't shake the irony of it all. Operating here in the midst of this splendid Nebraska farmland had been a force so evil it had brutally claimed two lives and tragically ruined the lives of several more.

Instinct told Becker no one could have prevented the events that had transpired at the command of Mike Ryan's twisted mind. Unraveling Ryan would be a terrible chore. But it appeared from what he had learned that the first seeds of destruction had been planted in northeastern Kansas, a few miles south of Rulo, perhaps two years earlier, in late 1982.

PART ONE

The Beginning

CHAPTER 1

The face of the town clock was weathered and faded. But from its position atop the spired tower on the corner of the town square, it still lent an air of respectability to the main street of Hiawatha, Kansas. It was 6:45 precisely; the clock kept perfect time.

An evening breeze stirred the tall pines on the lawn of the Brown County Courthouse across the street. Two traffic lights flashed routinely, though the downtown area was empty except for the parked cars of a few diners stopping in for the buffet at Danny's Restaurant, on the east end of the block. It was a typical, quiet, small-town Sunday night. But on this May evening in 1982, at a community hall a couple of blocks off the main drag, the scene was different.

"Look at that!" Mike Ryan exclaimed as he climbed out of the pickup truck and pointed to the cars parked on both sides of the brick-paved street. "They're backed up to the courthouse." His voice carried just a hint of drawl. Ryan crunched his 7UP can and tossed it on the floorboard.

Ryan, his brother-in-law Steve Patterson, and Steve's dad, Maynard, were fifteen minutes early—the lecture was set for seven o'clock. It appeared the Reverend James

Wickstrom, national head of the Posse Comitatus, would be drawing a full house tonight.

Impressed, the three men entered the hall and walked down the aisle between rows of tan metal folding chairs. They took seats on the right, halfway back from the podium.

As the minutes ticked away, more and more people filed into the auditorium, filling the seats. By seven o'clock, a number of people were standing up along the back wall.

Once settled, Ryan glanced around at the people who had gathered there. Nearly all were farmers with weathered faces and thick, callused hands. Tonight, most had traded their bib overalls and blue jeans for pastel Western shirts with mother-of-pearl buttons, string ties, double knit dress slacks with black belts and large buckles. Their worn, scuffed work shoes had been replaced by polished Western boots.

Ryan, a big, burly man, stood six feet, two inches tall; his two hundred twenty pounds gave him a bulging belt line. The dark mustache he wore blended into his closely trimmed beard, flecked with gray. In a couple of months, he would turn thirty-five. Tonight, Ryan wore a faded plaid shirt, blue jeans, and cowboy boots. He lifted the ball cap from his head and ran his thick fingers across the top of his crew cut; he settled the cap on his head again as he waited for the speaker to arrive. This is all right, he thought, feeling the excitement build in the hall.

Beside him, Steve Patterson felt the same excitement. Like Ryan, Steve was in his early thirties. At six feet, six inches and two hundred pounds, he could afford to be easygoing. Maynard Patterson, a reserved man, had been a farmer all his life.

For many of these farmers, their handshakes and smiles concealed a wrenching strain—the psychological chaos created by the possibility of losing their farms. This year's crop prices had not been enough to cover bank loans. Already they had seen land and machinery go on the auction block. In some cases, farms that had been handed down from generation to generation had been foreclosed on by banks. It was not a happy time for those who farmed and fed the nation. They were accustomed to the dignity of being able to work out their own problems. They had always believed that hard work would see them through. But now, that obviously was not true, and no one cared about them, they thought—least of all the bigwigs in Washington.

Promptly at seven o'clock the Reverend James Wickstrom, wearing a blue leisure suit, walked briskly to the front of the hall. Gripping the sides of the podium, he leaned into the microphone and announced in a calm voice, "All federal agents are asked to leave."

Three men in casual shirts and slacks, attire making them seem very out of place, stood up and walked from the hall.

Ryan snickered. This is going to be some meeting, he thought as he elbowed Steve.

Steve leaned over and whispered, "Those were FBI agents. They try to go undercover. They'll be outside now, taking down license plate numbers."

The Posse Comitatus was just one of several ultra-right-wing, paramilitary groups that the FBI had under investigation. Posse members had been known to flaunt weapons openly and spew rhetoric about a government conspiracy, masterminded by rich Jews, to destroy the American farmer. In short, the Posse, a largely rural movement in the plains states, was antitax, antigoverment, racist, and anti-Semitic.

In the late 1970s, law enforcement had begun watching these organizations in connection with replevin actions—bank repossessions of land and farm equipment. Activists had been known to show up at farm sales and auctions with nooses or guns, discouraging others from bidding. In western Kansas, a sheriff had turned in his badge over such threats. Law officials were concerned about the escalating potential for violence that seemed inherent in a religious crusade that preached hate and the stockpiling of weapons.

Likewise, the organizations Klanwatch and the Anti-Defamation League considered the Posse Comitatus violent and dangerous. Klanwatch, which monitored activities of the Ku Klux Klan and other white supremacy splinter groups, identified factions of the Posse in at least thirteen states. And, although the Posse boasted of a membership of two million nationwide, the Anti-Defamation League, a defense agency for Jewish citizens, considered this number a gross exaggeration, and estimated Posse membership at several thousand.

Steve had been attending Posse meetings and had been following Wickstrom for the past year, and Ryan had been listening to Steve talk on and on about the Posse. "Where in the hell are you getting all this crap?" he asked one day.

"Wickstrom," Steve said.

"Who the hell is Wickstrom?"

"The Reverend James Wickstrom, the leader of the Posse," Steve had explained. "He lives in Wisconsin. It's a national thing."

Steve, a truck driver like Mike, had picked up some pamphlets on a trip. For months now, Steve had talked about the Posse to Mike and Mike's wife Ruth, the gist of the talk being that taxes were unconstitutional, and that the Jews were screwing up the world monetary system. It looked to Ryan like a bunch of guys had gotten themselves into debt and were just looking for an easy way out. Ryan was attending tonight's meeting at Steve's urging, only because he had nothing better to do.

James Wickstrom straightened and gazed at the audience, seeming to penetrate each watcher with his intense eyes. Wickstrom's physical presence wasn't imposing. He was in his early forties, his face was round and unsmiling. Of medium height, he was a bit hefty with dark hair and dark-tinted glasses.

"I'd like all of you to stand and join me in the Pledge of Allegiance," he said. His voice sounded like it was strained through gravel.

The group rose as one and recited the Pledge. Wickstrom followed with a short prayer, then asked, "You're all hurting, aren't you?"

Heads nodded in response.

"You see friends losing their crops, their livestock, their property. Some of 'em are losing farms that have been in the family for generations. You're afraid your turn might be coming up.

"You're thinking what's happening isn't right. You know what? You're right there. What's happening isn't right. I'm here to tell you that God knows it isn't right.

"You people know the Bible. I know you do. You're good, hardworking Christian people. You know the Bible. But do you understand it?

"Some of you are nodding your heads. That's good. Then maybe you do know. It's good to be among God-fearing people. But, then again, maybe you don't know what the Scripture is saying.

"Being God-fearing Americans, wouldn't you figure that if the American farmer was in serious financial difficulty, the federal government would be rushing in to help? After all, the government trips over itself bailing out the Jew-owned airlines, tobacco companies, railroads, and steel industries.

"But then, you don't find too many Jews working the land, do you? No, you don't. Do you know why? Nobody? Not even you who thought you knew the Bible? Well, then, I'll tell you why.

"Almighty God put a curse on Cain, the father of the Jews. That's right. Genesis 4:12 says the earth would not yield her fruit to Cain and his descendants. Matthew 23:35 tells us that Cain is the father of the Jews.

"As a race, Jews cannot grow anything. Jews import Christian agriculture experts to the Middle East to supervise Arabs they have working their fields. Jews can't grow anything.

"But that wasn't the whole of Cain's curse. Now, God condemned Cain and his descendants to be vagabonds in the earth from that time on.

"We pay, you and me, over six hundred million dollars a year to support the Jew state. And you wonder why the federal government doesn't have any money for you farmers.

"The Jew-run banks and federal loan agencies are like a pimp and whore, working together as they foreclose on thousands of farms in America. Right now. As I speak!" he cried out, pounding the podium with his fist.

"Now the farmer is in debt up to his ears and the Jew banker, who had already gained real control over the land and money values, started to increase the value of farmland.

He fooled you, didn't he? Yes, he did. You believed you were getting ahead, didn't you?

"They GOT YOU!

"The Jew banks and federal loan agencies are committing treason, extortion, and outright theft under the guise of law and so-called human liberty, and they are doing this under the eyes of Almighty God, Jesus the Christ. We must rid ourselves of this wickedness!

"Yahweh is a god of war!" he grated. "He came not to send peace, but to send a sword." The suddenness of his declaration took everyone by surprise. "Soldiers of Yahweh are here to bring in a kingdom and destroy the wickedness in the land."

Wickstrom's reference to *Yahweh* was from the Old Testament. According to modern biblical scholars, the Hebrews had considered their real name for God, Jehovah, so sacred that they did not use it. Instead, they used the word *YHVH*. Wickstrom pronounced it "Ya-vay."

Wickstrom's message was aimed at preparing for the Battle of Armageddon—the final battle between good and evil. According to Wickstrom, believers in Yahweh would not be taken to heaven and spared the calamities of the final battle. Rather they would endure the destruction and should prepare by taking military and survival training, stockpiling food and weapons. "Every family," he preached, "should have weapons and several hundred rounds of ammunition put up!"

Meanwhile, "The battle is at the doorstep. It could come next week or in ten years. But it is time to prepare!" The Wickstrom forecast made sense to the farmers; the calamities he detailed certainly paralleled the strain they faced in keeping their land.

The battle, according to Wickstrom, would be against the sons of Satan; they would be killed during the battle in which "blood would flow as deep as the horse's bridle." This battle would not end the world, though. It would mark a new era in which the United States would become the new Jerusalem with a perfect, purified race made up of white Anglo-Saxons. "White Anglo-Saxons are the true Israelites of old—God's chosen people," Wickstrom said. No other race but Caucasian was capable of ruling the world. All other races would be returned to their original countries; they were of Satan.

"You will see tidal waves and earthquakes like you've never seen before when Yahweh stretches out his hand. Yahweh is a vengeful God. Sons of valor, soldiers of Yahweh, don't turn to your president, your governor, your state leaders. . . ."

Many of those in attendance nodded in agreement. What had Washington or anyone else done for them in these hard times? Nothing!

Unexpectedly, Mike Ryan discovered himself remembering some of the information Steve had passed on to him about Wickstrom. The guy was a hell of a speaker. He had his shit together, Mike decided. Tonight was proof of it. The man commanded the room; his delivery was just short of fire and brimstone. The man not only knew his Bible, he knew politics and economics, as well!

"Jews!" he shouted. "Jews are from the seeds of Satan. Jews are descendants of Cain. Most of the death, suffering, disease, and malice around the world we owe to them. Satan is against us. We are in a time of war!"

Here he lowered his voice, as if in conspiracy. "Jews control world banks. Jews screw others in business. Jews own all the distilleries. Distilleries make booze. Booze hurts people—people like you and me!" Jews were responsible for abortion. Jews were responsible for chemical dumps. "Jews don't read the Bible! Jews read something called a Talmud!" Did Jews produce crops? No! "Yahweh has said that the land will be barren at their feet!"

Mike Ryan nodded. He'd never liked Jews, although he'd never been sure why he disliked them—until now. Now he knew. He remembered an argument he'd had with a Jewish guy. He'd asked the guy for a job. The Jew had rubbed him wrong right off. The confrontation ended with Mike promising, "If you don't shut your mouth, I'll shut it for you permanent with my fist!" Yeah, Wickstrom's making sense, he thought.

Ryan straightened in his chair, listening carefully as Wickstrom drew from the Scriptures their true meaning—

his interpretation. "The Bible has had some twenty thousand mistranslations," he explained. "Jesus commanded us to search the Scriptures. Find the answer for yourself!"

Now he read from Ecclesiastes 3:1–8: "To everything there is a season, a time to every purpose under the heaven . . . A time to kill and a time to heal." He paused and stared at the audience, then began his interpretation. "Remember, Yahweh said it's okay to kill, but thou shalt not murder. You must kill the enemy of Yahweh—that is dictated!"

Suddenly, everyone was standing and the room was pulsing with excitement, applause, and shouts of "Amen!" It was a stellar performance in manipulating willing minds. Mike Ryan's heart was racing as he stood for the closing prayer.

The meeting at an end, the approving crowd gathered around Wickstrom to shake his hand. Ryan made his way through the crowd and stood before Wickstrom. Immediately, Wickstrom locked his eyes with Ryan's and offered his hand.

Ryan shook hands, saying, "You know, bud, you made a lot of statements up here. But how can you prove it?" He knew his tone was cocky, but he didn't care. "I was raised up a Baptist and everything you're saying is the opposite of what I was taught. How do you come up with all this crap?"

Wickstrom eyed him, his gaze unwavering. He smiled a small, satisfied smile. He had seen this "defiance" before. He knew it to be the final resistance of a true convert. "What are you?"

"What do you mean, what am I?"

"Do you know what your nationality is?"

"English. Maybe a little Irish. But I couldn't prove that part to nobody. What difference does it make?"

"White Anglo-Saxons are true Israelites!" Wickstrom said, delivering the final blow. "You are a true Israelite!"

Ryan stepped back, folding his arms before him, the idea soaking in: he was one of God's chosen people. It sat well with him; it was a powerful compliment. With a couple of simple questions Wickstrom had reduced Ryan from a challenger to an attentive listener. Ryan asked to see Wickstrom's Bible.

Ryan thumbed through the Bible, its pages thick with inserted notes, all Wickstrom interpretations. Ryan opened his mouth to ask a question. He never got the chance.

Wickstrom jumped in. "I had to look all this stuff up and now I've given you food for thought. So, you go look for yourself." He took the Bible from Ryan's hands. "Satisfy your mind on whether I've told the truth. I've given you enough to look for. If you can prove me wrong, forget it. If you can't, call me. Somebody here will know how to get hold of me. I'll talk to you any time at all." Wickstrom turned away to greet the other people who circled him, waiting.

Ryan lit a cigarette and hurried off to join Steve and his father in an adjoining room where there were tables full of Posse pamphlets and cassette tapes. Ryan picked up some pamphlets and left with Maynard and Steve.

As they got into the pickup, Steve said to Mike, "What do you think of Wickstrom?"

Ryan clicked his tongue. "At first," he said, "I thought he was a ravin', fuckin' maniac. Nuttier than a fuckin' fruitcake." Then he paused. "But he point-blank made a lot of sense on some things."

Steve smiled.

As they drove toward home in Whiting, Kansas, Mike Ryan had little to say. He smoked his cigarettes mechanically, staring ahead. He was thinking—about his heritage and Wickstrom's suggestion. Yes, perhaps he was one of God's chosen people.

CHAPTER 2

Wickstrom considered the evening a success. The response was clearly positive. But, like any good tent preacher, as soon as the last person left the building, he was already thinking about the next stop and the next group of converts.

Wickstrom had preached the Posse message from pulpits around the country since the early 1970s. Disgruntled with government and politics after his discharge from the army—which included duty in Vietnam—Wickstrom had sold his small tool business in central Wisconsin and drifted into right-wing politics. Already fueled by intense fundamentalist religious beliefs, Wickstrom had been ripe for the Posse. However, Wickstrom's real ministry was not a church of God but a church of hate.

His religious ideology came out of the Identity Movement, whose doctrine was common to many white supremacy groups such as the Ku Klux Klan and Aryan Nations. According to Identity, white Anglo-Saxons were God's chosen people. Jews were descendants of Satan. Identity followers accepted the Bible as the inspired, literal word of God; they believed in the personal return of Jesus to earth and in final battle between God and the enemies of Jesus.

Many Posse Comitatus members, embracing the Identity creed, had formed congregations of the Life Science Church; Wickstrom listed himself as a reverend in this church. Though not an ordained minister, his credentials were seventeen years of Bible research, he claimed. He'd become involved with the Posse Comitatus soon after it was founded by Henry L. Beach and William P. Gale in the late 1960s.

Beach, a former "Silver Shirt," a pro-Nazi organization in the 1930s, spread his ideological declarations around the country in a newsletter, *The Voice of Liberty.* "People will become so sick and tired of government officials that they will stage a rebellion," he said in the newsletter. He started the Citizens Law Enforcement and Research Committee, the Posse parent organization, from his home base in Portland, Oregon, in 1969.

That same year, retired army colonel William P. Gale launched the U.S. Christian Posse association—loosely affiliated bands of armed vigilantes and survivalists—from Glendale, California. Gale, a former aide to General Douglas MacArthur and director of guerrilla operations in the Philippines in World War II, stressed the importance of survivalist training and preached against income taxes. "It's unconstitutional to have a progressive income tax. It's communistic!" he'd said.

Gale tried unsuccessfully to take his antitax beliefs to the public by running for governor of California in 1958 and 1962. In 1983, he became chairman of the Constitution Party.

Wickstrom had emerged as a disciple of Gale; however, later in the 1970s, Wickstrom curtailed his frequent trips to visit Gale and hear his sermons when gasoline shortages hampered cross-country travel. Following Gale's advice, Wickstrom had gathered his own flock and struck out on his own.

"We will return the white Anglo-Saxon Christians to their rightful control of America," Wickstrom had said. The Posse Comitatus preached against state and federal government and believed that all government power was rooted at the county level; they sought the return of vigilante justice, organized in the county. They believed in self-sufficiency and self-rule, trusting no law enforcement officials except for the county sheriff—if he upheld their views.

Wickstrom insisted that a Jewish-inspired conspiracy of international bankers was at the heart of the faltering economy. The Posse's major targets were Jews, the IRS, the Federal Reserve banking system, firearm control, environmental protection, regional planning, and urban renewal.

Somebody had to be blamed for actual or imagined wrongs, and Posse groups had sprung up across the nation in the mid-1970s, associating themselves with the Life Science Church. Often members donated their land, their personal property, their guns. That done, those who donated declared themselves ministers, called their homes chapels, and wrote off all these donations as deductible religious contributions.

Meanwhile, Posse members filed countless lawsuits against businesses and state and local officials, seeking millions of dollars in damages for alleged rights violations. While they complained about and fought the government, they also made it a point to collect welfare and unemployment benefits. Evidently, drain the bastards one way or another was the key to success. The most fervent members of the Posse were armed survivalists whose stated goal was to be prepared for an eventual, and inevitable, catastrophe—a war or economic depression. Fundamental to the beliefs of the Posse was that only rural dwellers would survive a war and that unprepared urban individuals seeking food and shelter would become enemies. Accordingly, followers were instructed to collect arms and stockpile food.

In 1980, Wickstrom had attempted to take his political ideology into mainstream American politics. He ran for the U.S. Senate as the Constitution Party candidate; he pledged to "expose corruptive forces destroying our government from within and without, which have brought this once great nation to the brink of total destruction." Wickstrom garnered only 16,156 votes out of 2,104,202 cast. Then in 1982, he finished a distant third in a field of five candidates running for governor of Wisconsin. Despite poor showings in both races, his campaigns won him greater notoriety.

Now, in 1983, Wickstrom operated a paramilitary compound in Tigerton Dells, Wisconsin, and referred to himself as the national director of the Counter Insurgency of the Posse Comitatus and the high priest of the Identity Movement. James Wickstrom had strengthened his base and honed his message. As the farmers began to suffer greater economic hardship, he found a natural constituency.

There were a lot of distressed and angry people out there. People who would be receptive to his message of hate and blame. Mike Ryan was one of the angry ones.

CHAPTER 3

The day after he heard Wickstrom speak, Mike Ryan was off on a four-day run in his truck, heading to California. He drove an eighteen-wheeler. It was a 1981 Ford truck—dark blue with flashy light blue stripes. As driver, Mike and a friend leased the truck out to Trucker's Transport of Kansas City, and hauled butchered meat—large, swinging slabs of pork and beef.

Ryan reveled in the whine of the tires against the ribbon of black asphalt as the country passed beneath the truck. He liked the changing scenery. He even liked being alone for hours on end. No hassle, he told himself. And now, on this trip out, he used the time behind the wheel to ponder the things he'd heard.

Wickstrom's words kept coming at him, challenging him, irritating him. Outside the excitable atmosphere of the community hall, he had forced himself to make a cool appraisal of Wickstrom and his message. And it was true, he told himself—the Jews are a no-good race—yet Wickstrom seemed to twist the Bible, at least what Mike knew of it.

As a boy growing up in a Baptist home, the Bible message Mike had been taught was that Jews were God's chosen people. Now he had to contend with the Reverend Wickstrom telling him that Jews were to blame for many of the world's problems and that they had masterminded a conspiracy to destroy the American farmer.

What was he to make of these contradictions?

It was testimony to Wickstrom's power that Mike Ryan was still mulling over his message, was still troubled by it.

As the miles rushed by, he found himself falling into a deep quandary. He wanted to find some way to disagree with Wickstrom, he really did, but something inside of him was moving inexorably toward the leader of the Posse Comitatus.

About midnight, as he steered his rig west on I-70, he pulled into a truck stop outside Hutchinson, Kansas. The truck brakes hissed and squealed as he rolled to a stop in front of a blinking, blue and white fluorescent sign advertising rooms. He paid twenty dollars at the counter, went straight to his room, picked up a Gideon Bible off the dresser, laid down his key, and left.

As Ryan bore down on the road, he kept returning to the passages that Wickstrom quoted, hearing the preacher's voice explaining their true meaning. Wickstrom's gravelly voice was becoming more convincing.

At sunrise, Ryan pulled into another I-70 truck stop and found a stool at the counter.

"Coffee?"

Without looking up at the overweight, matronly waitress, Mike growled, "Yes." Then, he turned his attention to the Gideon Bible. He lit a Marlboro and turned to the book of Revelations: "The revelation of Jesus Christ, which God gave him to show his servants what must soon take place; and he made it known by sending his angel to his servant John, who bore witness to the word of God and to the testimony of Jesus Christ, even to all that he saw. Blessed is he who reads aloud the words of the prophecy, and blessed are those who hear, and who keep what is written therein; for the time is near . . ."

"Eggs?"

Annoyed at the disturbance, Mike glanced up. "Scrambled. And sausage."

When his breakfast came, Mike didn't lift his eyes from the pages of Scripture. He slurped his eggs down and gummed his link sausage toothlessly.

During an earlier road trip, he had bitten into a candy bar only to have a tooth come out in it. He put the tooth in his pocket and later, at home, went to the dentist. Several years earlier, when he had undergone back surgery, he'd been warned that the medication might damage his teeth. In the end, there was no saving them. The dentist removed them, but did such a poor job on the two sets of dentures he fitted for Ryan that they were too painful to tolerate. Unable to afford further treatment, Ryan simply went toothless. "Fuck it," he had said.

Surprisingly, the loss had little effect on his appearance. His full beard covered the outlines of his mouth and effectively hid the fact that he was without teeth.

Other than the slurping sounds of his eating, he was silent at the counter as he studied the pages of the Bible. It was the same at every stop he made. Oblivious to the chatter and the annoying trucker talk of weather, radar traps, and women, Mike Ryan studied his Bible. He even passed up the opportunity to flirt with the waitresses. And, when he hit the road again, he was thinking of what he had read.

His mind was a battlefield of conflicting ideas and feelings, not the least of which was that he wasn't ready to go home. He needed the solitude of the road to sort out his thoughts.

CHAPTER 4

Though he returned to Kansas after every trip, Mike Ryan, like a lot of truckers, thought of his truck as his home. He liked his wife Ruth and their three kids well enough, but sometimes it was all trouble—keeping them shaped up, keeping them in line.

To help make ends meet, the Ryans had moved into a vacant farmhouse on the edge of Whiting, Kansas, a few days earlier. It was now the middle of May 1982.

"This house suits the shit out of me," Mike said as he peered into the distressed rooms. "Feels sorta homey," he said, waiting for Ruth to echo his sentiments.

But Ruth wasn't so sure. She considered the surroundings with some doubt.

Thirty-one-year-old Ruth Ryan was a soft-spoken, plain-looking woman; her auburn hair, parted in the middle, hung limply at her shoulders. She wore faded brown polyester slacks and a white blouse. "The place must have been real nice at one time," she said, pushing her large, horn-rimmed glasses up from the bridge of her nose.

Indeed, the stately house had once been beautiful. Years earlier, it had belonged to a respected Whiting couple, and had reflected the prosperity of those times; the freshly painted white farmhouse was tucked into a green hillside at the end of a long lane. The carefully manicured lawn and neatly kept outbuildings, like the house, had reflected the owner's pride.

But now, the white, two-story frame house was on the down side of survival. Outside, the yard was littered with trash and the house was shabby—in need of several good coats of paint. Inside, it was no better—the beige wallpaper had yellowed with age and had blistered in the corners. The dining room linoleum was cracked and buckling. The woodwork had been coated with layers of paint as previous occupants had tried to refurbish the interior. The rooms smelled musty.

Ruth moved slowly from room to room, considering the prospects. "Well," she managed at last in her usual quiet way, "it sure needs some old-fashioned elbow grease." That was the best she could do under the circumstances.

Being alone here with three kids and Mike on the road so much would be an uneasy situation, at best. Still, the house was better than nothing; and to its credit, it did have electricity. But there was no running water.

"We'll have to bucket our water from the well out back," she said pointedly.

The boys, Dennis, fourteen, and Alvin, six, clamored to help with the water when the time came. Good-looking kids, who had their mother's easy disposition, they considered the old house an adventure.

But Ruth was reluctant. Baby daughter Mandy wasn't quite a year old. Washing clothes would be the worst of it—washing anything, for that matter—with no running water.

The boys raced off to investigate the rambling old farmhouse. Their footsteps and laughter echoed through the empty rooms. Suddenly the house felt more like home, just as Mike had suggested.

"It'll be perfect!" Mike insisted.

In fact, his enthusiasm made the rundown place seem inviting. His attitude about moving in caused Ruth to question her own judgment.

Maybe I'm being too negative, she thought to herself. So, as usual, she deferred. Anyway, the price was right. They could have the house rent free in exchange for cleaning it up and hauling away the junk in the yard. There would be no money for paint or redecoration. But Ruth was accustomed to having little money. After Mike covered his road expenses and made his monthly truck payment, there was barely enough money left to feed the five of them. Ruth had no choice and she knew it. So, the Ryan family made the move from Netawaka, Kansas, to Whiting.

The townspeople paid little attention to the new family. Neighbors who noted the comings and goings of the Ryans saw the children, well-mannered and clean, playing in the yard with their cousins, the Patterson kids. There was nothing about the family's behavior that drew the town's attention.

"Just good, small-town folks struggling to make a go of it," was the common judgment among those who bothered to judge at all.

Ruth didn't know if the move to Whiting was for better or worse, but at least she would know someone in the area. Mike's sister, Pat Patterson, and her husband Steve, lived in Whiting. They had moved there from Netawaka a few months earlier when their house had burned. In the past, the four of them had spent many evenings together, entertaining themselves inexpensively night after night, playing cards, Monopoly, Sorry, and Risk.

Ruth would try to change the subject when Mike told Steve of his fantasies about being a hit man for the Mafia or working for the CIA, assassinating people and blowing up government buildings.

"Those intelligence guys in the Pentagon oughta hire me to blow some of those motherfuckers away," Ryan would tell Steve.

Ruth didn't doubt that Mike could do it. "Do you guys always have to talk about such creepy stuff?" she would ask.

And always Mike dismissed her with a wave of his hand.

With the move to Whiting, Ruth now looked forward to spending time with Pat. Ruth could even ride into Holton with her and help out at Pat's Poodle Parlor. Ruth loved animals, and in the past had volunteered her help at the shop, bathing and clipping the animals with great care and pride. As Steve and Pat helped the Ryans move their belongings into the old farmhouse the very next day, Ruth felt encouraged—despite the chores waiting for her.

There was much to do—walls to scrub, furniture to arrange, boxes to unpack. Mike left the next morning on a four-day road trip in his truck.

While the boys tried to be helpful, Ruth carried the responsibility for the house. But as she worked, the old house took on an air of respectability. In the doing, though, she couldn't help thinking what a bit of money might do for the place. But, as always, she had to remind herself that there was no money.

In fact, there had never been money, since her marriage to Mike. Here she was, at thirty-one years old, and life— except for the kids she cherished—had not been generous with her.

Ruth carried a big, white enamel pot out to the well and filled it with water, then lugged it inside to the kitchen stove for heating. When the water began to simmer she poured in soap powder. Now with the hot suds she began to strip the grime from the kitchen windows and cupboards. The steam from the pot misted up her glasses, but Ruth was not a complainer; neither was she unaccustomed to hard work. This place is going to sparkle, she told herself.

Solitary hard work, though, left her too much time to think, and she didn't like to think about her past with Mike.

She was a sophomore at Anthony High School in Anthony, Kansas, the year they met. Her family had lived in nearby Bluff City, but had moved to Anthony about six months earlier to be closer to her mother's doctor. Her mom died of cancer in September and Ruth came down with mononucleosis and missed school during the months of November and December.

In January, she met Mike. He approached her under the guise of getting a date with Ruth's girlfriend, Carleen Mays, but Carleen's father refused to let his daughter go out with Mike Ryan. It was then that Mike and Ruth began dating.

Mike was older by three years, and he was a guy who lived outside accepted circles, but Ruth was willing to overlook his flaws. Like the time on their first date when he stole gas from a farmer. Lots of kids pulled those tricks, she told herself. He's just ornery.

Though Mike had a reputation as a drinker and motorcycle rebel, he had given Ruth what she needed most in those days—attention. Her father was dead set against Ruth having anything to do with "that Ryan boy." He had wanted better for her. Ruth hadn't listened.

Mike was so romantic, and he sounded so sincere. He would telephone Ruth late at night and sing to her. He liked songs by Jan and Dean and the Beach Boys. He was also partial to the Four Seasons; his favorites were "Sherry" and "Rag Doll."

In between songs, Mike murmured in Ruth's ear things she longed to hear. He loved her; he couldn't spend enough time with her.

In the beginning, Mike decided what they would do on dates. Usually they watched TV at his parents' house or visited his married sister, Pat, on Saturday nights. Or sometimes, Ruth would watch as Mike worked on his '57 two-tone blue and white Ford, making repairs after Friday night's drag racing on a straight stretch of blacktop outside of town.

Mike's affection and attentiveness made Ruth feel wanted and not so empty. Through most of her grade school and junior high years, her self-esteem had been virtually nonexistent. She had been fat—about fifty pounds overweight—and had never been able to fend off the cruel jokes by other kids about her appearance. But after her mother's death, her grief and the bout with mononucleosis made her lose weight. Now here she was, a slim teenager, and Mike Ryan, the sophisticated rebel, said he loved her and couldn't live without her. It was hard to resist when she had always felt herself so terribly unattractive.

"What do you see in that guy?" a girlfriend had asked.

"He cares about me," was the only response Ruth could come up with. A lonely, needy young girl, Ruth found a new sense of self-worth through Mike Ryan's admiration. However, her father and new stepmother still objected to her seeing Mike Ryan. Finally, one night, her stepmother told Ruth she was forbidden to date Mike anymore.

That set in motion something that Ruth and Mike had been planning for weeks. Ruth packed a few clothes, and she and Mike eloped to Miami, Oklahoma, just across the southeastern Kansas border. Neither of their families knew where the young couple had gone. Once in Oklahoma, however, Mike and Ruth found that the law was different from what they had thought—they could not marry without her parents' consent. They decided to stay on in Miami, though, and both got jobs at the Frontier Motel. Ruth cleaned rooms and Mike did odd jobs, keeping up the grounds and cleaning the swimming pool.

Mike and Ruth spent a couple of months in Miami before they met a young married couple. The four of them decided to see the country. They would get jobs and make enough money to travel on. Their sojourn took them to Springfield, Missouri, where Mike got a job first as a gas station attendant and then as a concrete worker with Rose's Pipe Company. So they decided to stay put for a while. The other couple moved on. Later, an incident with the police would take Mike and Ruth back to their hometown.

In Harper County, in north-central Oklahoma, as they prepared breakfast in a city park one morning, they were approached by police.

The officers had noticed that the couple was quite young and that they had out-of-state car tags. Perhaps they were runaways.

"Are you guys married?" one officer inquired.

"Yeah, we are," Mike answered.

The officers weren't so sure. These kids appeared nervous. "Do you have a marriage license or proof of your marriage?"

"No," Mike finally said. "We aren't really married, but we planned to be."

The police contacted Mike's parents and back to Anthony they went.

Ruth was glad to be going home. She was homesick.

Six months after their return a judge married them at the

Harper (Kansas) County Courthouse on November 19, 1968. Ruth was seventeen and Mike was twenty-one. Neither Ruth nor Mike finished high school.

As a result of the break with her father over Mike, Ruth and Mike spent most of their free time visiting with Mike's parents. She seldom saw her father in that first year of marriage. Then, her father suffered a heart attack and died.

Regrets were painful for her. Over the years she had come to understand her father better. But understanding Mike? That was not easy.

When he was home, arguments were frequent. "He had a terrible, terrible temper. He was brought up to never accept responsibility . . . nothing was ever his fault, to hear him tell it. Even if he got in trouble, it was always someone else's fault." There was no talking to him, no reasoning with him. What's worse, he tended to come out swinging with his fists. Ruth cowered before his temper, ending up with bruises and broken glasses.

Why do I stay with him? she wondered as she worked on the window of the Whiting farmhouse. It wasn't love. As she gazed through the newly cleaned window at her boys running in the yard, she knew the real reason. Fear. Mike had threatened her over and over: If she ever left him and took the kids, he would hunt her down.

"You'll never get away from me," he would say, his voice steely cold.

Knowing Ruth's deathly fear of knives, he would go into detail about what he would do if he found her, how he would torture her before he cut her throat.

Mike was six feet two inches tall to Ruth's five feet six inches. He was strong and he was big. Physically and temperamentally, he was not a man to cross. As the old midwestern saying goes, Ruth kept her place.

After their marriage, Mike worked construction, but had chronic employment problems. He was adept at getting jobs—he knew how to turn on the charm, the polite manners—but holding one was another issue. Ruth waited tables at the Silver Top Cafe in Anthony to pay their way. She gritted her teeth and hung on.

This went on for several months as Mike proceeded to

lose job after job; Ruth's income was all they had sustaining them.

"Stupid-ass bosses," Mike would complain, making it clear that he was smarter and bigger than any boss he met. "This place isn't for me. We have to go someplace where I can do something," he decided.

Although Ruth wasn't hopeful, she "kept her place." They moved on to Wichita, a city where expectations could take flight.

Mike found a job, but he didn't last at it—he encountered the same old problem with the new boss.

"Fucking asshole," he said. "Such a jerk." So they moved on—this time to Hutchinson, Kansas, where Mike worked first in a grain elevator and then in a gas station.

Next came a series of jobs in small machine shops in little towns around Hutchinson. It was touch and go all the way financially. Then, Mike fell ill. He had surgery for a bowel obstruction. He recovered, but now manual labor was not for him; he found a job driving a truck.

Driving a truck seemed more his métier. He was on his own—no bosses looking over his shoulder. He was king of the road. "The old nine-to-five grind isn't for me," he was sure.

He did fairly well. For the first time, they were able to begin saving some money. Then, one day in 1978, as he was putting a tarp over his truck in a windstorm, a gust of wind caught the thick canvas and billowed it out like a sail. Mike flew from the top of the truck to the hard roadway.

For several minutes he lay on his back, unable to move. He was afraid he had broken his back, but finally, he managed to roll to his side and get to his feet. He convinced another trucker to give him a hand with the tarp, and he got his rig going again.

Driving was excruciating, but he told himself to ignore the pain. Several weeks later, he slipped on a patch of ice, reinjured his back, and couldn't ignore the pain. He ended up having back surgery, and was out of work for eight long months.

Mike didn't convalesce well. He began habitually using marijuana to help him sleep. He became harder and harder to live with. His temper flared, arguments over sex were common. Mike wanted sex immediately and all the time; Ruth resisted.

"If you'd show me some consideration," she would tell him, gearing up for one more try at reality, "I might be more interested."

Mike didn't want to hear about it. They led their lives his way, and that's all there was to it. As often as not, she would tearfully submit to his desires.

Almost from the beginning, Ruth had known he had been unfaithful to her. Once she'd come home from several days at her sister's in Harper where she saw her doctor during pregnancy, and there were all the telltale signs of another woman having been in their bed.

"Who was it?" she demanded, more hurt than angry.

Mike didn't deny it. He just looked at her. "What are you making such a fuss about?"

"Was there another woman here while I was gone?"

He shrugged. "What if there was?"

Mike Ryan liked his women.

In 1979, Ruth and Janet Carter had become friends, spending time together while Mike was on the road. Mike had resumed driving a truck, even though long hours behind the wheel aggravated his back problem. Often they baby-sat each other's children. Janet, thirty-one, a petite, divorced blond, lived with her three kids a few blocks from the Ryans.

Mike was quick to express his attraction to Janet. He made sexual overtures toward her from the first time he met her. Finally, bored with his one-night stands on the road, he let Ruth know that he wanted to try a ménage à trois. Janet was the other woman who would be invited to their bed. Though Ruth was against it, she had no other choice—or so she thought.

Janet, alone and lonely in a small town, was at first easily lured. It would be all right, she thought—just for kicks, and just so the kids didn't know.

But Janet proved to be stronger willed than Mike Ryan expected. While she was willing to sleep in the same bed with Mike and Ruth, she would not tolerate Mike's abusing

Ruth. Far too often she had seen Ruth arriving at her house
with black and blue marks on her face and arms and her
glasses broken.

Though Ruth passed off these times as accidents, the
Ryan boys were quick with the truth: "Daddy hit Mama!"

Janet became a buffer between Mike and Ruth and the
ménage à trois continued, finally resulting in the Ryans
moving in with Janet. The arrangement lasted six months,
but Janet realized early on she'd made a mistake. Arguments between Mike and Janet became increasingly frequent. On one occasion Mike shoved Janet down on the bed
and tried to choke her because she wouldn't spend the day
in bed with him, while Ruth went to work.

And Mike accused Janet of sleeping with other men when
he was out of town. Then, he'd turn around and scream at
Ruth, "Janet's using us!" though Janet paid most of the
bills and purchased most of the groceries. Mike preferred to
spend his money on movies and dinners out.

"Can't you see how he uses people, Ruth?" Janet asked.
"He's a manipulator. He'll use anybody he can. He doesn't
care about anybody but himself. He's a goddamned con
artist," she told Ruth over and over.

Finally, Janet managed to get the Ryans to leave her
home—they rented a house nearby. Though she was trying
to detach from them, she helped them fix up the house. She
knew her pulling away angered Mike.

In August 1980, Janet was about to leave the Ryan house
after having dinner with them. Suddenly Mike grabbed her
and dragged her into the bedroom. There he held her,
ranting and raving at her, then knocked her to the floor,
straddled her, and hit her across the face.

In temporary remorse, Mike ran into the bathroom for a
washcloth. But then he started choking Janet.

Ruth fell upon Mike, hitting him and screaming,
"You've got to stop!"

"I'm going to kill the bitch!" Mike raged.

"Call the police!" Janet managed, nodding to her son,
who was watching helplessly.

Mike Ryan released Janet. But he didn't give up. He
began pushing her and her kids toward the door, Janet

kicking all the way, the kids crying, everyone terrified of Mike Ryan.

Once free of the Ryan household, Janet went to a friend's home nearby and telephoned police. Two months later, the Ryans moved.

Ruth imagined she could live with anything now, cope with whatever might happen. As much as she was hurt over Mike's episode with Janet and his affairs with other women, Ruth had learned that she could not stop Mike from doing what he wanted. And, she knew there would be other women in the future.

Still, she held onto hope for a better life. Maybe Mike would calm down. If he just wouldn't get angry—that's when his fists flew. Their son Dennis had also been a victim of his father's wrath. Ruth remembered the night Dennis was peacefully watching television while Mike and Ruth were in the kitchen. Mike shouted to Dennis, ''Stop watching television and do your homework!'' It was an order.

Dennis, like many teenage kids might, failed to respond.

Mike stormed from the kitchen into the living room. There he kicked and punched Dennis across the living room floor.

Ruth froze in the kitchen doorway. All she could do was stand there. She felt like such a coward. I don't have the guts to go in and help Dennis, she scolded herself. She had been treated that way, but it was different to see it done to her child. It was there, right there, that Ruth realized exactly how powerless she was against Mike Ryan.

CHAPTER 5

Mike, the eldest of five children, was himself the product of a difficult home life. Dissension in the family reflected early in his schoolwork. Though he didn't lack intelligence, Mike was never a good student. Academic troubles plagued him early on—he was held back in the second grade.

Later, at age fifteen, he missed most of his freshman year after he was injured in a hunting accident. It happened on Thanksgiving Day. Mike, his dad, and his grandpa were quail hunting. Mike was sitting in the backseat with his gun barrel down between his feet when it discharged. He lost the first and second toes of his left foot. He returned to class with only six weeks left in the school year.

"I talked to my teachers and they told me if I could pass the last tests, they'd give me credit for the year. I worked my hind end off and passed their tests, but they still said I was gonna take 'em over. I don't know why they had to lie to me."

Mike didn't have many friends. He went his own way. He was a country kid. He never studied. He accepted any grade he got—he didn't care.

When Mike failed to graduate at the end of his senior year, he tried bearing up to the humiliation of returning to Anthony High for a fifth year. Other kids picked on him. Some of the guys had a name for him. They called him "Dog Face," a jibe which referred to his problem with acne as a teen. He didn't talk much or trust much—he seemed to hold everything inside. Halfway through the school year, he dropped out. One day he just didn't show up anymore.

His poor academic record and foot injury dashed his hopes of going on to become an airline or air force pilot. Mike had desperately wanted to be in the military; he made one last effort to join the service. He got as far as the army's induction physical, but questions came up when an examining physician observed that one of his testicles had not descended.

"Does this ever bother you, cause you pain?"

"Hell, no," Ryan responded, not wanting to admit that at times he had pains low in his abdomen.

"What kind of physical work have you done in the past?" the doctor asked.

"I put up hay, lift bales, and lift weights. I can do anything your guys do in the army."

When his physical was over, Ryan and the thirty other guys in the line took the military oath. Ryan was in the army, he thought . . . until one of the sergeants told him that he should go home while additional paperwork was processed on him.

A few days later, Ryan received notification that he was classified as 1-Y, qualified for service only in time of war or national emergency. As far as he was concerned, he'd been jerked around, lied to.

Ryan's parents, Elsie and Gene, argued relentlessly. She frequently accused her husband of having extramarital affairs; at times they came to physical blows. To Mike, Elsie was a dominating woman; she controlled the family with an iron fist. Gene Ryan, a seemingly quiet man, also was known as a tough guy—a drinker and a fighter. With a few drinks under his belt, he'd take on anyone. Even so, he'd held a job as a lineman for the local telephone company for thirty years.

Elsie, a woman with unpredictable mood swings, had a way of placing blame when things went wrong, and Mike felt he often got the brunt of it. As a young boy, Mike was baby-sitting the family's sixth child, a month-old baby boy, when the child choked to death; it was Mike's fault. Mike would carry the destructive force of guilt and deep shame for the rest of his life.

In his adult life, only driving the truck had given him a life-style that he could contend with successfully. His personal life was more stable when he was on the road—he and Ruth fought less during the times he was home and his financial well-being was more secure.

In many ways, his self-esteem was intricately tied to his truck and his ability to be on the road. So, when he blew the engine right after his trip to California, he hit rock bottom.

Neither he nor his partner had the cash to make the costly repairs. Hard times were once again his constant partner. This time, he went into a downward spiral from which he couldn't extricate himself.

He felt powerless and angry. For a man like Mike Ryan, who struggled for control over even the most straightforward aspects of his life, going on welfare was a shameful admission of failure.

CHAPTER 6

On July 4, 1982, Steve and Pat paid a visit to the Ryans.

"Well, listen, why don't you come with us to Nate Babcock's? He's got one of the Reverend Wickstrom's videos," Steve said.

Mike perked up. During the long days of doing nothing, he often pondered Wickstrom's message. Facing another day of nothing to do, Mike agreed to go along. "See what the guy has to say this time," he mumbled.

They parked on the gravel driveway in front of Nate Babcock's home southeast of Hiawatha. The white, two-story farmhouse was surrounded by a dairy barn and several outbuildings. A pet peacock strutted across the yard, flapping its wings and squawking.

Nate Babcock was seventy years old. He'd lived on this farm all his life, had taken it over from his folks. Fortunately for him, when hard times hit, he sold thirty-five acres to the government for part of a new highway running along the edge of his land. That's what saved Nate Babcock.

He'd seen the fortunes of the local farmers rise and fall. Through most of his life, he could attribute the success or failure of a crop on the weather and the determination of the farmer. But now he saw something different happening. The government was putting farms out of business.

Fueled by his anger, Babcock attended a number of Wickstrom's meetings and was impressed with his message. "We need a strong voice telling those idiots in Washington that we know what they're up to."

Babcock held Posse meetings, which he called Patriot meetings, at his home and participated in the national tractorcade on Washington, D.C., in 1978.

When the Ryans and the Pattersons arrived, Babcock greeted them at the back door, off the kitchen. He wore faded navy blue Big Smith bib overalls; his gold, wire-frame glasses suited his oval face. He led them into the living room.

"You know, the people in charge of the world today operate using fear . . . that's the only way they can control people," he said, dragging in a chair from the kitchen so they'd all be able to gather around the television comfortably. "And, in my estimation, creating fear is one of the biggest sins you can commit. The source of all put everything out here for us to use and then here comes the Antichrist. We don't have a damn bit of freedom left. We think we do, but we don't."

With that, he pushed the play button on the VCR and left the room to join his wife in the kitchen where they'd been playing cards.

As soon as Wickstrom's image filled the screen, Ryan felt his heart quicken. At the sound of the gravelly voice, he found himself leaning forward, determined to catch each word. As Wickstrom spoke, Mike followed along in his Gideon Bible.

Babcock might have been attracted to Wickstrom's political message. Steve might have appreciated having someone to blame for hard times. But Mike was drawn to the religious message.

Ruth noted the change in her husband with interest. There was a fire in his eyes she'd never seen before. As he absorbed the Wickstrom message, she turned her attention to the man on the television, wondering what he had that could light such admiration in her husband's eyes—eyes that had seemed dead to any emotion save anger for years.

Although she'd never seen Wickstrom himself, Ruth had heard much about him and his ideas from Steve and Pat during the past year. When they played cards together, the small talk was often about Wickstrom's message—the way Washington and those "Jew bastards" were destroying the farmer's way of life.

She glanced at the others from the corner of her eye. Steve and Pat were as enthralled as Mike. Maybe he does have something worth listening to, she thought.

Wickstrom railed on, picking the Bible apart verse by verse, amending it with his own interpretations. She was startled by Wickstrom's words about the story of Adam and Eve.

"That bit about Eve eating an apple? That's a fairy tale!" Wickstrom thundered. "There was no apple. How could a piece of fruit have such knowledge? That's the most ridiculous thing I've ever heard!

"Do you want to know what happened in that Garden of Eden? Eve did beguile Adam all right, but not with an apple. She beguiled him with sex. She had sex with Adam.

"He took something from her but it wasn't a piece of fruit.

"And you know what? That experience changed both of them. Really changed them."

What Wickstrom was preaching was the "two-seed theory," common to white supremacist groups. According to the theory, when Eve, in the garden of Eden with Adam, took a bite of the forbidden fruit, she actually had sex with the serpent—Satan in disguise—and was impregnated. This seed eventually became Eve's son, Cain. Then, after she mated with Adam, his seed became their son, Abel. The story went that after Cain killed Abel, he ran off to propagate with various tribes, spreading his demon seed. Accordingly, all Cain's descendants were an impure race— blacks, Orientals, Hispanics.

"However, Cain also spread his seed among white tribes, so just because you're white doesn't mean you're a true Israelite," Wickstrom explained smoothly. "Remember the passage in Luke that says, 'Slay thy enemy at my feet.' You're not murdering a human being if you kill these impure breeds, those who are not true Israelites. They have the demon seed of the devil in them!''

Mike struggled to keep up with Wickstrom, following verse by verse and chapter by chapter. As Wickstrom spoke, Mike nodded his head. Ruth, who had started out more amazed by Mike's reaction than by the message, was now glued to the television set. She was scribbling notes, trying to keep up with what Wickstrom was saying.

As she wrote, Ruth thought about all the people who listened to Wickstrom and who respected him. They couldn't all be wrong. Of course not.

Then, as if the preacher hadn't convinced them enough, he topped off his sermon with a word on the ''dualism theory,'' another common thread among white supremacists and a concept that fuels their belief that they are a superior race.

According to Wickstrom, God and Satan had a battle in the heavens. God won the battle and cast Satan down to earth. Satan was not allowed to leave the earth until he had performed certain deeds—namely, tricking people to join his side. He would do this with the help of his evil allies, the Jews. It was to be a test of the people.

''The final battle, the great Battle of Armageddon, will be the final battle between good and evil! Are you ready for it?'' Wickstrom said, lowering his voice to a whisper.

It was almost enough to raise gooseflesh. As the sermon came to a close, the Ryans had become like sponges, soaking it all up.

Ryan dropped back in his chair and left the Bible open on his lap. ''The thing that pisses me off,'' he said, ''is why does everyone have to lie to you? Dammit, I've been lied to all my life. Now I'm learning that they even lied to me about the Bible!''

Quickly he jotted down some notes to which he could refer later.

Steve rewound the tape. As he did, Pat tapped Ruth on the shoulder. ''What did you think?''

Ruth raised her eyebrows and let out a low breath. "I liked it."

"It makes sense to me, point-blank," Ryan said. "The lies started right there in the beginning—in Genesis."

Ruth looked at Mike, waiting to hear what he was going to say next.

Mike saw that they were all waiting. He cleared his throat. "It was in the beginning that Satan started getting his fingers into it. Don't you get it?" he asked, leaning toward the others. "That's where it had to start!" Then he straightened. "Yahweh says we have to find the truth."

He took a deep breath. "It's out there, but it's up to us to search it out." He shook his head. "If we don't go out and find it for ourselves, we'll end up listening to some son of a bitch preacher go on and on from the pulpit every Sunday—and even though we'll think we've been hearing the truth, we'll be listening to lies.

"Damn!" he said, slapping his fist down on the arm of the chair. Finally, Mike believed he knew the truth.

The defeats, the criticism, the sense of never making it he'd endured over the years, all returned to him. The hurt he had buried was now exploding through his being.

"Why did I lose my toes in that hunting accident?" he asked, returning to the time he had become disenchanted with God and the Baptist church. That injury had changed all of his plans for what he'd wanted to do with his life.

For the first time in months, his grandfather's face appeared before him. He had been very close to the kind old man.

He remembered the last time he'd visited him. Three days later, the old man was in a casket. As he stood before his grandfather's corpse, he had felt the life drain from him. He cried angry, bitter tears—the last tears he cried.

Next, he remembered working in the fields for his mother's brother-in-law, only to have the brother-in-law take all of his summer's earnings for room and board. Stuff like that, crap like that, he had had to take it all!

Mike looked at Ruth, Pat, and Steve. "People are always saying one thing to you and then something else behind your back. If you make two cents, they'll give you the

shaft." He shook his head. His whole life seemed to have
been one long series of psychic wounds. Wickstrom's words
had opened those wounds.

As they bumped over the dirt lane leading out of Nate
Babcock's place, they were quiet. Steve negotiated the
sharp turn from the dirt road onto the gravel country road
that led to the main highway.

Once on the main highway, the four compared their
feelings about Wickstrom's lecture. Steve and Pat had been
enthusiastic about the Posse for a long time. Most of Steve's
comments were to the effect of "I told you so," or "Didn't
I tell you you'd be impressed if you'd only give him a
chance?"

Ruth was quiet. Something had jelled inside her. Wickstrom's words had had a profound effect on Mike, certainly
enough to impress her. But there were other things that
attracted her.

Mike hadn't been the only one in the room who had
suffered a difficult life. She'd lost her parents and now
struggled to keep her family going. She'd had a painful
childhood, having been teased mercilessly by classmates in
school. Now, like Mike, she had someone to blame. "I got
my work cut out for me," she said finally.

"What do you mean?" Pat asked.

Ruth lifted several sheets of paper. "I got some notes
here with a lot of ideas I have to sort out. I don't think that
it's something that I want to do overnight. The reverend's
message is going to have to sink in."

"You're right there," Mike said, agreeing with Ruth for
one of the few times in their marriage—a fact that didn't
escape Ruth's notice. "I have chapter and verse to go over
in this," he said, lifting the now worn Gideon Bible.

Once home, the Ryans set to their task with a vengeance.
For the next three days, they pored over the pages of the
Gideon Bible. It seemed they didn't sleep at all. They were
too excited about what they were piecing together. The only
time they took from study was to eat and feed the kids.

So much of what they'd never understood was being
made clear. The sense of being victims, of never having a

chance, was being replaced with a sense of empowerment. Mike understood now that being on welfare was not a personal failure but the result of a carefully played out strategy of the Jews.

Ruth and Mike were closer during those three days than at any time since their courtship. Mike didn't utter a cross word to Ruth. They were partners in this new endeavor.

After all the lies they had been subjected to throughout their lives, they were finally working together and learning the truth.

CHAPTER 7

NOVEMBER 1982

A wheat field, now reduced to dried stubble poking through a light blanket of snow, stood across the road from the Best Western Motel on the southern edge of Hiawatha. Here, tonight, would be another meeting between Mike Ryan and the Reverend James Wickstrom.

Steve had visited the Posse compound in Wisconsin several months earlier, before Mike's truck had broken down. Steve had asked Mike to go with him, but Mike had a road trip to make.

Wickstrom, who had recalled the urgency in Ryan's eyes after that lecture down in Kansas, had asked Steve about his brother-in-law.

"Why didn't you bring him along?"

"He couldn't come," Steve explained honestly. "He's on the road."

Wickstrom had nodded his head with the certainty of a man who had been through this many, many times. "Don't worry," he said with conviction, "he'll come around."

Now, as Mike and Steve walked through several inches of fresh snow, bundled against the cold, it seemed that Mike had indeed come around.

"How do you know Wickstrom'll talk to us?" Mike asked, rubbing his hands together.

"Don't worry," Steve replied. "He'll be only too glad to talk to us."

Mike was elated. Meeting Wickstrom personally the night before the meeting was an honor. Mike walked straight and proud.

As the two men entered the lobby of the Best Western Motel, they were approached by Wickstrom's bodyguard and right-hand man, Fred, or "Dead Fred"—so called because of his alleged expertise in weaponry and explosives.

"Hey," Fred said, recognizing Steve.

Steve led Mike over to Wickstrom's man. "Mike Ryan, this is Fred." Fred was middle-aged, plain-looking enough.

The two shook hands. Then Fred motioned them down the hallway. "The reverend is waiting for you."

As he went up the stairs, Mike tried desperately to remember everything he had been studying in the Bible. Like Wickstrom, he had been making his own interpretations. In addition, he had been praying.

What he didn't realize was that he had primed himself perfectly for Wickstrom.

Suddenly, they were in the inner sanctum—Wickstrom's room in the motel. Wickstrom greeted both men. Mike had the feeling that Wickstrom had been looking forward to this meeting as much as Mike had.

"Have a seat," Wickstrom said, motioning the two men to the edge of one of the double beds in the room.

Immediately, Steve and Wickstrom struck up a conversation having to do with some of the training Steve had received at Wickstrom's compound. As they spoke, Wickstrom continually glanced over at Mike, who was engrossed in a conversation with Fred.

A thin smile showed on Wickstrom's lips.

"Check this out," Fred was saying to Mike, showing him a listening device.

Ryan put on the headphones Fred offered him. Fred opened the motel room door and stuck the microphone outside, pointing it in the direction of a man sitting in his parked car about sixty feet away.

Mike watched out the window, seeing the man had the window cracked about half an inch. The smoke curling from his cigarette wafted out the window.

Fred smiled and turned on the device. Ryan's eyes lit up. He chuckled as he listened to the man's car radio.

Mike was smiling as he took off the headphones. "Pretty slick."

"If you like, I can sell you one tomorrow night after the meeting. Fifty-nine dollars."

Mike glanced at Wickstrom. Their eyes locked for a moment. "Okay, yeah. I'd like to have one. Just for the hell of it."

Wickstrom nodded. "So, have you been reading your Bible and checking things out like I told you to?"

Mike paused, suddenly wary. "Yeah," he said after a moment, "I've been checking some things out."

"I hear you lost your truck," Wickstrom said.

Mike's eyes narrowed. "Yeah. Damnedest thing, too. That engine blew and I thought it was running good, better than ever. That baby would walk right up a hill with a full load, right before she blew . . ."

"Did you ever think that maybe you were spending too much time and energy on that rig?"

Mike shrugged. "I thought about it. But a man's got to make a living."

"You're not starving now, are you?"

Mike let out a snort. "You're right there. Here I am without a job, and I have more money in my pocket than I can ever remember having." Ryan tapped his pocket. He had picked up eight hundred dollars in welfare money, including some money for his dental work. And Steve had paid him four hundred dollars for a paint job they'd worked on together.

Mike chuckled. "I even went out and bought me a Ruger Mini-14. I figure the feds'll be coming after me and Steve sooner or later, and I want something to shoot back."

When their laughter died down, Wickstrom was looking Ryan squarely in the eye. "I want to show you something," he said. "I'm going to test you for fasting and repentance."

"What?"

"It's time you got straight with Yahweh."

Mike shrugged. "Okay."

"Good. Put your arm out, your right arm. That's all you have to do. Don't try to hold it up and don't press against me. Just hold it steady."

Wickstrom faced Mike, putting his left hand on Ryan's extended forearm and his right hand on Ryan's left shoulder. Following Wickstrom's example, Mike lowered his head in prayer.

Steve looked on and felt a twinge of envy. Wickstrom had never treated him this way and he had gone clear to Wisconsin, to the compound.

"Yahweh God," Wickstrom began, "are Mike Ryan and James Wickstrom clean enough to speak with You?" Wickstrom pushed down on Mike's arm but it wouldn't move. It remained extended in spite of the pressure Wickstrom put on it.

Mike chuckled to himself. What the hell did he do to my arm? he wondered.

"Yahweh God, is Mike Ryan in need of five days of fasting and repentance?"

Ryan's arm dropped like a brick.

"What the . . . " Mike sputtered. The dropping had felt totally involuntary.

"Is Mike Ryan in need of more than five days of fasting and repentance?"

Mike's arm went limp. Mike stared at it as if it belonged to someone else.

"Is Mike Ryan in need of more than two days of fasting and repentance?"

Mike's arm began to rise.

"Is Mike Ryan in need of three days of fasting and repentance?"

Mike's arm continued to rise. He held a nervous grin.

"Is Mike Ryan in need of four days of fasting and repentance?"

Mike's arm dropped.

Wickstrom looked at Mike. "Three days of fasting and repentance, according to Yahweh," he intoned.

Ryan dropped to the bed. "What the hell did you do?" he asked suspiciously.

"I communicated directly with Yahweh God," Wickstrom said. "It's not something I show just anyone, either," he added.

Ryan practically glowed. Not only was he impressed by the special treatment, he felt special, chosen.

What Wickstrom didn't explain was this. In his use of the arm test, he was modifying an ancient custom used by some religions to test the purity of food. According to the Old Testament, the Israelites followed dietary laws that prohibited them from eating pork or other meat from animals considered scavengers—catfish, rabbits, and anything with cloven hooves. Using the arm test, a person would hold out the food; if it was impure, it would sap the body of its electrical strength and the arm would drop. If the food was pure enough to eat, the arm would rise.

Now, used in this fashion by Wickstrom, the arm test was a self-sealing ritual. Regardless of whether the arm rose or fell, Wickstrom could interpret or give reason to an answer in any manner he wished.

"When do I do this fasting and repentance?" Mike asked.

"Whenever you want to," Wickstrom replied. "When you decide it is time. Remember that while you cannot eat solid food, you can drink fluids.

"Yeshua fasted for forty days on the mountain, according to the New Testament," Wickstrom said, using the Hebrew word for Jesus. "Moses fasted for that long on Mount Sinai. Yahweh God didn't make either of them fast. They chose to do it. They gave themselves freely and willingly. Do it when you're ready and ask Him for forgiveness."

Mike was speechless. Wickstrom had given him a way to "get rid" of all the things in his life that hurt him. There was no question in his mind that he would do exactly what Wickstrom suggested. Me, Jesus, and Moses . . .

When Mike and Steve departed, they both assured James

Wickstrom that they would be at the meeting the following night.

"Wouldn't miss it for the world," Mike said.

"Good," Wickstrom replied. "Good. I'll be looking for you."

Light snowflakes spit into the beam of their headlights as the Wickstrom converts traveled home. Steve was silent as he drove. He was still a bit ticked off by the special treatment Mike had received.

Mike was oblivious to Steve's feelings. He was on an all-time high. "This is one of the most important things to happen in my life," he said, his eyes lit with enthusiasm. "I am beginning to see what I need to be here in this life."

CHAPTER 8

The following evening, people started arriving early for the Wickstrom lecture. Mike Ryan also arrived early. If his position in the front row wasn't enough to mark him as a true believer, the fact that he had brought his entire family should have been. Ryan felt reborn.

He sat straighter as Wickstrom took the podium. When Wickstrom glanced down, he looked on Ryan. Mike was aware of the silent and strong bond between them.

"Tonight we have a study very appropriate for the times," Wickstrom began. "It is entitled, *To the Drunkards.* Yahweh said that His people and His new Jerusalem would be a nation of drunkards in the latter days."

Wickstrom paused. "Go to the bars any night," he challenged his listeners. "Not just Friday night, any night. You'll see the bars filled to overflowing with fools out whoremongering. Drunks," he shouted, spitting out the word. "They're lost in the fantasy land of blinking lights. They have their filthy jokes and their filthy language.

"But let me tell you something. The Bible said that on that day the drunks shall perish. Jesus says it's so . . ."

Wickstrom kicked his sermon into high gear. "Yes, we

are coming to the end of days!" he said to his rapt audience. "Look to the heavens to find out. The planets are aligning for the first time in two thousand thirty-six years. Why? To foretell of the destruction of the age, of this system of the Antichrist which has been foisted upon us!"

Under Wickstrom's "tutelage," his followers dismissed the authority of the Bible, relying instead on Wickstrom's bizarre explanations, connecting the Zodiac to the final days on earth. Facts were no longer important; reason was no longer relevant. They were hooked on the skewed logic of Wickstrom's hatemongering.

"What were Jesus' words? 'I come not to bring peace, but I come with a sword,' and 'I come not to bring peace but to divide . . .'"

Wickstrom gave them the one thing that their churches could no longer give them—a sense of worth in the midst of crashing self-esteem. He told them they were the chosen of God and that their earthly failures were the failures of demonic strategies beyond their control.

His was a call to action, a call to arms. He wanted them to prepare to fight in the final battle—the Battle of Armageddon. They were part of an elite corps of mankind. Banding together for this noble cause, they had a new sense of purpose surging through them. They were inspired with the rightness of some of their basest hatreds.

After nearly two hours, Wickstrom closed his lecture with a message to the "drunkards." "I hope you've enjoyed yourselves! Because you're not going to be around when the smoke clears and the brimstone and the heat dissipate.

"To those of you who have heard what I've said—get off the booze. You know all you do is go to the bathroom after a half hour and whiz it away anyway. Buy food, instead!

"The time is drawing nigh!"

Then it was over. The audience, chilled to the marrow with his doomsday message, sat in stunned silence. Everyone seemed to be examining himself, asking himself if he would be ready for the coming battle.

Wickstrom looked out upon the sea of faces and he saw expressions that he had come to know intimately.

Ryan was sold. He had known that something had been

against him his entire life. But Wickstrom had put that lie to rest. Now he knew where to place his blame. With that revelation, he was suddenly head and shoulders above those who had run over him in years past. Now he had the answers he needed. Now he, not they, stood among God's chosen.

Ryan, with baby Mandy in his arms, led his family toward the podium. He wanted Ruth to meet Wickstrom.

Wickstrom reached for Mandy and she held out her arms. "That's quite a young lady you're got there," Wickstrom said, bouncing the child on his hip.

Ryan beamed with pride; Mandy was the apple of his eye, and she rarely went to strangers.

"Whatever you do, never break her spirit," Wickstrom said, handing the little girl back to Ryan. Wickstrom shook Ruth's hand, according her just the right amount of attention to impress her. A moment later, he had turned away, to convince someone else of the importance of his soul.

The Ryans stopped at a table covered with Wickstrom's pamphlets and audiocassette tapes. Tapes were available for three dollars; pamphlets were marked fifteen cents. Mike bought several of Wickstrom's recorded sermons, then moved through the crowd as they headed for the exit.

"Mike!"

Mike looked up to see his brother-in-law. He waved and began moving toward him.

"Mike, this is Jimmy Haverkamp," Steve said, introducing a young man of about twenty-four, small build, with a ruddy complexion and sun-faded, light brown hair.

Mike extended his hand.

"Jimmy here just got himself a Mini-14," Steve said.

"Yeah," Jimmy said, "one of those ranch models."

Mike looked into the younger man's eyes. "Haven't picked up one of those ranch models yet. I hear they have a nub on them with a clip that's different than the one I just got."

Jimmy nodded enthusiastically. "Yeah, that's right."

Ryan nodded. "That's a good gun," he added as he and Steve joined the crowd moving toward the exits.

"I'll talk to you," Jimmy called to them as they flowed out with the rest of the crowd.

As anxious as he was to continue their discussion about guns and about Wickstrom's message, Jimmy knew there would be time. They would meet again the next night at an overnight survival training camp being put on by Dead Fred.

CHAPTER 9

Jimmy Haverkamp, like most of Wickstrom's followers, had been lured into the fold as a result of hard times. He was struggling to keep his hog business going—he raised and sold purebred breeding stock—in Mercier, a town of thirty, in northeast Kansas, where he was born and raised.

Unlike many of Wickstrom's followers, Jimmy had a year of college to his credit. He had taken a year of agricultural studies at Highland Junior College after he graduated from high school. Still, he was barely getting by financially.

Jimmy had gotten in over his head. When he'd started raising purebreds, business was good, and he had borrowed money for a new hog shed. Now, hog prices had dropped and farmers weren't buying breeding stock. Jimmy was fifty thousand dollars in debt and saw no light at the end of the tunnel. He worked twelve and fourteen-hour days and still could barely make his bank payment—six thousand dollars every six months. "Too many farmers are going under," Jimmy told his dad. "This can't be a coincidence. Something's going on." Jimmy prayed and spent hours reading the Bible late at night.

His work was taking a toll on an already unstable marriage. Jimmy's long hours and increasing attention to the Bible seemed to alienate his young wife. Jimmy felt them drifting apart; he knew the marriage was in trouble. A sense of impending doom had drawn him to Wickstrom's bizarre message of ultimate war as hope. Although he had been raised a Catholic—he had been an altar boy and there was a time he never missed a Sunday mass—he was now a Bible-thumping, born-again, Christian Wickstrom follower. And he was trying to convince his parents and two sisters, Cheryl and Lisa, to convert. His motives were as sincere as they had been when he was a devout Catholic. He wanted desperately to save his family from eternal destruction.

Finally, he'd gotten his parents, Norbert and Maxine, to lend him an ear. If nothing else, they were curious about the zeal with which their son had thrown himself into this new religion. Yes, they'd agreed that maybe sometime they would come to one of the Bible studies Jimmy held at his home; he lived just a block from them.

Jimmy's older sister, Cheryl, had gradually begun to respond, too. He could read it in her face; she was no longer as quick to argue with him.

"You're nuts," she'd said at first. "All this talk about guns and fighting is a bunch of bull. Leave me out of it."

But now, her tone was different; she was more open-minded when she talked to Jimmy about it. "Jimmy," she said one night over coffee at his kitchen table, "do you really think that this Battle of Armageddon is coming?"

He looked her straight in the eye. "You bet I do. There's no doubt about it."

Those attending the survival training parked their cars and pickups in the driveway of a farmhouse near Westmoreland, in northeast Kansas. For the fifty bucks they'd paid to attend, they'd been promised an information-packed weekend. Although there were only seven of them, what they lacked in numbers they made up for in dedication.

As Mike Ryan came down the basement steps of the house into the room where the meeting was getting under way, he recognized only Fred and young Haverkamp. "Hi, Jimmy," Ryan said, taking a seat. Ryan thought he recognized two other guys from the Wickstrom lecture, although he'd never met them.

Indeed, both young men had been at the Wickstrom meeting. They were David Andreas and James Thimm, both from Beatrice, Nebraska, in the southeastern part of the state. David and James were best friends. They'd met several years earlier through the Mennonite Church both had attended in Beatrice.

David was thirty; his chiseled features and dark hair made him a handsome man. Attracted to the Posse because of the poor financial shape of his own farm, David had first heard the Reverend Wickstrom eleven months earlier, in January 1982, at a meeting in Lincoln. In March, he'd attended his second lecture in Grand Island, Nebraska, and had taken James. Since then, they'd become full-fledged Posse followers.

James, twenty-four, was soft-spoken and shy. He too was good-looking—six one, with deep-set blue eyes and soft brown hair. James acknowledged Ryan with a smile.

Dead Fred was into his spiel on survival. "Think of your families! How will you survive and take care of them? We need bomb shelters and bunkers to protect ourselves. And, after the Battle of Armageddon, the world as we know it will be destroyed. There will be no conveniences, no electricity, no grocery stores, no hospitals—nothing that we have come to rely on.

"We will have only ourselves. Success will depend on how well we've planned ahead."

With that, he described his agenda, which concentrated on weaponry and explosives—the best kind to use, the prices, and how to acquire them.

According to his reputation, Dead Fred was so good with explosives, he could wire your mouth and blow out your teeth one at a time without ever hurting your lips.

"Food, too," he emphasized. "Stockpile now! Once the battle begins, you can forget about supermarkets."

He outlined the staples to store, how to store them, and where to store them. "Make sure you know how to hunt wild animals, too. There won't be any frozen meat to be had from the grocery store. Remember, you can eat a lot of wild animals—even sparrows or blackbirds, if you have to!''

Ryan spoke up. ''Well, let me tell you this . . . if you're going to have food stored, you sure as shit better have your weapons, too. If you haven't got anything to stop people from coming and taking your food, you're going to lose it. I've seen a lot of movies made about how those things can happen. People try to write them off as science fiction, but just wait and see what happens.''

David Andreas and James Thimm had kept an eye on Ryan from across the room. Now they nodded in agreement.

Point well taken, Dead Fred said, and talked on about first aid. ''Use Vaseline to clean wounds and cayenne pepper to stop bleeding.'' He paused for a moment. ''It stops bleeding for damned sure.''

The camp gave Mike Ryan and Jimmy Haverkamp a chance to become better acquainted. Fred's emphasis on weaponry was to their liking.

''I tell you,'' Mike noted to Jimmy during a break, ''all hell's going to break loose in the world.''

Jimmy nodded. ''Yahweh's wrath will be unbelievable.'' He was grim as he said it. He didn't doubt the ferocity of Yahweh's anger. He only hoped to be able to save his family before the final days.

They talked about guns, and Mike's knowledge impressed the younger man. ''I've always liked guns,'' Mike told him. ''Guess I take after my dad. He was sort of a gun nut.''

But more than his knowledge, Jimmy was impressed by Mike's toughness and sense of certainty, which became even more apparent that night when the group went to turn in.

Instead of rolling his sleeping bag out on the basement floor, Mike insisted on sleeping outside. ''Fuck it,'' he said. ''I'm not sleeping with a bunch of pansies.''

Jimmy watched Mike as he took his sleeping bag and half tent down by the pond, in spite of the thirty-degree temperature. Jimmy shook his head in admiration before climbing into his truck and driving home for the night.

The next morning, Dead Fred summed up the points he had made the day before. With each word, he emphasized the urgency of their task.

"Want a ride?" Jimmy called to Ryan as they were breaking camp.

Mike shrugged. "Sounds good to me."

Jimmy nodded his head. The drive to Whiting would give them more time to talk, more time to plan.

Before they left, James and David approached Ryan. "I'm James Thimm from Beatrice. This is my friend, David Andreas," James said.

Ryan shook James's hand. "How you boys doin'?"

"All right," James said.

"Say, what do you know about getting an HK 91?" James asked.

Mike frowned. "You can get one for about seven hundred dollars, but it's a piece of shit. Unless you're willing to spend twelve to fourteen hundred, you won't get much." He paused. "You need to know someone who can get you the military version."

"Makes sense," James said.

Then, Andreas handed Mike a slip of paper.

"What the hell's this?"

"Our names and phone numbers," David explained. "Wickstrom told us to contact you if we had any questions or if we wanted to get together to talk about things."

Ryan sucked in a deep breath. "Okay, if you want to find me, you can go through Steve Patterson, because if you come driving into my yard at night, you're liable to get your dicks blown off. I live out by myself and I don't appreciate any surprise visits."

"You got it," David said. He was, at least, impressed with Ryan's no-nonsense approach.

To Mike, the admiration in the young men's eyes was further proof that Wickstrom had confidence in him and that the confidence was well placed. The weekend had been a huge success.

CHAPTER 10

Mike returned home to the Whiting farmhouse shortly after noon. "I'm not eating for three days," he announced to Ruth. "I'm going to fast."

"Why?" she asked.

For a moment, he almost lost his temper. He wasn't going to win the admiration of such people as Haverkamp, Thimm, and Andreas, only to be challenged by the doubts of his wife. But he took a breath. "Because I need to," he said.

He didn't explain. He was ready to do Yahweh's will. "I can't go on without doing it," he said. That night, Mike Ryan prayed like he hadn't since he was a boy. He gave himself over to Yahweh's will wholeheartedly. If he was indeed chosen, he wanted to find out for sure.

The following morning, Ryan rolled out of bed at seven thirty. His first thought was of his fast. Since he could take liquids, he gulped down a cup of black coffee. A moment later, he was out the door and headed toward Maynard Patterson's farm to help chop down some trees. The wood would be used to stoke their wood stoves.

Ryan and Maynard pulled their pickup into a grove on the edge of Maynard's property and set about their task. Ryan yanked the cord on his eighteen-inch chain saw. The power tool growled to life. Its deafening roar echoed through the pasture.

Planting his feet firmly on the ground, Ryan angled the saw and pressed it into the soft bark of the elm tree. The churning steel teeth ripped through the bark, spitting wood chips back into his face.

As he worked throughout the day, Mike Ryan took time out to sip coffee from his thermos, nothing more. He was amazed at how much more time and energy he seemed to have when he didn't have to bother with food.

Even as he concentrated on the job at hand, he tried to keep his thoughts on Yahweh and the purpose of his fast. He was repenting. Images—often of his being unfaithful to Ruth—flashed through his mind, images of the past.

The first two days of the fast went well. Ryan managed to keep up his end of the work even without food. He was, in his mind, being nourished by Yahweh's power.

By the third day, he and Maynard were finishing up the work. Ryan was glad for that. He was beginning to feel weak.

"One more to go, Mike," Maynard said.

Mike smiled. He had done it!

He cut through the final tree. As he got down on his knees to finish out the cut, he suddenly felt faint.

At that moment, Maynard glanced up and saw Mike collapse. "Hey, Mike!" Maynard reached for Mike, but not before he had fallen forward on the ground, the grinding chain saw between his knees.

Maynard feared for Mike's leg as the saw danced into the ground, choking, spewing dirt and wood chips.

Maynard scrambled to the saw and switched it off. As he looked down, he was surprised to see that Mike's legs hadn't been touched. There was only a tear in his pants.

"Hey, Mike, wake up," Maynard said as he propped Mike against a stump. "Come on. I think we'd best get you something to eat. You're too weak to work."

Though still groggy, Mike was determined. "No," he said firmly. "I'm not eating anything until tomorrow morning."

Maynard shook his head. "Well, at least come up to the house and have something to drink," Maynard said.

Ryan sat at the kitchen table while Maynard boiled water and stirred in a cube of chicken bouillon. Mike didn't pay any attention to the older man. He was running his finger along his thigh through the tear in his jeans.

Maynard glanced at him. "You could have lost your leg. Ever think of that?"

Mike nodded.

"Maybe someone upstairs is trying to tell you something."

Ryan looked at the old man and smiled. "Maybe you're right."

Mike Ryan drank three cups of chicken broth before returning to the grove with Maynard to finish up. The next day, he woke up and felt deeply and genuinely spiritual. Yahweh had heard him and had accepted his fasting and repentance.

There would be no turning back for Mike Ryan now. He believed he had received the blessing of God himself.

CHAPTER **11**

J ames Thimm folded the top of the brown paper
bag and slid the sack of nails across the counter toward his
customer. "Two pounds, sixteen smooth box. Three dollars
plus tax," he said, sounding indifferent.

The customer, a local man, picked up the bag, tipped his
cap, and walked out the front door of Sack's Lumber Yard
in Beatrice, Nebraska.

As the door closed behind the customer, James leaned
over the U-shaped counter, rested his chin in the palms of
his hands, and gazed out the plate-glass windows of the
storefront.

At first, James didn't notice his boss, Allen Schroeder,
coming down the back hallway from the offices to the front
of the store. Schroeder stopped for a moment and eyed
James. What's gotten into that kid? he wondered.

James had been working at Sack's for almost four years,
and he'd been one of Schroeder's best employees. He had
been an eager worker, quick to smile and help a customer.
But lately, Schroeder had noticed a dramatic change in him.
Somber and always preoccupied with religion, James had
lately become an employee who simply put in his time.

Schroeder was at a loss as to how to handle the situation. Anyone but James he might very well have threatened to fire. But James had been with him so long . . . Besides, Schroeder felt a bit parental toward the young man. James's parents had left two years earlier for a three-year tour as missionaries in Africa. And being alone for the first time in his life had rendered James vulnerable, Schroeder thought.

As a result, Schroeder found himself treading a fine line between being James's employer and trying to be his friend. "James, I could use your help out back on a delivery," Schroeder called to the front counter.

"Oh, okay," James said, slowly turning to face his boss. "Sure, no problem," he said without enthusiasm. He followed Schroeder to the yard, toward the shrill sound of buzz saws and the smell of fresh sawdust.

As James listened to his instructions, Schroeder felt troubled for the young man. He was convinced that many of the changes he was seeing were the result of James's involvement with the Posse, which Schroeder knew little about beyond the fact that it was a religious-political fringe group.

That Schroeder knew little about the Posse was not James's fault. He would gladly have shared information with anyone about the group, any time.

As he completed his task, James approached Allen Schroeder. "By the way, I was wondering if I could get this Saturday off. I have an important meeting . . . uh, the Reverend Wickstrom is going to be speaking . . ."

Schroeder made a face. It wasn't the first time James had made such a request. "That's a bit awkward for me," Schroeder replied honestly. "You know everyone's on a five-and-a-half-day work week here. Saturday's a busy day. If I let you off, it'll mean more work for the other guys." Schroeder hoped that by appealing to James's sense of community he might convince him not to want the day off.

"It's real important," James insisted.

Schroeder lowered his eyes. "Yeah, James, I suppose it'll be all right."

"Thank you."

"Listen, James, I know it's not any of my business, but

I'd hate to see a good guy like you get hurt. Watch yourself with these groups, okay? Make sure you know what they're up to before you do anything they're going to regret.''

"I have to place Yahweh God first in my life, even if that's difficult for others to understand.''

"James, you're a great kid, a damned good worker. Whatever it is you're getting into, you must see that if it was genuinely good it wouldn't damage other parts of your life . . .''

Schroeder's words and concerns fell on deaf ears. The dramatic change in James's attitude had begun some nine months earlier. That was about the time James had begun hitting the surrounding towns to hear the Reverend Wickstrom preach. James had also regularly attended local Posse meetings. In short, he was hooked on the word. Schroeder knew he could no longer count on James to be on time. He was curt with customers. He no longer seemed anxious to learn.

Schroeder shook his head as he watched James leave that afternoon. He just didn't see how much longer he was going to be able to protect the young man.

James drove a few blocks from his work to his home on North Fourteenth Street, pulling up in front of the single-car garage and getting out. A small, hand-painted sign over the doorbell read, BLESS THIS HOUSE AND ALL WHO ENTER. James picked up the newspaper from the porch and went inside.

The modest yellow house had been home to James since he was eight years old. The neat, middle-class home reflected the character of the family who dwelt there— conscientious and hardworking. James's mother was a registered nurse and his father had been a farmer before going to work for a Beatrice farm implement dealership.

As he sat down, James glanced at the black-and-white family photos on his mother's antique organ. The house was well-kept. As usual, James had the basement to himself. He spent most of his time there.

Visiting the house, one would have no trouble imagining the kind and gentle young man who had first started working for Sack's Lumber Yard. The household was deeply religious—they were Mennonites. In fact, James was actually a foster child whom Carl and Hilda Schmidt had adopted from a family in their local church.

James's real parents, Frank and Betty Thimm, were also members of the Mennonite Church in Beatrice. Although she'd already had four children, James's mother had been institutionalized for chronic mental illness when she was pregnant with James. It was clear that she would be unable to care for her child when he was born.

Having a caring regard for Betty Thimm, the Schmidts inquired about taking the baby to raise. With the help of their minister, they took James home from the hospital.

James always knew that he had a second family. He knew that, if his mother recovered, he would be free to return to his "natural family." In the meantime, the Schmidts loved him as their own, doted on him. "He's brought such joy to our home," they'd told their friends and family.

But by early 1982, with his parents in Africa, the house was quiet, the entire family gone. Karen, ten years his elder, was teaching grade school art in Manhattan, Kansas. His brother, Melvin, had a Ph.D. in physics and was working on research in Indiana. His youngest sister, Ruth, was married and living in Washington state.

James had not gone on to college like his siblings, although he had been an above-average student at Beatrice High. He'd been fairly active, too. He participated in German Club and the Madrigal Singers; he had a lovely singing voice—perfect pitch, they said. He simply had no interest in striking out on his own after high school.

He'd seemed happy, working at Sack's and living in the basement of his parents' house. After their mom and dad left for Africa, Karen had teased him, "I've never heard of the parents leaving home and the kid staying."

In spite of the teasing, the others knew how difficult it would be for James to be alone in the house. Karen called frequently and visited whenever she could—especially on holidays.

Not only did she feel this was her duty as the eldest child, but she wanted to stay in touch—she'd always enjoyed being around James. She'd been his first baby-sitter; they had a special bond.

But now, the pleasure Karen had always felt in her brother's company was becoming strained. Like Schroeder, she recognized that James was going through some difficult and unpleasant changes. But, unlike Schroeder, she had no fine line to walk. She was concerned when she realized that something was very, very wrong.

CHAPTER 12

Karen Schmidt had a gnawing feeling in the pit of her stomach as she headed for Beatrice to visit her brother James. She was anxious to get there—she desperately wanted to know what was going on with him. She'd been so taken aback by the prophecies of gloom and doom he'd rambled on about over the phone—the Antichrist, weapons, and violence. This wasn't the James she knew.

Karen, an intelligent, attractive woman, thirtyish, with her mother's brown eyes, wore her shoulder-length dark hair in ringlets around her face. Arriving at the Schmidt house in the late morning, she bounded up the sidewalk, looking forward to seeing her brother. But James greeted her with an unenthusiastic hug. She found him to be almost totally preoccupied.

At first, she tried to act like everything was normal and brought up interests they shared, but it was as if she was talking to a stranger.

"How about a walk in the country?" she asked.

He shrugged. "No, thanks."

"A game of Monopoly?" James loved board games and always played competitively.

He shook his head.

She was at a loss for what to do. "James, what's going on with you?"

"Karen," he said, coming closer to her and beginning to talk with a sense of urgency, "you have to understand. The Jew-run banks are out to take the farmers' land away and there are secret organizations out there that are planning to overthrow the government. The odds are, they'll succeed within the next five years."

"What are you talking about?" she asked, hearing only paranoia.

"Karen, the Jews are the Antichrist. It's not like we were taught. Jesus wasn't Jewish. He was from an Israeli tribe, but he wasn't Jewish. He was a white Anglo-Saxon. So were his disciples . . ."

James was as frustrated as Karen. He wanted her to know the truth, but it was plain to him that she was resisting. She kept asking strange questions. She doubted what he was saying.

"We have to be ready to make America the New Jerusalem," he said. "The whites should not mix their seed with other races. Jesus came only to save his own people—the white Anglo-Saxons.

"We have got to purify America . . ."

"James, James, listen to me!" she cried, taking him by the shoulders and shaking him. "What you are saying is making no sense."

She was frightened by the expression on his face and the way his eyes glazed over.

"True believers must be prepared for war," he declared. "We must gather with people of like minds and collect our weapons and stockpile food."

"James!" she cried, losing control. "What's happened to you?" Mennonites were conscientious objectors to all war. They would never pick up a gun. One of the basic tenets of their faith was nonviolence. To hear James preach war and violence was more than she could handle. "Where are you getting these ideas?" she asked.

"James, I can understand your concern for suffering farmers. Dad was a farmer once. But all this . . . I don't get it."

"We have to protect our families and our land. A man who doesn't take care of his family is worse than a viper. With this country's government more crooked than ever, we each have to be prepared to fight. We must be ready.

"And don't believe what you read and hear in the papers and on television. That's all a lie.

"And why should Mom and Dad have gone to another country to help people when we have people starving right here in America? Who cares about what happens to those jungle bunnies in Africa . . ."

"But James," Karen countered, "you mean to say I shouldn't have black friends? You've met some of my black friends . . . how can you say that?"

"They're an impure race. Jesus came for the true Israelites, the white Anglo-Saxons," he insisted.

Karen tried to reason with her brother, but her logic wasn't getting through to him. She talked about their faith and their religion, about the values they'd shared their entire lives, but it was as if she was talking to the wall.

The more they talked, the worse it got. Karen feared that their relationship was deteriorating, along with the conversation. She tried to think of what she could do. He's angry with our parents for leaving him alone, she thought. This is his way of rebelling and I'm getting the brunt of it.

The more she considered this, the more sound it appeared. She remembered her own rebellion in her late teens and early twenties, around the time of Vietnam; she'd done the things that she knew would irritate her parents the most.

She hoped that getting James out of town might help. They would be leaving for Africa to visit their folks in a couple of months. They already had their tickets. In fact, the visit had been planned long before their parents' departure.

Karen was excited about making the trip. She had already had her shots and gotten her passport. But James had been procrastinating and hadn't gotten anything done.

"Maybe I can go with you to get your passport pictures taken," she suggested later.

James didn't respond and went down to his room in the basement. Karen retired to her old bedroom. She tossed and turned most of the night, worried about James.

Karen left the next morning. Again trying to act as if everything was normal, she climbed into her car and waved good-bye.

She was really worried now—scared was more like it. What in the world was James into? What was he talking about? Why was he so paranoid, especially about national issues? And what was this talk of violence?

She wondered if there could be a connection to the war games he'd gotten hooked on. She knew he'd been driving to Lincoln weekly where he met a group of guys in the back room of the Hobby Shop. From what she understood, they played complicated board games in which historical battles were simulated; players moved little figurines across battlefields and followed intricate rules for troop movement and battle strategy. A game could last over several evenings.

Whatever had happened, Karen was stunned at the contrast between the James she'd known and the one she'd just left. She flashed on old images of him—the jovial, easygoing James. She remembered him in the blue bathrobe that she'd made for him, sitting in the living room rocker, listening to the Beatles and singing "Yellow Submarine" at the top of his lungs, tapping his bare foot in time with the music. When Karen had teased him about his long feet, he'd laughed and replied, "God bent my ankles too soon."

She remembered how much fun he'd had just a Christmas ago, when he had made building blocks for his nephew. He'd been painstaking in cutting the wood, sanding and painting the blocks himself. Mostly, he'd enjoyed the giving.

What had happened to that James? Now, it just didn't make sense. What had crawled inside James's mind and taken over, she wondered. One thing was for sure. She was going to find out. Maybe she should consult a psychologist.

Meantime, she was not altogether surprised to hear from James by mail several days after her visit.

Dear Karen,

This will be the hardest letter I have ever written in my life.

As you hmay have possibly noticed, I've been a little

depressed in the last month or so. I have received a lot of bad information about our house. I cannot leave until it is cleaned up.

What I mean to tell you is that I'm not going to Africa this summer or ever until my house is cleaned up. This is why I've not gotten my shots. I knew this even before your visit . . . I know you may think I'm crazy but if the world would know what I know, you wouldn't think so.

Karen, I do love you very much but I just can't go to Africa with anyone. I love Mom and Dad very much, too, but I love God, Jesus the Messiah, more. We had a good talk and we decided I should not go.

Please read the following verses in the King James version: Matthew 15:24, Matthew 10:6, Matthew 10:34, Matthew 10:21, Luke 19:27. Please read these in order. I'm also writing to Mom and Dad. I still love you very much.

Love,
James

Karen read and then reread the letter before running to her bedroom to get her Bible. The letter still in her hand, she sat on the edge of the bed and quickly flipped through the pages, searching out the Scripture James had instructed her to read. Perhaps she'd get a clue about what he was thinking.

The first verse in Matthew read: "But he answered and said, I am not sent but unto the lost sheep of the house of Israel." The second verse read, "But go rather to the lost sheep of the house of Israel."

"The house of Israel, the house of Israel," Karen muttered to herself. This house of Israel, she surmised, might be what James meant in his letter when he talked about getting his house in order. For him, maybe it was like his spiritual house. That might be it, she decided.

Karen closed the Bible and reread the letter.

CHAPTER 13

Mike had known Steve for a long time, since high school, and could tell that Steve had felt slighted by Wickstrom. Mike figured Steve was jealous that he and Wickstrom had hit it off.

Both Mike and Steve had strong egos, and since the meeting with Wickstrom, Mike could feel the tension mounting. Now, they never missed an opportunity to disagree with each other. As a result, their relationship was gradually disintegrating. The final break came in the spring of 1983.

The Pattersons and the Ryans had planted a garden. They had agreed to share the garden's produce, but the Pattersons had taken all the potatoes.

"I can't believe that son of a bitch would do something like that!" Mike descended into the kind of violent rage he'd avoided since his fast. "I should destroy him! I swear, I will never, ever have anything else to do with that bastard."

But a couple of days after his anger had subsided, Ryan began to question his judgment about Steve. Perhaps he wasn't right to shut Steve out of his life. After all, Steve was his brother-in-law. He wasn't sure if he was doing the right thing.

Ryan walked into the kitchen. "Ruth, you're not on your period, are you?"

Ruth looked up from the sink. "No."

Mike thought for a second. She was physically and spiritually clean, then. "Let's see what Yahweh has to say about Steve."

"Okay," Ruth said, drying her hands and coming over to Mike.

Although Mike had spoken to Yahweh a number of times through the arm test with Steve, this was the first time he had used Ruth as a partner. "Stand here and face me," he said, directing Ruth. He brought Ruth's arm out with his own hand on her wrist. "Yahweh, Heavenly Father, are we clean enough to speak with you?"

Ruth's arm stayed up.

Mike looked her in the eye. He was pleased. "Yahweh, Heavenly Father, should I try to correct things with Steve Patterson?"

Slowly, Ruth felt her arm descend.

Wanting to make sure, Mike addressed another question to Yahweh. "Yahweh, am I asking the correct question?"

Ruth's arm rose.

"Yahweh, was the argument with Steve my fault?"

Her arm dropped.

"Should we be friends again?"

No.

Mike Ryan thought quietly for a moment. He felt he had to be sure. "Yahweh, are you happy with the way things are?"

Yes.

"Will I understand the reason for all this later on?"

Ruth's arm jerked up, almost pulling her over.

Ryan looked at his wife and nodded his head. This arm test worked; he liked it.

Ruth felt vitally connected to both Yahweh and to Mike. "I can't understand what made my arm move," she said, truly mystified. But whatever the force was, she liked this bond between her and Mike.

The arm test was based on faith—a faith that became an important facet of the Ryans' lives. They came to depend on it.

Mike listened to the Wickstrom tapes over and over again. Soon he had memorized the Scriptures and could quote them with the ease of a scholar.

Steve Patterson was finished with Mike Ryan . . . though not because of the argument over potatoes. Steve saw Mike going off on a new power trip—one that Steve didn't want to be a part of. Mike was headed for trouble, Steve told his wife.

CHAPTER 14

Comfortable in his faith now, and considering himself a true believer, Mike Ryan began attending a series of weekly Bible studies at the homes of area Posse members.

Ryan saw more and more of Jimmy Haverkamp, David Andreas, and James Thimm at these meetings. They also showed him deference and respect. Sometimes they met at Nate Babcock's; other times, the four of them got together at Jimmy Haverkamp's. The "Bible" meetings focused more on everyone's gripes about taxes and the Jewish conspiracy to screw up the economy than religion, but Ryan attended them purely out of interest and commitment to Yahweh. There was not enough talk about the calling of Yahweh in these meetings. He remained unmoved by talk of the Constitution, government loans, the crooked banks, and the Jews.

The farmers in the group tolerated Ryan's indifference to their problems. Ryan didn't seem to understand or care about their going under. In earlier years, when land values were high, farmers had borrowed heavily. But now, as land prices declined sharply, federal land banks were calling in debts, and a lot of farmers couldn't make it. In the past two years, four thousand farms in Nebraska and Kansas had gone out of business; about half of those were forced out because of the economy. To make matters worse, drought during the past couple of years had cut corn yields nearly in half.

As Ryan became increasingly bored with the farmers' talk of agricultural and constitutional issues, his attendance at the meetings dropped off. It was no disappointment to the older men in the membership. They'd seen right through Mike Ryan. "He never cared about fighting taxes like the rest of us, who wanted to save ourselves. He just cared about getting next to Wickstrom, being a big shot," Ted Stone remarked. "He was just a windbag," one member said. "Yeah, I got tired of all his tales about being a mercenary and about his women," said another. Nate Badcock was glad to see him go, too. "That guy had an ego," he told the men. "He wants to be an authority, control everything."

Ryan's break with Steve had left him isolated. Mike and Steve had known each other from high school days. Now Ryan no longer had someone he could discuss his ideas with, and he felt the loss of that kind of companionship acutely.

The following morning, Mike made the fifteen-mile trip from Whiting to Mercier. When he pulled his pickup into Jimmy's yard, Jimmy came out on the porch to greet him. "Come on in."

"No. Thanks. All I know is that Yahweh instructed me to come down here and tell you that if you want to come and talk to me, it's okay."

"Oh," Jimmy said, neither surprised nor disturbed by the message.

"If you want to talk to me, you can come see me," Ryan said. Then he jumped back into his truck, backed down the driveway, and returned home to Whiting.

Two days later, Jimmy Haverkamp came knocking on Mike Ryan's door. He had thought a great deal about the short visit. "If Yahweh's telling him things, he must be special," he concluded.

Mike invited him into the house. They sat in the kitchen. "What's on your mind?" Mike asked simply.

Jimmy knotted his hands on the table. "Steve Patterson is saying some wild stuff about you," he said straight out.

"Really?" Mike said, bristling.

"Yeah, he says that you've got the demon seed of the devil in you and that we should be careful about being around you."

Jimmy expected Ryan to explode. Instead, Mike reacted calmly. In an almost amused tone, he said, "Well, if you believe that, then you better get out of here or I'll corrupt your ass."

Jimmy looked up to see Mike Ryan's eyes boring down on him. "It sounded strange to me," he confessed, once again coming under the influence of Mike's dominating personality and his certainty. "Why would Steve say that about you when he knows that Wickstrom makes a point of seeing you when he's down this way? Why would he think you're evil?"

"Why do you think?"

"I don't know. Unless someone's not telling me the truth."

Ryan didn't say anything. He didn't like learning that Steve was saying things about him, but there was nothing he could do about it. Besides, it only went to prove that Yahweh had directed him well—they were done, he and Steve. "I have more important things to tend to than Steve Patterson's bitter feelings," he said calmly. "Yahweh said, 'I came not to bring peace but to send a sword.' Everybody's running around talking about peace, but there isn't going to be any peace. There's a lot of shit about to come down in this world, pure and simple. As you know, our beliefs don't put us in the majority."

Jimmy had arrived with a mind filled with confusion. He'd wanted to get to the root of whatever the conflict was between Mike and Steve. Instead, he found himself no longer caring. It was clear that Mike had the direct line to Yahweh.

When Steve said those things about Mike, he was angry, blustery. Mike simply dismissed them outright. And Jimmy thought, we do have more important things to worry about. The world's coming to an end as we know it.

"You're right," Jimmy said. "Us with like minds should stick together." He said this as much to cement Mike's regard for him as make an observation. If Mike was ready to fight the Battle of Armageddon, he wanted to be a soldier beside him.

"You know, that battle is going to break out right here in Kansas," Mike told Jimmy. "*Armageddon* means 'battle of the wheat fields.' We're right here in the middle of it all."

"Yeah, that's right," Jimmy responded.

"I figure there'll be invasions on us from the north and from the south. It's going to be a hell of a battle."

Weapons would be of the utmost importance; their discussion turned to the guns they'd begun collecting. Jimmy had been spending every spare dime on guns. They talked about strategies for the battle. "Mike, you sure have a lot of ideas on what we need to do," Jimmy remarked.

"Yeah, a lot of these ideas I pull from my time in Vietnam. Spent a lot of years in the military," Mike told him.

Jimmy was impressed.

"I was in the Green Berets. That's how I lost two toes on my left foot—in Nam. Hurt like hell, but it didn't keep me out of action."

Jimmy leaned forward. Mike had never talked about being in Vietnam before. "What did you do in Vietnam?"

Mike paused. A lump came to his throat. "It hurts to talk about it," he said. "At one point, I was discharged for taking down a lieutenant I was mad at. A military psychiatrist had them put me in a straitjacket. I was pretty mad, I guess. Later on, I was with the CIA; I can't divulge too much about that, though. But I'm proud of my service, I'll tell you that."

Young Haverkamp was overwhelmed. He had no idea Ryan had been in Vietnam. As a war hero in their midst, Ryan could understand the urgency of the times. "We really need to start preparing," Jimmy admitted. "I don't worry about myself so much . . . it's my family—Mom, Dad, my sisters and little brother—I worry about.''

''Yeah. I'm not worried about myself, either.''

Jimmy glanced at his watch. He had to be moving along, he told Mike.

''So, long, bud,'' Mike said.

Jimmy smiled as he drove off. He was proud to have Mike Ryan as a friend.

CHAPTER 15

Zeal for Yahweh and trepidation at the coming Battle of Armageddon cemented the relationship between Mike Ryan and Jimmy Haverkamp. They dropped by each other's house at least once a week. Sometimes Mike would spend a couple of days at Jimmy's, helping with chores. Other times, Jimmy would visit Mike and Ruth, the three of them visiting late into the night, often over games of Yahtzee or cards. Jimmy, now divorced, found that his new friendship with Mike took the edge off his loneliness, and he appreciated Mike's insights about life.

Jimmy could tell that Ryan understood his anguish over his marriage breaking up. Often in the course of their long talks, Jimmy saw that Mike Ryan was the kind of guy who cared deeply about his friends. When one of them hurt, Mike hurt along with them. Jimmy, who'd been relatively happy-go-lucky prior to this point in his life, was grateful for a friend who understood the kind of pain he now suffered.

Ryan predicted that Jimmy's wife would leave. He was right—she did.

"I hope the separation is just temporary," Jimmy said sadly. "I keep thinking she'll come back."

"Maybe Yahweh is trying to tell you something—that she's not the right woman for you, pure and simple," Ryan said, sure of himself.

"Maybe so," Jimmy said, warming up to the idea. "Maybe so." Surely God's plan for him was all powerful, he thought.

"I sorta know how you feel," Ryan said when the two of them were alone. "I'm praying for change in my life— trying to give up smokin' dope and runnin' around with other women. We've got to trust Yahweh."

"You make a good point," Jimmy said. Mike's trust in Yahweh and desire to do His will were the things that had most impressed Jimmy.

But their personal problems were not their only topic of conversation. Jimmy and Ryan discussed endlessly the way the Russians or the Chinese would move against America, precipitating the end.

"The Russians can move a whole division of airborne troops anywhere you want inside of twenty-four hours," Ryan explained to Jimmy. "They've got a million troops sitting up there in Siberia. They're ready to go any time. Look what they did to the Germans."

Jimmy didn't know his history well enough to challenge Ryan's facts, but Ryan sounded like a man in the know when it came to military strategy. As Mike drew Jimmy closer to him, he also drew James Thimm and David Andreas into the relationship.

All four of them had a serious interest in weapons by now. Haverkamp had already amassed a number of guns, including an automatic AR-15, the civilian version of the M-16. He wasn't going to be caught unarmed when the final battle came.

Mike became their leader. By virtue of his age, his intelligence, his preferred relationship with Wickstrom, and his knowledge of weaponry and survival techniques, he drew the three younger men into his aura. They respected him. There could be no doubt who controlled their discussions and who led the way in devising strategies for the Battle of Armageddon.

Mike was also their spiritual leader. Increasingly, they

admired his unshakable confidence, his faith in Yahweh. He had communicated directly with Yahweh and he had studied the Bible thoroughly, as well as listened to Wickstrom's cassette tapes over and over. The three men looked to him for substantive answers to their concerns.

From what they'd learned, they knew that the Battle of Armageddon was imminent. It could come this week or the next, or next year, or in the next decade. No one could know for sure when the first shot would be fired. But it was at their doorstep.

Weeks later, as they sat around Jimmy's kitchen table, they knew they had some plans to make.

"The name *Armageddon* means 'wheat field,'" Mike reminded them again. Based on this etymology, he concluded that the Battle of Armageddon would take place in Kansas. He had no trouble convincing his friends of this. There was no one among them who was aware that there was such a field near Megiddo in Israel where scholars believed the battle was envisioned.

They wouldn't have cared about what the scholars had to say in any case. Knowledge wasn't what they thirsted for unless it was knowledge that further "proved" what they already believed.

Who among them could challenge Ryan's assertion that the battle would take place in Kansas because it was one of the nation's top wheat-producing states? To them, it was as clear as crystal.

"According to the Old Testament," Ryan taught them, "one hundred forty-four thousand Israelites will fight in the battle, twelve thousand from each of the twelve tribes. Of that number, seven thousand will be an elite corps."

Considering themselves part of that elite corps, the four of them found a sense of purpose. Indeed, it was a noble cause. They planned to do battle with Satan's forces and they planned to kick ass.

As time went on, Ryan took on a more and more dominant tone. One afternoon, he and the group got down to some serious discussion about preparing for the battle.

"You know, we're going to need a hell of a lot of things to get ready," Jimmy said. "Not only guns, but food, clothing, all kinds of supplies—utensils, canteens, flashlights, batteries . . ."

"I been thinking about all that," Ryan interrupted.

"It all costs money," David offered. "It would cost a fortune to get all that kind of stuff together."

The others agreed.

"If we had some calves to raise, we could sell them," Jimmy suggested. "Trouble is, we don't have any livestock."

Ryan let them go on for a few minutes. "I've already thought of that," he assured them. "There is a way for Yahweh to get us what He wants us to have, if we're going to get ready for the battle.

"Stop and think about it. When Moses led the Israelites out of bondage in Egypt after four hundred and thirty years, they just took what they needed."

Ryan opened his Bible to Exodus, chapter 12, and ran his forefinger down the page as he read: ". . . And the children of Israel did according to the word of Moses; and they borrowed of the Egyptians jewels . . . and clothing . . . and the Lord gave them favor in sight of the Egyptians, so that they lent unto them such things as they required."

"So, see," Ryan said, closing the Bible, "the Israelites had been slaves so long, they had the things they took coming to them. They needed it and they deserved it. It's the same kind of thing with us. It's all for a greater cause. And besides, everything on this earth belongs to Yahweh."

The three young men sat in silence, pondering Ryan's proposal. Simply put, they should steal what they needed.

"But why take my word for it?" Ryan asked. Ryan positioned Jimmy in front of him, face-to-face, putting his hand on Jimmy's wrist.

Within moments, they were relieved to learn that Yahweh agreed with Mike. Even better, according to Yahweh, they should take things only from people who were not true Israelites.

"And, is it so, Yahweh, that insurance will cover the loss of property we take?" Ryan asked.

Again, the answer was yes.

Jimmy and the others were fascinated by the arm test. They had been confused by it at first, but they'd come to develop a gut-level trust in it. "It's the darnedest thing," Jimmy had said. "I can't figure out what makes my arm move." But now, it was faith—faith in the arm test that convinced him and the others of Mike's true connection to God.

In the beginning Mike had used the arm test to ask simple questions—about fasting and repentance; then, he'd begun using it to check their faith in Yahweh, even pinpointing what members of the group had been thinking. "Yahweh knows you're having doubts about your faith," he'd told each of them more than once. Each time, he'd been right. Later, through the arm test, Ryan had shown an uncanny knack for predicting future events. Baffled by the ongoing accuracy of the arm test, their reliance on it became absolute. "I believe it," David had told the others. "I've seen too many things happen that Mike said would happen."

Ryan increasingly provided the assurance and affirmation they so desperately needed at this point in their lives—a time of great vulnerability brought on by losses, both financial and personal. They had come to believe that, indeed, Ryan was a divinely inspired prophet of Yahweh. "God's will is the most important thing to Mike. He understands the truth," Jimmy had told David.

Now, as Jimmy lifted his arm to the heavens, little did he or the others realize that by surrendering to Yahweh, they were, unknowingly, submitting their minds to the control of Mike Ryan. What felt like surrendering to Yahweh was actually an extreme dependence, deepening psychologically and emotionally. Their personal identities were eroding as they sank deeper into Ryan's power. As their old sense of themselves diminished, they emerged with new identities, soldiers of Yahweh, ready to do whatever it took to please their God.

Their faith empowered Ryan. He was impressed with

how easily he'd convinced the young men. In fact, he convinced them so easily that he was beginning to become convinced himself. Wickstrom had been right. The answers he needed could be found, if only he looked hard enough.

As Ryan considered his three associates, he felt more than pride—he felt the euphoria of power.

CHAPTER 16

A light rain was falling as Ryan, Jimmy, and James parked in front of the St. Marys Surplus Sales, a bright yellow corner building on the main street of St. Marys, Kansas, a small town about seventy miles south of Whiting.

A copper bell, tied with twine to the front door of the shop, clanged as they entered. The place was chock-full of army surplus goods. Shelves went to the ceiling with clothing, blankets, and field gear. Floor racks were packed tight with pants and shirts—army tans and greens.

"Mornin'." Mike nodded to the woman running the store.

Pat Wiltz and her husband had run the store for years. "Help you?" she asked.

"We need gear," Mike told her. "Uh, for starters, we need combat boots."

"Right this way." Mrs. Wiltz directed them toward the rear of the store. She'd been out of combat boots but had received a huge box of assorted boots that very morning. "You're in luck—we got a big shipment in just this morning."

Ryan grinned at Jimmy and James as they followed her to

the shoe section. "See, Yahweh's taking care of us," Ryan said.

Both Jimmy and James agreed. Things were happening for a reason, they knew.

"We need field gear, too," Ryan told Mrs. Wiltz.

She led them to the field gear racks, where they picked up complete field packs: ammunition pouches, boot knives, canteens, and eighteen-inch military machetes, pistol belts, and butt packs.

In the next aisle, Ryan eyed a pile of fake hand grenades with childlike fascination. "Got any more of these?" he asked.

"That's all we have," Mrs. Wiltz replied.

"We'll take 'em."

"We'll need some of this," Ryan exclaimed, picking up a tube of camouflage face paint. Ryan pointed to the sleeping bags stacked up along the wall. "Yep, we need several."

Pat Wiltz pulled five bags, olive drab, from the shelf. As she totaled the sale, Ryan looked over a rack of military insignias. He'd take several insignias, including some sergeants', he decided.

Ryan pulled a wad of cash from his shirt pocket and paid the bill.

Pat Wiltz watched from the store window as Ryan and the two young men loaded the gear and drove off. For the life of her, she couldn't figure out what they were up to.

CHAPTER 17

M ary Babcock, Nate's wife, was breathless as she dialed the operator. "Give me the Brown County sheriff—this is an emergency!"

"Brown County sheriff," the dispatcher answered on the first ring.

"This is Mary Babcock, southeast of town. We've been robbed. Our home has been ransacked!" Her voice quivered.

"We'll send someone right out, Mrs. Babcock."

Mary Babcock hung up the phone and joined her husband as they examined the broken glass of the back door. It was about 10:30 P.M. Whoever had broken in had done so sometime between two o'clock that afternoon and just now, when the Babcocks had come home.

"I guess it wasn't too hard to get in, huh?" Nate said, observing how they could have reached through the broken window and unbolted the door. He tried to stay calm.

"For God's sake, who could have done this?" Mary said. "Nate, all your guns are gone!"

"I know," he said. As he looked at his gun case, he noticed that about six cases of shotgun shells were also missing.

The house was a mess. Not a room had been left untouched. Cabinets, desk drawers, and dresser drawers had been left hanging open in each room. The mattresses had been thrown off the beds.

"They did get about a hundred dollars' worth of silver quarters I had rolled," Nate said, "but look here." He pointed to a closet shelf. "They missed these rolls of half dollars and silver dollars." He forced a chuckle.

"Oh, Nate," Mary said, "they took the VCR and a bunch of your tapes, too." She sat on the sofa; the sense of having been violated was soaking in.

Nate put his arm around Mary. "Don't worry, it'll be okay. We'll be okay," he consoled her.

Just then, they saw the headlights of a car coming up the lane. It was the Brown County sheriff. As Mary walked through the kitchen to meet the sheriff at the back door, she paused as a piece of material on the floor caught her eye. She reached down and picked it up. She turned the patch of material over in her fingers several times. It looked like military stripes off some kind of uniform.

CHAPTER 18

Rick Stice trudged through the mud, lugging two more buckets of feed out to his hog shed. Eager sows snorted and squealed as they crowded to the trough. Emptying the last bucket, Rick pushed his way through the hungry sows and over to the other end of the shed. He dropped the buckets and leaned up against a farrowing crate. He was exhausted, physically and emotionally. His wife was dying and he was going broke. He looked out over the farmstead, wondering if he could ever get his life together again.

He looked older than his twenty-seven years. Stress was taking its toll. He removed his cap and pushed back his mop of dark hair, exposing a band of pale skin at the temples, shaded from the sun by his cap. To judge by his lean body and solid arms, he'd been a hard worker.

Rick lived on the eighty-acre farm near Rulo, Nebraska, with his wife Sondra and their three kids. They lived in a trailer house—white with faded brown shutters. Rick had married Sondra, his high school sweetheart, in 1976; they had been sixteen. The first of their three children, Ora, had been born a few months later. Barry had been born in 1978 and Luke had come along in 1980. By the time Luke was born, the family was struggling to make ends meet. No matter what they did, they seemed to lose ground rather than gain it. To economize, the Stices lived modestly and entertained themselves inexpensively. They'd quit going to movies. They participated in community catfish fries and other such events. The children wore hand-me-downs.

Since high school, Rick and his dad had farmed the place, fifty-fifty. But since Rick had taken over almost four years ago, when his dad had retired, he'd struggled to make ends meet. Rick farmed ten acres—corn, mostly. But for the past two years, the crop had failed. Last year, he'd planted in May, but heavy rains had flooded the fields, and the corn had only grown to five feet. He never harvested the crop. This year, rains had washed away the herbicides. The field filled with weeds; by July, the crop was ruined.

Thanks to the hog business, it seemed for a couple of years that they would be able to survive, but now escalating costs and reduced profits were making it tough to meet living expenses and make the bank payment.

By spring 1982, they had dropped their health insurance to use the money to cover their loans from the Richardson County Bank. They lived from day to day, keeping their fingers crossed.

Rick wasn't good at dealing with stress. There were times when he would stay in his fields and gaze out at the horizon, wondering how he was ever going to get through these trying times.

They did take some solace in the fact that they were not alone in their troubles. Many of their friends and neighbors were suffering similar difficulties. Then, Rick was dealt a hand he couldn't cope with.

A month after canceling their health insurance, Sondra was diagnosed as having Hodgkin's disease—a deadly form of cancer.

Rick argued with his former insurance carrier, trying to convince the company to take the family back on, but to no avail. There would be no insurance to cover the expensive treatments that Sondra would need.

The Stices had hit rock bottom.

"What're we going to do?" Sondra would ask tearfully after the children had been put to bed.

"I don't know," he'd whisper. "I don't know."

Becoming more and more terrified, Rick and Sondra began to attend meetings of the Posse Comitatus after a former state senator had given Rick a brochure about a Wickstrom lecture. Given their financial desperation, it didn't take the Stices long to embrace the Posse's antitax doctrine.

Eagerly attending the ongoing Bible studies, they first met David Andreas. Somewhat of a self-proclaimed health nut, Andreas had visited Dr. John Ray in Wisconsin, a holistic doctor, and was on one of his vitamin programs. Ray was a friend of the Reverend Wickstrom.

Encouraged by David's regard for the doctor, Rick and Sondra visited Dr. Ray. He talked about using body electronics and acupressure.

"You have to be very careful about what you eat," he told her. "Cancer feeds on cells."

Sondra, whose disease was progressing rapidly, did not feel up to undergoing Dr. Ray's full treatment. But they thanked him for his advice and traveled back to Nebraska.

About six weeks later, Sondra's health was deteriorating rapidly. She had undergone chemotherapy, funded by welfare. But the treatments had made her violently ill and she had vowed never to repeat them if her cancer progressed. Now, she was dying.

It was Easter weekend. Sondra, too weak to sit up and in pain, was confined to a reclining chair in the living room of the trailer. Rick carried food to her, helped her onto the portable commode beside the chair, and tried to make her as comfortable as possible.

Rick, lying on the couch beside her, fell asleep watching television shortly before two o'clock in the morning.

Around four o'clock she called his name. "Rick. Rick, Rick, wake up." Her voice was faint.

Groggy, Rick slowly realized she was calling him. He bolted upright. "What is it, honey?"

"I've got it figured out," she whispered. "I've got it figured out."

"What, Sondra? What do you have figured out?"

"I've got it figured out," she said, closing her eyes.

"Yes, Sondra, but what have you got figured out?" he urged her gently. "Have you got the pain figured out, is that it?"

"No. The master plan. I've got it figured out," she said, drifting off to sleep.

"That's good, honey. I'm glad," Rick said, stroking her forehead lightly. "That's good." He lowered his head to the pillow and dozed off.

Two hours later, when he awoke, Sondra was gone.

Rick was left with a failing farm and three small children. There were days when he didn't think he could go on—days when he wanted to lie down and die himself. Fortunately, he had some new friends. David Andreas introduced him to James and Jimmy and Mike Ryan. It seemed that whenever he was as low as he could get, he would hear from one of the guys.

Vulnerable and beaten, Rick became totally immersed in the group.

CHAPTER **19**

$\mathbf{M}$ike and Ruth Ryan sat glued to the television set. They'd waited all week for this moment. Ryan gently removed daughter Mandy from his lap, giving the television his full attention. Then, all of a sudden, there he was—the Reverend James Wickstrom—in the middle of their television screen. Ryan swigged down the last of his 7UP and watched in amazement as the famous, white-haired talk show host came striding down the aisle of the packed television studio.

The Reverend Wickstrom was on *Donahue*.

Phil Donahue raised his microphone, looked directly into the camera, and introduced Wickstrom as the national director of the Counter Insurgency for the Posses of America, the Posse Comitatus.

The Posse, Donahue explained in his introduction, had been making headlines after Posse member Gordon Kahl of North Dakota had killed two federal marshals; Kahl had not yet been arrested and the case had sparked one of the largest manhunts in the history of the Dakotas.

The network cut to a commercial.

* * *

"Hot damn!" Ryan said, leaning toward the television screen. Wickstrom was on national television.

Ruth was excited, too. "I can't believe Reverend Wickstrom is on national television," she said.

"Oh yeah, I can. Jim knows what he's doing," Ryan said.

Indeed, James Wickstrom had made it to network television. As national leader of the Posse, he was responding to Gordon Kahl's shootout in North Dakota ten days earlier.

Kahl, a sixty-three-year-old retired farmer and tax protester engaged in a gun battle with six officers serving a parole violation warrant near his farm home in Medina, North Dakota. When the shooting stopped, a U.S. marshal and his deputy were dead, three other officers were wounded, and Kahl was at large.

Although Wickstrom didn't know Kahl, he seized the opportunity to defend the man and, in the process, be catapulted into the national spotlight. Kahl wasn't running from anybody, Wickstrom told Donahue, referring to the day Kahl was approached. According to Wickstrom, the U.S. marshal's office in Fargo knew that Kahl was living with his daughter, and that he was speaking at a meeting that evening. Wickstrom's point was that Kahl could have been arrested, perhaps peacefully, under other conditions.

Donahue agreed that strategies for making arrests could have been reviewed, but argued that Kahl had no right to fire random shots from inside a car at police officers who were walking along the road to make an inquiry.

With that, Phil Donahue segued to another commercial.

"Hell, yes, they could have arrested him different," Ryan told Ruth. "They didn't need to go off half cocked, shootin' at anyone up there. It could have been different. It just shows you what we're all up against."

For Mike Ryan, the Gordon Kahl incident was a signal. Satan was at work. The battle was drawing near. More than ever now, they were paranoid about evil forces in their midst.

*   *   *

The subsequent media attention heaped on the Reverend James Wickstrom only served to heighten the respect accorded him by his followers.

Two weeks later, some fifty reporters, including members of the national media, flocked to Tigerton Dells when Wickstrom called a news conference. He'd received a sixteen-page letter from Gordon Kahl, still at large, outlining Kahl's account of how and why the shooting had taken place.

Among those media representatives attending the news conference was Columnist Bill Stokes of the *Chicago Tribune*. He wrote on March 15, 1983, "It was a strange sensation to be part of the press contingent that gathered before this self-righteous bigot. You could feel terribly manipulated on the one hand and even angry that members of your profession had assembled like a pack of trained circus dogs to the bidding of this outrageous buffoon . . . Such people as Wickstrom and the gun-toting macho fuzzheads who follow him around thrive on attention. While they say they want to be left alone, they are forever devising ways to get publicity." Stokes closed his article citing one Posse member who said he felt the Second Coming of Christ would take place in Tigerton Dells. That, Stokes said, would be the only story he would go back to cover there.

Gordon Kahl died nearly three months later in a shoot-out in Walnut Ridge, Arkansas, where he had holed up in a house with two sympathizers. Unfortunately, one of Kahl's bullets took the life of a local thirty-eight-year-old sheriff.

CHAPTER 20

Increasing alarm that James Thimm was falling deeper into the clutches of the religious cult prompted his sister Karen and members of his birth family in Beatrice to consult a psychotherapist. They feared some cult indoctrination was responsible for the dramatic changes in James.

Each time Karen had tried to talk sense to him, the conversation degenerated into his attacking her. He chided her for being divorced and for being part of the public school system. God did not approve of these actions, he insisted.

"And you have black friends. Blacks are an impure race!" he scolded.

"James, there's nothing impure about being black. You took biology class. You know there's no difference," she tried.

"It's a lie. It's all a lie. They lied to us!" That had become his standard response any time she hit him with logic he couldn't refute.

At her wit's end, Karen agreed with James's sister Miriam and his father, Frank Thimm, that they should seek help. They met with a psychotherapist in Beatrice, hoping for advice—something they hadn't thought of to get James away from the cult.

The therapist, a tall, dark-haired man in his thirties, offered them chairs at a table in his office.

"Our brother James has been pulled into a cult, we believe," Karen started, "and we're having no luck getting him to leave it. We're really worried about what could happen . . ."

The therapist listened closely as Karen and Miriam described the changes in James's behavior over the past months—the talk of guns, violence, and secret government schemes.

"What kind of help can we get him?" Karen asked. "Is there any way we can get him into counseling?"

"How old is your brother?"

"Twenty-five," Karen replied.

"Well, legally, since he's over the age of twenty-one, you can't force him into any kind of therapy unless you can prove that he's dangerous to himself or others. That's the law."

"What about deprogramming?" Karen asked.

"Again, the problem is, with an adult, you literally have to kidnap these people. First, that's not always easy with a grown man, and second, it's not always successful."

"Not successful?" Miriam asked.

"Yeah. Part of the problem is that those who are forced into deprogramming often become angry or hostile toward you for doing this to them and in the end, they can turn on you."

"What happens to all the people who get pulled into cults?" Karen asked. "Do they stay in them forever?"

"No. I'd say in the majority of cases, they eventually get tired, become disillusioned, and begin to see through what's going on. Many times, they end up leaving of their own free will . . . once they're fed up."

Karen and Miriam had discussed that prospect before. They had hoped that James would eventually come to his senses and leave the group.

"What can we do?" Miriam wanted to know.

"Is James holding down a job and maintaining relationships in the community?"

"Oh yeah," Miriam said. "He goes to work every day and he does stay in touch with us and other friends. A couple of my parents' friends have him over for dinner on Thursday nights."

"Well, then, it's very positive that he's maintaining relationships," the therapist said. "Try to keep as much contact with him as you can."

Satisfied with what the psychotherapist had told them, Karen, Miriam, and Frank stood to leave.

"Thank you," Karen said.

"I wish you the best," he said with a warm smile.

It was a brief session—only about thirty minutes—but the therapist had affirmed for them that, at the present, they were doing all they could.

Karen, Miriam, and Frank resolved to stay in contact with James and let him know he was loved. And pray. They would pray a lot.

The next day, Karen called a priest she knew whose sister had been sucked into a cult. He was very understanding and recommended that she contact the Citizens' Freedom Foundation in Virginia. "They have a lot of information about cults. You really should contact them."

That she did. Karen wrote the organization, enclosing notes which detailed the rhetoric James spewed about Jews, the Antichrist, government conspiracies, and unfair taxes. Days later she got a letter and packet of information from the Citizens' Freedom Foundation.

Posse Comitatus. Hate groups. That's what they said James's rhetoric was all about. Karen devoured the packet of background information on the Posse.

She began trips to the library to research cults. She read everything she could get her hands on. She began to understand what was happening to her brother.

From the research, she learned that recruitment techniques varied, but in most instances, members were approached at vulnerable times in their lives. Stress could be due to major transitions in financial stability, job changes, breakups of relationships. When defense mechanisms were overloaded and weakened, certain people were easy prey.

Delving further into mind control, she found that most emotional control was done through fear. Groups were bound by fear in two ways—fear of an outside force that the cult proclaimed as evil, and fear of a leader who would punish group members for showing signs of weak faith.

Under such mind control, an individual's identity was replaced with a new one. In most cases, it was one that the original identity would strongly object to, if it knew in advance what was in store.

In destructive cults, members believed that the ends justified the means. Members believed that they were above the law as long as they believed that what they were doing was right. Lying, cheating, and stealing were justified.

Cults produced psychosis early with vulnerable people and a state of extreme dependency was created. The leader of such a cult was in total control, telling people what to wear, what to eat. The group became dependent on the leader's absolute authority.

Most destructive cults had a persecutory delusion—that someone was after them, be it Communists or Satan. It was always good against evil; all issues were black or white. This impending doom created a state of chronic fear and destabilized the normal personality. The good versus evil dichotomy kept people from reasoning, thinking clearly. Most groups of this nature had messianic goals and derived a sense of being noble for being chosen to save the world.

As her field of knowledge grew, Karen prayed that James would snap out of it.

AUGUST 1983

Carl and Hilda Schmidt completed their three-year missionary tour of Africa and returned home to Nebraska. James and Karen met them at Epply Airfield in Omaha.

Hilda, a tall, slender woman with coal black hair and friendly brown eyes, rushed down the exit ramp. ''James!

Karen!'' she exclaimed, her excitement overriding her exhaustion. She threw her arms around James. ''It's so good to see you, kids!'' she said, her eyes welling with tears.

''Good to see you, Mom,'' James said, smiling broadly. He hugged her, then turned away long enough to greet his father. ''Hi, Dad! How you doing?''

Carl, a soft-spoken man of medium build, wrapped his arms around James and hugged him to his chest. ''I'm just fine, Son, just fine!''

The four of them talked nonstop as they loaded luggage, then stopped for dinner before making the ninety-minute drive back to Beatrice.

James seemed to be himself, Hilda thought. He was genuinely happy to see them. Maybe Karen had exaggerated in her letters when she wrote on James's behavior.

But the months ahead revealed many unsettling changes in James. His talk of war and weapons baffled his parents. And he had a new diet regimen. He would not eat sugar or pork—or the meat of any cloven-hoofed animal. To eat such meat was to take the devil inside of you—to be, in effect, consumed by the devil.

''Okay, James, if you don't like pork, you don't have to eat it,'' Hilda said. ''If I fix pork chops, there'll be something else on the table as well.'' She tried to accommodate rather than provoke.

He didn't like chlorinated tap water. Too many chemicals in it. He took vitamins by the mouthful.

James would not go to church with them. His Sabbath was now on Saturday. He would leave on weekends and not return until the early hours of Monday morning. Some Mondays he would be late for work—very late. But at least he was going to work every day at the lumberyard. That was a good sign, they thought.

They listened to James when he wanted to talk about religion. Carl would open the Bible to discuss Scripture that James recited. But there was no convincing him to abandon his beliefs.

His mother confronted him on his views about blacks being an impure race. ''James, do you think that the black people we worked with for three years in Africa were not Christians? Do you believe that they cannot be saved?''

On that one, James had finally relented. ''Well,'' he said, ''maybe if they truly believe, they can be Christians.'' He sounded sad and confused.

At rare moments like this, Hilda could tell that somewhere, deep inside, James remembered the teachings of his earlier faith.

Hilda knew her son was of a passive nature. She'd seen that side of him many times. Like the time he quietly walked off a job after high school because the machinery was squirting oil all over him. He went through several pairs of gloves and then just walked away. No confrontations, no demands that the employer repair the faulty equipment—he just left.

Also, she remembered the evenings she'd ask, ''James, are you going to young people's meeting tonight?''

''I don't know,'' he'd reply. Then, he would finally say he guessed it was too late to go. He decided by not deciding.

It was a Monday in January 1984 when Hilda rose and noticed that James was not getting ready for work. She went to the top of the basement stairs. ''James, are you awake?'' she asked.

''Yeah.''

Perplexed, Hilda walked down the stairs and over to the side of James's bed. ''James, are you going to work today?''

''I don't have a job anymore,'' he said, staring blankly at the ceiling.

Hilda paused. ''James, are you saying you've been fired?''

''Yeah,'' was his reply.

Hilda said nothing. She leaned over, kissed her son on the cheek, and went back upstairs.

James moved out of the house and in with David Andreas on his farm at the edge of Beatrice. David's parents had moved to town. The Schmidts figured it logical that James would want to move out of his parents' house, although they were concerned that he was not looking for work. Trying to stay in contact with James was frustrating—David had no phone. And when they'd drive out to the Andreas place to see him, they usually found that he was not there. David would tell them he didn't know where he was. They usually left disappointed.

"David's lying," Hilda told Carl. "His face gives him away. Carl and Hilda, in past weeks, had picked up something about a farm in southeast Nebraska, but that's all they knew.

When they did find James at the Andreas farm, he was distant. They felt him slipping away from them.

CHAPTER 21

Rick Stice hustled out the door of his trailer; Jimmy Haverkamp, Mike Ryan, and James Thimm waited in the driveway. They had invited Rick, their newest member, to accompany them to Tigerton Dells, Wisconsin, for a weekend retreat at the Posse headquarters. The free retreat was to focus on tax protesting.

As they transferred green canvas duffel bags to Rick's Toyota Celica, Rick's youngest son, Luke, ran to the edge of the drive.

"Good-bye, Daddy!" The blond-haired boy waved, his brown eyes sad.

"Good-bye, Luke. You be a good boy and mind your grandma while I'm gone," he instructed.

The forlorn four-year-old kept waving as the car pulled away. Still grieving over the loss of his mother, Luke didn't like his dad leaving. His lower lip quivered as he watched the car disappear.

"This is goin' to be some motherfuckin' good weekend," Ryan said. It was a chance to rub elbows with James Wickstrom, star of *Donahue*, and since then, the Larry King radio show.

Mike talked on and on about the eminent catastrophe, the battle. He talked of weaponry and what it was going to take to survive. And pussy. Mike Ryan liked to talk about pussy, and he'd had a lot of it, to hear him tell it, including some high-class prostitutes. He had skill, too. "Some guys need a choke chain to get their women to move in bed. Not me!"

Once in Tigerton Dells, the four were impressed with the dells—the river sliced through the outcroppings of rock some one hundred feet high. It was hilly, rocky, tree-covered terrain.

Wickstrom operated the Posse compound on nearly six hundred acres along the scenic banks of the Embarras River. The landowner, a local member of the Posse, had donated the land as a tax write-off. Formerly the Tigerton Dells Resort, the tract perfectly suited the Posse's needs for a home base; the Life Science Church, trailer park, and guerrilla warfare training camp blended into the landscape.

A sign at the main gate warned, "Federal Agents Keep Out. Survivors Will be Prosecuted!" Two unsmiling men in camouflage uniforms motioned with their rifles for them to park. The main building, the former dance hall and bar, was surrounded by cars. At least two hundred people were expected, and it appeared they'd all shown up. Most everyone was in army fatigues or camouflage. It was a strange psychological blend of paramilitary, Ku Klux Klan, right-wing radicals, white supremacists, and anyone else who had a beef with somebody.

Ryan and the three young men hurried into the meeting hall, squeezing into the back of the room, which was already filled with the weekend's participants. Wickstrom was at the podium, winding into a sermon. His backdrop was a three-by-four-foot photo of a smiling Senator Joe McCarthy and a forty-eight-star American flag. The Posse did not recognize Alaska and Hawaii because they did not have contiguous borders. And Wickstrom had called McCarthy "one of the greatest Americans who ever lived."

"We are the Posse Comitatus—the power of the county!" Wickstrom shouted. "We will return the white Anglo-Saxon Christians to their rightful control of America!"

The crowd thundered with applause and shouts of "Amen!"

Ryan was busy watching the crowd, only half listening as Wickstrom roared on about unfair taxes.

"It's unconstitutional to have a progressive income tax. It's communistic . . ." Wickstrom shouted.

One man in the audience jumped to his feet, unleashing his anger. "If you look at the way the Constitution was written, our forefathers never meant for us to have to pay these kinds of taxes!"

"Amen!" another man shouted, waving his fist.

The gist of the Posse antitax rhetoric was that the nation's income tax was a plank of the Communist manifesto. To pay these taxes was to tithe Satan. The Posse insisted that the country had no enforceable laws mandating the payment of income tax.

As Wickstrom stepped down from the podium, Ryan elbowed his way through the crowd and greeted the preacher. "How ya doin', Jim," Ryan said, making sure he was the first in his group to approach Wickstrom.

"Hello, Mike," Wickstrom replied. He turned and shook the hands of Jimmy, Rick, and James. "Let's get together some time this weekend and talk," he suggested as he rushed off to another session.

Ryan and the guys sat in on the tax meetings, but Ryan was bored with this talk about protesting taxes and Farmers Home Administration foreclosures. The survival training he'd heard about at the compound would have been infinitely more interesting.

"Eighty percent of Posse members are prior veterans of either World War II, Korea, or Vietnam," Wickstrom had bragged. "The majority of our trainers are former Green Berets and army rangers."

When Posse members did offer their survival training sessions, the day was a smorgasbord of violence. They taught members how to use combat gear, tear gas, gas masks, explosives, and fuses, and how to make homemade bombs. Frequently, classes taught by a veteran of Vietnam special forces focused on guerrilla warfare—how to assemble killer teams, how to harass and demoralize the enemy, and how to organize hit-and-run operations. There had been classes on the use of barbed wire, booby traps, land mines, and pungi stakes, and the use of knives, needles, and spray bottles to administer poisons. Posse training had also covered night patrols, setting up ambushes, knife hunting, hand-to-hand combat, sighting devices, and first aid.

"Too bad they're not teaching survival stuff this weekend," Jimmy said, noticing that Ryan was bored with all the tax talk. "I'll bet you could teach them a thing or two, Mike."

"Oh, hell yes," Ryan replied. He'd heard enough griping over taxes from these farmers.

On Sunday morning, Wickstrom wrapped up the weekend with a sermon from his pulpit, where he preached most Sundays. Usually, he had a following of fifty or sixty show up.

Eager to see Wickstrom before leaving, Ryan and the others walked a quarter mile deeper into the woods to Wickstrom's modest trailer, set among seven other mobile homes arranged in a semi-circle.

His wife of fifteen years, Diane, greeted them at the door and invited them in. She was a tall, slender woman, her brown hair cropped short.

Wickstrom met the men in his living room, comfortably furnished with overstuffed chairs; a bay window overlooked a timbered ravine. The recording equipment Wickstrom used to make cassette tapes was shelved at one end of the room.

"Did you fellas learn something this weekend?" Wickstrom asked.

"You bet we did," Ryan answered.

"You can't be overprepared. And, it's absolutely vital that people of like mind stick together."

The four men assured him that they were doing just that. They told him of their preparations down home—their collecting weapons and gear.

Wickstrom encouraged them.

As they bid Wickstrom good-bye, Ryan hung back.

Wickstrom shook hands with Ryan. He looked Mike right

in the eye and said, "You know, Mike, it's time to gather
your own flock."

Ryan squeezed the preacher's hand tighter.

Rick Stice had been impressed with Ryan before he'd met
him, based on the tone the others used when they spoke of
him. Ryan the Vietnam vet, with CIA and Green Beret
experience. But now that he'd seen him with Wickstrom's
crowd, he realized just how well Ryan fit in.

They'd motored down the highway for about forty-five
minutes. Then, Ryan asked Rick to pull the car over.
"Jimmy, I need to talk to Yahweh."

The two men stepped outside the car onto the grassy
shoulder of the road.

Ryan faced Jimmy for the arm test. Jimmy extended his
arm and Ryan wrapped his hand around Jimmy's wrist.

"Yahweh, Heavenly Father, is there something You want
me to tell these men?"

Yes.

"Yahweh, Heavenly Father, shall I tell them your plans
for me?"

Yes.

Ryan crawled back onto the car and shared his news. In
recent days he'd learned that he embodied the spirit of the
archangel Michiel, the warring angel of God. And in due
course, Ryan told them, he would lead the Battle of
Armageddon.

PART TWO

The Deterioration

CHAPTER 22

Indian summer brought the Midwest harvest to a close. Farmers worked from sunup to sunset, their combines rolling across rows of corn, soybeans, and milo, stretching out like tightly woven tapestries of gold and copper threads. Soon, the harvest would be complete and the landscape would be transformed into the barren, icy fields of winter.

Mike and Rick had become close friends. Mike made frequent visits to Rick's, often staying overnight and helping around the farm. On one occasion, Mike helped him haul hogs to market; another time Mike helped him load grain. At the end of their long days, they'd talk—about life, about the battle—until late at night. Mike Ryan was just about the best friend Rick ever had. Rick liked the fact that Mike was "of like mind" and that he had the common sense and experience of a good leader. He was about to see that leadership in action.

The next night was to be the team's first big mission— "night work." Stealing in the name of God. They were after cattle and a backhoe they'd spotted at a bridge construction site six miles south and a mile east of Hiawatha. They needed a backhoe for digging a bunker for the Battle of Armageddon. The cattle they'd sell for cash.

For weeks now, Yahweh, through Mike Ryan, had been instructing them to randomly take pieces of equipment that could be used in their base camp. In these parts, where farmers trusted most everyone, snatching equipment had been easy. They cased farms forty or fifty miles away by day, and returned under cover of darkness.

In years past, none of these men would ever have considered such acts. But now, they were part of the group think. As soldiers of Yahweh, the action was more than justified—it was demanded.

At midnight, all five of them—Ryan, Jimmy, Rick, James, and David Andreas—met at Rick's farm north of Rulo and donned their military gear. Nervous with anticipation, they dressed from head to toe in the mottled greens and tans of camouflage. They snapped ammo pouches, canteens, and machetes into their field belts and suspenders. Each carried a loaded pistol and some ninety rounds of ammunition. "Never be taken alive," they'd solemnly pledged.

As they began smearing dark green camouflage paint over their faces, David paused for a moment. He looked at the others and then at himself in the mirror. It seemed sort of silly, he thought, dressing up in this garb, but he kept his thoughts to himself and covered his face with the paint.

James, in contrast, was excited by the mission ritual. This was the real-life version of the war games he'd played so often. It was like acting out the board games, he told David.

Once ready, they took off in Jimmy's one-ton Ford truck, pulling a trailer behind them for the backhoe.

Jimmy turned off on the road to the construction site a few minutes after one o'clock in the morning. He killed his headlights. A half moon provided enough light so that he could easily follow the tire tracks down the gravel road.

Jimmy's heart throbbed as he pulled up to the secluded bridge. The orange backhoe was parked on the south side of the bridge, next to a crane. A pile of lumber was stacked next to it. He scanned the surroundings. Not a soul in sight.

He knew a farmhouse sat just over the next hill, out of the line of sight. The only other farmhouse in view was two cornfields away. The house was dark.

Now, they fitted earphones to their heads. The sophisticated walkie-talkies had microphones extending from the earpieces—they could communicate with one another throughout the mission. Headsets in place, Yahweh's soldiers went to work.

"We'll work in pairs," Ryan ordered, whispering into his mouthpiece. "Thimm, you go back up the road and watch for cars. Make damn sure you warn us if you see anyone coming." Ryan's tone was condescending. He was still pissed at James. Some nights back at Ryan's house an HK 91 had gone off in James's hands. The bullet ripped into the ground, missing Ryan's daughter Mandy by only three feet. Ryan had raged at James and threatened to beat him to a pulp if he was ever careless with a gun again.

James, now eager to get back on Ryan's good side, nodded obediently and strode briskly toward the intersection a quarter mile away. Once there, he crouched alone in the dark, watching for approaching headlights.

Jimmy and Rick fumbled to hot-wire the backhoe. It chugged and sputtered, but they managed to load it onto the flatbed trailer. Then they began loading lumber—two-by-fours and two-by-sixes.

"We sure as hell can use the lumber," Jimmy grunted as he shoved several planks onto the trailer bed.

"Yeah, boys, but we may be looking at three to five if we get our asses caught," Ryan snickered. The backhoe alone was worth about thirty thousand dollars.

They worked quickly.

"Okay, we got all the shit on there we can. Let's get the fuck out of here," Ryan said. They were on a roll.

Jimmy and Ryan piled into the cab of the truck; everyone else jumped on the back for the ride to a farm that bordered Norbert Haverkamp's property for the cattle.

"Damn. I can't believe we got that backhoe loaded that easy," Rick remarked. He breathed a sigh of relief.

"Just shows you, somebody above is looking out for us," Ryan said.

Forty-five minutes later, Jimmy parked the truck across the road from the cattle pasture. In the darkness, they could see the white faces of the Herefords, huddling together. Stice's pickup was already parked in waiting by the loading chute. Quickly, Rick backed his truck up to the fence gate. They set up a portable corral, which they'd stolen days before, and started herding the cattle into it.

"Get the cattle and the calves in the corral," Rick whispered, "then we'll load the calves and let the cattle out."

The calves scampered up the loading chute and into the truck. They had twenty-eight calves when the truck was full. Seventeen calves came from the Haverkamps' neighbor. They also took nine from Norbert Haverkamp, to eliminate Jimmy and his friends as possible suspects. They had executed the mission with precision. Everything had gone according to Yahweh's plan—the plan Ryan had outlined—so far. Ryan and Andreas loaded the corral, hooked up the portable chute, and headed for David's farm near Beatrice, where they would keep the calves until they sold them under David's and James's names over the next few days. They had stolen about six thousand dollars' worth of cattle.

Jimmy, James, and Rick struck out for Rulo, where they would store the backhoe temporarily. Eventually they'd hide it in western Kansas, near Norton, on a farm belonging to another of Jimmy's sisters and her husband.

They drove northward, toward Rulo, staying on lonely back roads. It was the safest route. If they made it across Highway 36, the main east-west highway, they'd be in good shape.

But luck was running short. The weight of the backhoe was too much strain on the trailer tires. And then . . . Pop! Thud! The right tire blew. The wheel hit the pavement.

"Oh, shit!" Jimmy yelled, gripping the wheel as he felt the truck pull to the right. He jerked around to see the backhoe still riding on the lopsided trailer bed.

"Damn, what do we do now?" Rick asked, also watching the backhoe through the rear window.

"Pray to Yahweh to get us through this," Jimmy replied. They still had to cross Highway 36.

Meanwhile, the iron rim of the truck wheel chewed into the blacktop, spewing bright orange sparks like a Fourth of July pinwheel.

James prayed silently. Straining his neck, he watched the backhoe teeter in the darkness.

As they approached the main intersection, Jimmy saw traffic coming from both directions on Highway 36. He prayed they'd get across the highway undetected. Then, as he rolled to a stop, the traffic disappeared. It was as if his prayers had been answered. He looked to the east and could see only one car coming from the distance.

"You've got time to make it. Go!" Rick said.

Jimmy gunned the truck and the vehicle chugged across the highway. Sparks still spun off the tire rim.

"Whew! I think we made it okay," James said. He looked back at the approaching car, wondering if the driver had paid them any attention.

"Yahweh was taking care of us on that one," Rick said, his heart pounding.

Once across the highway and up the county road a half mile, Jimmy pulled over. They couldn't make it another twenty-five miles to the Rulo farm; the other tire would blow any second. The solution: unload the backhoe.

"We'll road it the rest of the way," Rick said.

"I'll drive it," Jimmy offered. He jumped on the piece of machinery and once he got the lights on, pulled out in front of the pickup. Rick and James followed.

Dawn was breaking as they pulled into Rick's farmstead.

The theft of the backhoe went undetected until the next Monday morning when the bridge crew reported for work. "A crew foreman discovered the theft and called the Brown County sheriff," so said the morning newsman on KNZA radio.

Mike Ryan chuckled to himself as he listened to the broadcast.

Meanwhile, the sheriff immediately sent out a teletype to surrounding county law enforcement offices:

REF: Stolen loader with backhoe.

We have a report of a backhoe stolen from a bridge construction site south and east of Hiawatha, Kansas, sometime over this past weekend. 111 Model 580 C Case backhoe, orange in color. Only info we have is that a flatbed trailer was possibly used.

Please check with service stations in your area to see if anyone has had a tire fixed on a flatbed trailer. A citizen advised a vehicle pulling a flatbed had the vehicle and they went up into Nebraska on U.S. 73. They would need a new rim and wheel since the old one was bent.

If any info of this vehicle or about the case, please contact the Brown County sheriff's office in Hiawatha.

"The reason you had that blowout is because you were having doubts! You angered Yahweh, Jimmy!" Ryan growled.

Ryan tried to regain his composure. He had not meant to let his anger show. "You see, Jimmy," he now said in a normal tone of voice, "Yahweh just knew that you were having some kind of doubt about His will for us and that's why He punished you."

Jimmy dropped his gaze in shame, feeling both surprise and hurt at Ryan's attack. Jimmy sensed Ryan's faith in him had been dwindling. He wanted Ryan's approval.

"Yeah, I guess I can see that now," Jimmy admitted.

Ryan was more than sure of his assessment. He knew he was right. He'd heard the voice of God.

CHAPTER 23

Ryan was alone in his living room late at night
the first time he heard the Voice. A voice. Loud and clear.
It frightened him. He remembered Steve Patterson accusing
him of having the demon seed of the devil in him. He
wondered whether the Voice he had heard might have been
the voice of Satan.

But, as the Voice sought him out, it spoke in soft and
gentle tones. "Son, I love you," the Voice said. It was the
voice of Yahweh!

Spiritually stirred by the experience, Ryan's fear gave
way to euphoria. In the past he had communicated with
Yahweh through the arm test, but this was different—
powerful, overwhelming.

Soon, the Voice had other things to say, to teach, to help
him understand.

The Voice told him why he was the chosen leader for the
Battle of Armageddon: the Reverends Wickstrom and
William Gale, Posse co-founder, would be killed during the
next seven years, and only Ryan would survive to lead
Yahweh's soldiers against the forces of Satan. The Voice
told him to take command of his band of people and prepare
them for the final days.

In no time Ryan began making sense of everything that had happened to him. A fragmented life of ups and downs was now fitting into a pattern that he could understand. He'd always imagined that he had special powers of the mind.

He remembered in his mid-twenties, how he had dreamed that his grandfather, the person he was closest to, would be killed in a car wreck. A week later, his grandfather had died in a traffic accident.

Later, he had had another unforgettable vision. For three nights in a row he had dreamed that his father was injured in a car crash, and that, too, came to pass. His father suffered minor injuries in an automobile accident.

Then, he recalled the night in 1969 when Dennis had been born. Ryan had learned of his son's birth when he had called home from a truck stop in Pennsylvania. He had bolted from the phone booth to share the news with a fellow trucker. A few minutes later, the trucker had been crushed to death in a freeway accident. Ryan worried that he might have somehow influenced the friend's death. It had troubled him for years.

To Mike Ryan, the spiritual mysteries in his life were finally making sense. All that had happened to him in the past few months was part of a greater plan, he reasoned. He did have special powers and, just like Moses in the movie, *The Ten Commandments,* Ryan had been brought to earth for a reason. "I was born to this world for a special purpose," Ryan whispered as he heard the voice of Yahweh.

Moses had led the Israelites out of bondage in Egypt, and Ryan would lead his band of followers through the destruction of the apocalypse. And Ryan knew that he, like Moses, would one day suffer for the transgressions of his people. Like Moses, he would remain steadfast during the time of testing for fear he would invoke the wrath of Yahweh.

CHAPTER 24

The fine, powdery snow formed a swirling mist over the surface of the highway as February squalls fell across the Midwest. The milk white fields stretched for acres, blurring at the horizon. The winter scene offered little variety—only the jagged line of a barbed-wire fence, the hoarfrost on naked tree lines, and a solitary windmill.

A red-tailed hawk glided through the gray skies, then circled and plummeted toward earth, tucking its wings to hush the sound of its approach. In an instant the bird of prey flapped its wings and hovered close to the frozen earth, snatching up an unsuspecting field mouse with its sharp claws.

Jimmy drove over the hill of the country road in the early afternoon. Ryan had told him that Yahweh had picked a farm in this area, just north of Seneca, Kansas, where they would find more calves. The calves would be the right size and would be there for the taking. Jimmy had departed that morning and was growing more frustrated by the minute as he tried to find them. He drove slowly, scanning the icy horizon. Nothing met his eye but the fields of winter, and it was three o'clock in the afternoon. He was positive that he must be lacking in faith again.

He sighed with frustration. Finally, he pulled to the side of the road and prayed to Yahweh. "Please, Yahweh, Heavenly Father, help me do my work. Help me find the calves. Lead me."

He drove on. Then, thirty minutes later, almost on impulse, he made a turn to the west and headed down a road he had not taken earlier. A barn and silo beckoned in the distance.

"Son of a bitch!" he said, chuckling as he rounded a curve and saw an eighty-acre pasture full of cattle . . . and calves. "I can't believe it," he muttered to himself. The calves were about a week old and there were so damn many of them, no one would miss a few. He checked for landmarks so that he could remember the exact location and turned the truck around, heading home, eager to report his success. "Thank you, Yahweh," he sighed.

Jimmy made another trip by the farm during the next week. He observed that the owner had stopped by the cattle lot only twice a day—once in the morning and again in the evening.

Ryan and his men wrote down all the questions they needed to ask Yahweh about taking the calves. No detail went unapproved by Yahweh. The team wasn't going to risk getting caught rustling cattle.

The following weekend, Jimmy, Ryan, David, and James outfitted themselves in camouflage and returned for the calves. Turning out the headlights of his '72 Ford station wagon, Ryan pulled up to the edge of the cattle pasture; the stink of manure cut through the chilly night air. Ryan sat on the fender of the car and watched as the three young men went after the calves.

The cattle stirred, swishing their tails nervously, as the thieves crept into the lot. The calves darted under their mothers as the men pursued them. Jimmy almost had one, but it slipped away. David and James were trying, unsuccessfully, to corner a calf. "Grab those little farts," Ryan said under his breath as he watched the free-for-all inside the cattle pen.

Finally, Jimmy got one of the calves down. It let out a bleat. Jimmy scooped up the calf and carried it to the car. Ryan dropped the tailgate on the station wagon and Jimmy pitched in the calf. "Those suckers are hard to catch!" he exclaimed.

Then, they watched David catch a calf. He pulled it to the ground, then lugged it to the car.

But James was having trouble. He couldn't get his calf. Ryan watched as he slipped and fell in the mud. "Fuck, that guy can't catch that calf," Ryan whispered to Jimmy and David. "Look at him." Ryan folded his arms and leaned back against the pickup.

On their return home, the calves tied securely in the back of the station wagon, Jimmy and David said that once they asked Yahweh for help, it was no time before they had the calves down.

"James, what the hell happened to you out there? Did you think taking the cattle was wrong?" Ryan asked.

"No," he said, trying to reassure Ryan. "Once Yahweh told us where the cattle were, I knew it was okay to take them, but I just wasn't sure He was going to help me when I asked him to," James said thoughtfully.

Ryan scowled. He knew James was in for trouble with Yahweh.

The next day, the rustlers were hauled to Norbert's pasture. They'd be fed and raised there, until it was time to sell.

Several nights later, the guys struck again, only this time the prize was hogs—ten of them taken from a farm near Robinson, Kansas.

The stealing continued at a feverish pitch, all at Yahweh's command. Just as the Israelites took what they needed when they left Egypt, Ryan and his followers took what they needed from this earth.

The livestock-rustling business was profitable. So far, stealing cattle had brought in several thousand dollars. They had divided the cattle they'd stolen and sold them under different names at various sale barns in Nebraska, Kansas, and Missouri.

The money went to buy more guns, ammo, and supplies.

They stored equipment that they'd taken in the three-state region at Rick's farm. By now, their list of hardware included: riding lawn mowers, yard wagons, radios, hard hats, buckets of bolts, spools of wire, chain-link fencing, shovels, sledgehammers, and more. Rick's farm was becoming a heavily armed, well-stocked encampment.

JUNE 19, 1984

Ryan, Dennis, and James walked into the H & E Body and Gun Shop in Seneca, Kansas. Their obsession with guns had brought them here three or four times a week, ever since Jimmy had bought his first Ruger Mini-14 here in December 1982.

Ignoring the strong paint fumes seeping in from the adjoining auto body shop, the three of them browsed through the store. Ryan eyed the bulging breasts of the bikini-clad poster girl on the wall as Dennis quickly turned his attention to the rifles stacked against a pegboard rack.

Dennis now understood the importance of guns; he knew a well-stocked arsenal was their only defense against enemy attack. He feared the nearing battle. And steeped in Mike Ryan's rhetoric, young Dennis was beginning to parrot Ryan's messages of Yahweh's wrath and impending doom.

At first, Dennis had been shocked by his dad's ability to speak directly to Yahweh through the arm test. But, like the other young men, Dennis was sucked in. He both feared and idolized his dad, and would do anything to please him. Dennis was learning to hate Jews and blacks and anyone else his father hated. "That's the way it is," Ryan had told him. "Believe what we believe or you won't eat at our table."

Only months earlier, Dennis had been much like any fifteen-year-old—a carefree teenager. He went to school and made good grades, mostly As and Bs; his favorite subject was science. The Otis-Lennon Test of Intellectual Ability placed his IQ in the average to high-average range. He was a quiet student who never presented discipline problems. Dennis loved sports, especially baseball, and played saxophone in the school band.

As a younger boy living in Anthony, he had demonstrated his sensitive nature, working for an elderly woman who was confined to a wheelchair. Dennis did odd jobs such as working in the yard, planting flowers, cleaning the refrigerator, dusting and running the vacuum cleaner.

"You couldn't ask for a nicer boy," the woman had told her neighbors, explaining that Dennis always did a good job and followed instructions. She was touched by his concern over her finding a replacement for him when he knew his family was moving.

But the gentle side of Dennis Ryan was becoming deadened by the paranoia and impassioned belief that enemies of Yahweh were out to get them. They had to stay on alert. That's why guns were so important.

"Hey, Dad, look at this," Dennis said, picking up a .22 rifle.

Ryan headed over to Dennis just as Randy Engelken, the shop owner, came in from the body shop.

"How you guys doing?" Randy asked. He was a small, wiry guy, about thirty, with thinning blond hair. He was eager to help Ryan and his guys; they'd spent thousands of dollars with him in the past two years. He figured Mike was in to pick up the new 9-mm pistol he'd ordered.

"Gettin' by," Ryan told him. "I came to pick up my pistol and I need to order a gun stock for my AR-15," Ryan said. His tone was one of disgust. "Fuck-up here shot a hole in it." He nodded at James.

James, his head down, would not look Randy in the eye. He attempted a brief smile and nodded his head as if to confess. "Yeah, but it was an accident," he said, as if to soften Ryan's assessment of his shortcomings.

"Yeah, but now we're going to have Dennis kill him for fucking up my gun stock," Ryan snapped.

Randy knew Ryan was cocky and outspoken, but the comment took him by surprise. He leaned across the counter toward Ryan. "Ya know, Mike, I don't think I'd talk that way around your boy."

Ryan shrugged, took a deep drag off his Marlboro, then

stepped behind the counter and held a .45-caliber pistol to Randy's head. "If anyone ever comes around here asking questions about me, don't tell 'em anything. Don't ever tell anyone where I'm at or I'll blow your fuckin' head off," Ryan warned.

"Knock it off, Mike." Randy was more than a little offended by Ryan's actions, though he didn't feel really threatened. Ryan was acting just to impress the two younger men. And from the looks on their faces, they believed in Mike's theatrics.

What did impress Randy was the wad of money that Ryan always had. He paid cash for every gun they bought. Randy especially noted the day Ryan and his gang ordered fifty cases of .223 ammunition, a total of fifty thousand rounds in all. It was PMC .223—Korean-made ammunition. Randy had ordered it for them. He could get a better price—$140 per case—on the Korean-made goods than on Winchester or Remington, which went for $150 per case.

The wooden cases of ammo came by UPS one Friday afternoon. "Ryan and the boys picked it up around eight o'clock that evening. The bill came to $7,780.03. Ryan flipped through his wad and plunked cash on the counter."

Randy marked the invoice "paid in full."

The men, Randy knew, were survivalists and were wrapped up in some kind of religion. But he didn't know exactly what they were up to and didn't particularly want to know. Although their transactions with him were legal— they always filled out the yellow forms required to register their gun purchases, Randy sensed they were converting their weapons to fully automatic, which was illegal.

In fact, they had converted about a dozen of their .223-caliber rifles—the Mini-14s and the Colt AR-15s. The Mini-14, a semiautomatic weapon, was the civilian model of the military's fully automatic M-14. The AR-15 was the civilian model of the military M-16 automatic machine gun. Buying parts for the military versions of these weapons, they'd easily convert them to automatic.

Ryan knew what he was talking about when it came to converting the weapons. "You get your military bolt and your parts, your trigger mechanisms—the whole inside.

You just yank the guts out of it and put the new ones in. A little sanding here and there, a little red cloth. Then, you test it till it works.

"Of course, now we're just buying the parts to convert them," Ryan had once told Randy. "We won't actually convert them until the Battle of Armageddon begins." Ryan winked.

"Hey, if you get caught converting weapons to automatic you could go to prison for that shit," Randy had told Ryan.

Meanwhile, Ryan and his men had several HK 91s— German-made, .308-caliber rifles. They had KG 99s, 9-mm pistols; the latter they also converted to automatic. The collection they'd amassed also included .22-caliber rifles and pistols. In all, they had about sixty weapons. Ryan hid his guns in the wall, behind the TV, at the house in Whiting.

The Ryan gang also had several thousand rounds of .308 ammunition, about two thousand rounds of .45 ammunition, and several thousand rounds of 9-mm. They had bricks— five thousand rounds per brick—of .22 ammo.

Later, Randy learned about Ryan's fascination with homemade explosives. Ryan told him that he had made a dozen hand grenades out of the charcoal briquettes and drums of potassium chlorate they'd collected.

Randy didn't question these cash-paying customers. But he wondered how all these guns fit into any man's religion.

In Tigerton Dells, Wisconsin, James Wickstrom—the man who had preached guns and religion—was in jail. Wickstrom had run afoul of the law when he had issued documents as though he held public office. What had Wickstrom done? He had declared himself a municipal judge of what he considered the Constitution Township of Tigerton Dells and called a grand jury to investigate what he called "corruption in county government."

As a result, the Wisconsin attorney general had filed two charges against him for impersonating a public official. The attorney general said the township had not been created under statutory procedures, that the township was fictitious, and that actions taken by its purported officers had no legal effect.

Initially, Wickstrom considered the charges another instance of government imposing itself unconstitutionally, just causing trouble. Upon arrest, he had posted a two thousand dollar cash bond and appealed the charges; he claimed that the state statute was vague and allowed for "political representation of groups like the Posse Comitatus." However, Wickstrom had lost his appeal and had begun serving an eighteen-month sentence—nine months on each count—in the Shawano County jail in Shawano, Wisconsin.

Wickstrom had long been a thorn in the side of Wisconsin law enforcement officials. Run-ins had included armed Posse members blocking a public road that ran past the Posse compound, and the Wickstrom clan had been cited for violating zoning laws; the former resort, on which their mobile homes were parked, was not residentially zoned. When the county sheriff had served papers ordering that the trailers be moved, the Posse had refused.

However, Wickstrom had no previous criminal convictions on record. When the Shawano County sheriff ran a background check on him through the National Crime Information Center, he found nothing.

CHAPTER **25**

His head bowed, Mike Ryan prayed aloud to
Yahweh over the muffled twang of Loretta Lynn on the FM
radio in the next room. Jimmy's sister Cheryl now joined
Ryan and his men for Saturday Bible study at Jimmy's
house. Cheryl was twenty-nine and attractive—she had
green eyes, and auburn hair she wore in bangs with soft
curls framing her oval face. Her parents, Norbert and
Maxine, her sister Lisa, and her little brother Danny joined
the circle, too. They had become believers.

His prayer finished, Ryan sucked in a drag off his
Marlboro and chased it with 7Up. "The Antichrist is
here . . . here on earth, now," he said in hushed tones.
"He can count every hair on your head." Ryan was seguing
into one of his favorite sermons—the Battle of Armageddon. "The Antichrist shows us the final days are here. The
battle is at the doorstep," he whispered, locking eyes with
Cheryl. "It could happen next week or it could happen in
ten years. The sons of Satan will fight the sons of light, and
we must be ready." Ryan jumped to his feet and moved
around the room as he preached.

Cheryl sat quietly, drinking in the truth according to

Ryan. After months of Ryan's persuasion and Jimmy's enthusiasm, the conversion of Cheryl Gibson was complete. Of a trusting nature, she had gradually subscribed to the concept of Yahweh and she shuddered at the thought of the Battle of Armageddon.

Ryan stooped and narrowed his eyes at Maxine, Cheryl's mother, preaching in her face. "The Catholic church is wrong! All churches and preachers are wrong. Yahweh's way is the only way and Armageddon is coming!"

Maxine nodded that she understood. She knew the battle was a time bomb ticking at their feet. A small woman with a thin voice, Maxine was a young-looking fifty-two, pleasantly attractive and neatly groomed.

"We can't wait to get ready!" Ryan ranted.

It was this magnetism—the way Ryan had drilled his message in, over and over, with such intensity—that had drawn Maxine in, made her a believer. What if he's right, she'd kept asking herself. Just months before, she had worshipped in the Catholic church where for years she'd been a member of the Altar Society and taught Sunday school and vacation Bible school.

At first she'd been skeptical about Jimmy's new religion; she'd even read some articles about cults and warned Jimmy of the possible dangers. But as Mike Ryan's eyes bore into her soul, she'd gradually accepted his preaching.

Norbert, a dark-haired man of fifty-two, listened carefully as Ryan preached. Norbert had lent a listening ear, mostly believing because everyone else did. He had come to believe that Mike Ryan was an emissary of the Lord and embodied the spirit of the archangel Michiel. Norbert had been the least likely convert, but Rick had gotten into Norbert's good graces by convincing him that he and Ryan were interested in working for him. Norbert was self-employed. He traveled the Midwest selling feed additives for livestock, and made a decent living. He had one other man who sold for him, and the prospect of having a couple of other guys covering some of the territory had appealed to him.

Jimmy's other sister, sixteen-year-old Lisa, was the easiest conversion. Having had a religious upbringing by her parents, she considered the new interest in Yahweh a natural extension of their beliefs. She liked the newness of it, the urgency of it all.

And, for all the Haverkamps, it was the arm test that sealed their faith. At first they were skeptical about it, but their skepticism gradually turned into reliance. They were overwhelmed by the arm test, totally incapable of explaining it. When they did have questions about vague answers they'd get from Yahweh, they found Ryan adept at interpreting. Soon, though, the arm test was part of their collective wisdom. They never stopped to question its validity.

"Remember what Yeshua said," Ryan preached, using the Hebrew term for Jesus, "I came not to bring peace, but to send a sword!" Ryan tapped down his cigarette and lit it.

This afternoon's Bible study at an end, Ryan approached Cheryl. He took her by the arm and, pulling her along with him, said, "I'm worried about you. I need to talk to you now." His tone was urgent. "Yahweh is very concerned about you."

Ruth watched as Mike led Cheryl to the next room. Though quick to embrace Cheryl as a close friend, Ruth was edgy about their friendship so far as Mike was concerned. Mike had told Ruth that Yahweh wanted Cheryl to be one of his wives during the Battle of Armageddon. "I don't understand why Yahweh chose me when we've got these other men in the group," he'd told Ruth.

Ruth suppressed her jealousy as best she could. She remembered the experience with Janet Carter and resigned herself to the fact that Mike would do as he wished.

Now, Ryan called Jimmy into the room. He wanted to use Jimmy's arm to confirm the message he had been pounding into Cheryl for the past five weeks: "You and Lester are not married in Yahweh's eyes. Lester is living the way Satan wants him to. You and the kids have got to get away. You've got to." He sounded impatient, frustrated that she did not understand the spiritual danger she faced by staying with Lester.

According to Yahweh, Cheryl should leave Lester at once

and turn her life over to Yahweh. "At least save yourself and the kids. Think of your kids!"

"But I'm not sure what to do, where to go," Cheryl said, confused. "I've got a lot on my mind that . . ."

Ryan hushed her by standing up and pulling Jimmy over in front of him. "Let me ask Yahweh one last question." Jimmy eagerly lent his arm.

"Yahweh, is Cheryl Gibson supposed to come by our house in Whiting after she leaves here tonight?" Ryan asked.

Jimmy's arm remained stiff; Yahweh had said yes.

"Yeah, okay, I'll come by," Cheryl responded.

Ryan and Ruth departed immediately. Ryan wanted to make sure he was there when Cheryl arrived.

Cheryl bid her brother and mother good-bye. She loaded the kids in her old car and took off for Whiting, ten miles south of Jimmy's home.

Initially, Cheryl had been lured into Ryan's group purely for the purpose of the Bible study. For years she had wanted to join a Bible study but had never found the time. When she'd read the Scriptures alone, she'd had trouble understanding them. "I wished I had been able to learn these things years earlier," she told Ruth. "Maybe life would have been easier." Here, for the first time in her life, Cheryl could discuss religious beliefs she'd questioned from her Catholic education.

As Cheryl became closer to Ruth, she found herself sharing secrets she'd never told anyone. She confided in Ruth about the tension in her marriage with Lester; with Lester's short temper, they'd had some screaming matches. Financial pressures fueled many of their arguments. In spite of both of them working full-time, they strained to make ends meet. Cheryl was exhausted—drained by the stress of the marriage, working overtime, and raising five small children, all under the age of eight. Cooking . . . cleaning . . . laundry . . . finding baby-sitters.

For Cheryl, the world of Yahweh was an escape. Cheryl desperately wanted the uncomplicated life-style these people seemed to be living. They were like a happy, closely knit family. Never once did she see the seeds of hate that were sown at the base of the Posse religion or the dangers of tangling with Mike Ryan.

Cheryl kept her attendance at the Bible studies a secret from Lester. He considered her brother and his friends religious fanatics. And, when he questioned her about the food she was stockpiling at home, she tried to pass it off as taking advantage of sales.

Cheryl's parents had been the deciding factor in her conversion. They'd been lifelong members of St. Leo's Catholic Church in Horton, and once Jimmy had recruited them, she figured it was okay.

When she arrived at the Ryan house, Mike was waiting for her at the door. He started in on her again, telling her more forcefully than before that she should leave Lester. And, he added a few new twists—not only was Lester not living for Yahweh now, Ryan reported, he was running around with other women, cheating on her. Ryan insisted that eventually Lester would beat her and the children, causing serious injury or even death. Lester was possessed by Satan.

To drive the point home, Ryan positioned Ruth in front of him for the arm test. Ruth's arm did not fall when Ryan asked Yahweh to prove him right.

Browbeaten and vulnerable, Cheryl was resigned.

Ryan took full advantage of his self-serving arm test ritual. Just a few more questions for Yahweh, but Ryan already knew the answers.

Again, Ruth faced Ryan and put her left hand on his right shoulder, while extending her right arm toward the ceiling.

"Yahweh, is it true that Cheryl Gibson is not to go home to her husband tonight?"

Ruth's arm did not budge. Yahweh was telling them that Cheryl should not go home. Ruth wasn't sure why her arm responded as it did.

"Yahweh, is it true that if Cheryl leaves this house tonight, her children will be killed in a car wreck?"

Yes!

Cheryl gasped.

Ryan penetrated Cheryl with his eyes. Inwardly, he tingled with excitement as he inched closer to dominating her.

CHAPTER 26

From a distance, Lester Gibson couldn't tell that his farm home was dark and deserted.

Exhausted, he rumbled homeward down the two-lane gravel road, his left arm hanging out the window of his silver '62 Plymouth; a trail of dust streamed behind him. His sweat-soaked chambray work shirt flapped in the breeze.

At last, he had reached the end of another long week of work—seventy hours—loading fertilizer onto barges at the White Cloud Grain Elevator along the Missouri River. He was glad to get off early this evening. He leaned forward on the steering wheel, yawned, and gazed off to the west. The descending Kansas sun poked through clumps of cottonlike clouds, and cast amber beams across the freshly disked fields.

Lester, twenty-nine, was six feet two, two hundred pounds. His blond hair was thinning. He liked living in the country; it was peaceful and private. Raised a farm boy, he had known farm work all his life—from throwing bales of hay on work crews in the summer to milking cows by hand in the dead of a Kansas winter. Now he and his wife Cheryl lived on a small acreage in northeastern Kansas. Cherry trees lined the dirt driveway up to their white, two-story home.

They'd been married eleven years; they had met in high school. He had asked her for a date during a teen dance; five months later they were married in a large Catholic wedding. The marriage had given them three sons and two daughters, ranging in age from nine years to nine months.

Tonight, Lester knew he and Cheryl needed to talk. Their marriage was strained, but with their hectic schedules, months had passed since they'd even tried to sit down and talk things out. Lester was working long hours, and so was Cheryl; her job as a family service aide with Head Start had turned into a full-time proposition and she traveled between two counties. Ignoring their problems would not make them go away, Lester realized.

Two miles from home, his neighbor waved from his barn lot; Lester returned the greeting, raising his forefinger from the steering wheel. Seeing the neighbor reminded him that he had promised Cheryl the day before that he would borrow the neighbor's disk to work up the garden spot. Now was as good a time as any. He'd come back for the disk after supper.

Lester turned into the driveway only to notice that Cheryl's car was gone. There were no kids on the swing set. A tricycle sat in the middle of the yard. Quickly, he scanned the length of the house, looking for signs of activity. Then it dawned on him—Cheryl had gone to visit her parents, although she should have been home by now.

He decided to go ahead with plowing the garden. Lester returned to borrow the tractor and disk before dark set in and went to work on the garden. From time to time, he glanced down the gravel road, expecting to see Cheryl's car top the hill. But it was nearly eight o'clock when he finished disking, and Cheryl still wasn't home. Anxious now, he waited.

At nine o'clock there was still no sign of her. He always worried about her and the kids on the road with their old car. The odometer on the '70 Chrysler Newport had long since rolled over a hundred thousand miles, and the car had generator problems.

Positive that something was wrong now, he dialed her parents. "Norbert, has Cheryl been there?"

"Yes, but she left two hours ago."

The words sent Lester into a near panic. Two hours? She should have been home an hour ago, then. My God, she's had a wreck, he thought.

Frantically, he dialed his parents; they hadn't seen Cheryl. He called the Brown County sheriff. The sheriff's office had no reports of area traffic accidents that evening, but a deputy would start checking the county roads.

Sensing Lester's concern, his parents drove over from Highland, about twenty minutes away.

"There's probably some explanation here," his mother said. "They'll be all right."

"What do you want to do, Lester?" his father asked.

"I think we should go out looking for them. Maybe they're sitting on the side of the road somewhere with the car broke down."

"Lester, you and your dad go, I'll stay here by the phone," his mother offered.

"Okay. Dad and I'll cover the roads between here and Cheryl's parents' house."

Lester and his father headed south on Highway 73, looking for skid marks or tire tracks leading off the shoulder. Logic told Lester his wife and kids must have had an accident.

Lester slammed on the brakes and stopped the car next to a ravine. His father jumped out and shined his flashlight into the gully, fearing that he might find the mangled wreckage of the light blue Chrysler. But he encountered only darkness and the cadence of chirping crickets. He climbed back in the car and they hurried down the empty highway.

Driving through Horton, they scanned the side streets, hoping to see Cheryl's car pulled over somewhere. Nothing. They drove on to the Haverkamps' house. The brown-shingled bungalow was dark. No sign of Cheryl's car. Despairingly, they returned to Hiawatha.

Lester turned onto Oregon Street, Hiawatha's main drag, and drove to the police station. Inside, the dispatcher, who happened to be a friend of the family, looked as worried as Lester when they walked in.

"Lester, I've been listening to police monitors. They've got a make on the car and are searching county roads for Cheryl and the kids. Highway patrolmen are being sent from Topeka. They'll do everything they can," the dispatcher said, trying to reassure him.

It didn't seem real—a swarm of officers fanning out at midnight, looking for a missing woman and her children. The chatter on the police radios sounded impersonal. This was his family.

Dazed, Lester's mind raced wildly. What could possibly have happened? The phone rang.

"It's for you, Lester," the dispatcher said, handing him the phone across the counter.

It was Lester's mother.

"We've found Cheryl," he heard his mother say.

CHAPTER **27**

Lester instantly felt a wave of relief come over him, but there was something in his mother's voice—she didn't sound as relieved as she should. "Found her? Where?" he demanded.

"Cheryl's dad just called. He said that Cheryl and the kids are okay, but . . . Cheryl has left you."

Lester was speechless. Then: "What does that mean? Why?" Lester sank into a chair next to the counter.

"Her dad only said that Cheryl was in a safe place. He won't say where she is or what she's doing."

"But I've got to talk to her about this," Lester pleaded.

"That's all he would tell me, Lester."

Now Lester's fear turned to anger. "We're going to Norbert's," he told his mom. "I've got some questions I want answered."

"Lester, you and your dad come home now," his mother cautioned. "You're asking for more trouble if you go down there. Please come home." She knew her son's temper all too well. Like his father, Lester had a short fuse.

"Sorry, Mom. We're on our way!" Lester dropped the phone on the counter, and he and his father slammed out of the police station.

By the time Lester stepped out of his car in the Haverkamp driveway, Norbert was at the front door in his stocking feet and white, ribbed undershirt.

"Where the hell is Cheryl?" Lester demanded angrily.

"You better get out of here before I call the law!" was Norbert's only reply.

"I want to know where Cheryl is!"

"Why do you give a damn? What are you worried about? You never worried about her before. I don't have to tell you a damn thing about where she is!"

Just then, Cheryl's sixteen-year-old sister Lisa darted from the house and onto the front porch. She strongly resembled Cheryl, except her hair was cut shorter; she wore summer shorts and a T-shirt. "Lester, if you'll just listen and understand, everything will be okay. You don't understand what's going on. We're trying to help Cheryl."

Norbert shoved Lisa back into the house, admonishing her to keep her mouth shut.

"You're not helping anybody. Now, I want to know where my wife and kids are." Outraged, he considered grabbing the claw hammer he saw lying on the porch and burying it between Norbert's eyes. But common sense prevailed; Lester returned to his car.

"Where do you think she is?" Lester's father asked.

"You know," he said slowly. "I have this strange feeling that I know exactly where she is. She's with Jimmy's group—that Mike Ryan group—down by Whiting. It's the only place that makes any sense!"

"What makes you say that?"

"Mike Ryan is a friend of Jimmy's. They were all mixed up in some sort of religion, the Posse Comitatus," Lester explained. "I had a suspicion that Cheryl was getting mixed up in it, and that fucking Ryan is crazy, Dad! He's a big guy, a redneck. Strange guy, Dad, maybe even dangerous. Ryan was laughing about having threatened to shoot a utility man who'd come out to turn off their electricity because the utility bill was past due. He said the man shimmied down the pole and ran for cover."

"Jesus!"

"The guy's nuts, threatening to shoot people off utility poles." Lester shook his head.

As they drove home, Lester became more depressed. Cheryl's attitude had changed recently—she'd been aloof, detached, irritable. She had been reading the Bible a lot and had begun defending Jimmy's new religion. "If you'd just listen to what Jimmy has to say, you'd understand and wouldn't be so against him!" she'd say, looking at him like he was on the outside of something looking in.

CHAPTER **28**

Just before morning, Lester crawled from bed, thinking he might find a clue to Cheryl's reason for leaving. He ran his fingers between the mattresses, thinking he might find a letter or note. Nothing. He rummaged through their bedroom closet; all of Cheryl's clothes were there—not even an arm load missing. Two suitcases sat in the corner of the closet.

Next, he went across the hall to the boys' room. He found drawers full of pajamas, socks, and underwear. Nothing missing. Even the baby's diapers were there.

Cheryl had taken nothing.

Downstairs, he shuffled through the papers in Cheryl's desk. Perhaps she had started a letter to someone, outlining her plans to leave. The desk held no evidence.

He dumped the trash from the small wastebasket. Pausing, he found a picture of himself in the trash. She'd also tossed away a stack of their wedding invitations. Lester sat down, the old invitations falling from his hand. Cheryl had always said the invitations were keepsakes. Where had she gone?

Lester left the trash where it had fallen and crossed the

red shag carpet of the living room to the buffet in the dining room. In the top drawer, he discovered a stack of cassette tapes—six or seven of them. He picked one up. It was labeled: "YHVH is God, Rev. James Wickstrom. Mission of Jesus Christ, P.O. Box 94, Newton, WI 53063." Lester slapped the cassette into a small Sony tape recorder on top of the buffet and listened.

It began with a group of people saying the Pledge of Allegiance. Then Wickstrom began, "Gladly cut off the head of a Jew," he preached. "They are Satan's people."

Lester fast-forwarded the tape. Wickstrom criticized the nation's tax system, asking his audience if they were tired of being taxed, paying property taxes, paying for everyone else's way. He blamed the Jews for the nation's problems because "they controlled the world banks and the currency . . . be it nickel, gold, or dog turds!"

And then, Lester heard the word *Yahweh*, Wickstrom pronouncing it "Ya-vay." "All who don't cross over to Yahweh shall die!" he declared. Yahweh. Lester had heard Jimmy refer to Yahweh when he'd come to their house preaching his religion.

Lester ran upstairs and grabbed Cheryl's Bible from the nightstand. He opened it and flipped through the pages, stopping when he caught a glimpse of blue ink in one of the margins. Cheryl had marked verses in Matthew 10:34–36 with fancy parenthetical marks. Lester pored over the words: "Think not that I am come to send peace on earth: I came not to send peace, but a sword . . . And a man's foes shall be they of his own household."

Lester riffled through the pages, finding more verses marked in the book of Matthew, chapter 25. As his eyes moved down the page, goose bumps rose on the back of his neck. "And many false prophets shall rise, and shall deceive many . . . but he that shall endure unto the end, the same shall be saved . . . Let him which is on the housetop not come down to take anything out of his house: Neither let him which is in the field return back to take his clothes."

Lester closed the Bible and put it back on the nightstand. He fell across the bed, bouncing lifelessly.

CHAPTER 29

It was light at last.

Lester was on the phone to a couple whom he'd known to be associated with local Posse Comitatus meetings. The woman had been one of Lester's teachers in school. Perhaps they knew something of Cheryl's leaving.

"Yes, Lester, we knew that Cheryl had left. We heard it at a meeting last night," his former teacher said.

"Well, do you know where she is?" Lester asked.

"No, we don't, but let me take your number and maybe I can have someone call you who knows something."

About an hour later, Lester's phone rang. Steve Patterson was on the other end of the line. Patterson and a man by the name of Ted Stone, who lived in the area, were among the leaders of the area Posse members. They knew all the players in Ryan's group.

"I know where your wife and kids are. They're down at Mike Ryan's house on the edge of Whiting. I'll see if we can send some of our people in to check for sure."

Lester had been right. "Should I call you back?" Lester asked.

"No. We'll have one of our people stop by your house and visit with you tonight."

At seven o'clock that evening, Ted Stone knocked at the door. Lester knew Stone—he only lived a few miles away. Lester had known of Stone's involvement with the Posse— trouble with the IRS and fear of losing his farm had sucked him in, he suspected.

Stone, in his fifties, wore blue jeans, and black military boots. He first explained how Mike Ryan had been a part of his own Posse membership but had broken away and started his own group, taking some of the original members. The rift had created some bitter feelings. Stone disliked Ryan.

"So, what do you want to do?" Stone asked, cocking his head to one side.

"Well, I want my wife and kids back, dammit. This is a bunch of . . ."

"I think we can go in the morning," Stone broke in. "I think we can get the kids out, but I can't guarantee we can get Cheryl out."

"What do you mean?"

"We've called our people together and we'll go in and surround the house in the morning. We'll tell them to send out the women and children . . . and whoever doesn't come out, we'll kill the rest of them." He sounded dead serious.

"What the fuck are you talking about?"

"We know Ryan. He'll shoot back. Whoever doesn't come out will die. We'll give them a certain amount of time to come out, and if they don't, then we fire."

"Hell, no, you won't! Jesus, Ted, that's my wife and kids in there. You can't send a bunch of guys in with rifles and start shooting the place up. Are you crazy? This isn't some neighborhood game of cops and robbers. Absolutely not. Don't go in there. Get off this shootout kick. Just tell me what's going on. How did this all happen?"

"It's simple. They brainwashed her."

"Then they're holding her against her will."

"No," Stone said with a wry smile. "They just changed her will. It's a slow process . . . it doesn't happen all at one time. But once she started coming around, and the more she believed, the easier it was to control her. Our group has done it quite a few times to quite a few people." He explained that Cheryl's job, initially, had been to recruit Lester into the Posse. "But you're damned hardheaded, Lester. You wouldn't listen."

"They also pumped Cheryl full of some pretty wicked information about you, Lester. They told her that you had been running around with other women and that you were going to beat her and the kids."

"Ah, shit, Ted," Lester said, then looked up sharply. "Ted, promise me you won't go in there with guns tomorrow!"

Stone backed off, promising a cool head and no guns the next morning. Then Stone left, giving Lester one last, stern instruction. "Whatever you do, don't ever go near Mike Ryan by yourself. He's well armed and he'll kill you. I'm not kidding."

That night was the second sleepless night for Lester. At one o'clock in the morning, Lester got up, dressed, and drove to Hiawatha . . . up and down the main street, thinking as he drove. The two traffic lights on main street were flashing yellow. The town clock on the corner said 1:10.

Lester turned off main street and headed down the side streets of the sleeping town; the street lamps bathed the residential area in a soft glow. Occasionally he passed a house with a light in the window. It all looked so normal!

Lester was too wired to go home and sleep. He drove on to the Haverkamp house. No sign of Cheryl's car. Wearily, he turned his car around and went home.

When the sun rose on Monday morning, Lester still hadn't slept. He rolled over and looked at the alarm clock. It was 5:30. His head throbbed. In the bathroom, he caught a glimpse of his bloodshot eyes in the mirror. He looked pale and haggard. A quick shave and he was off to work.

Somehow, Lester made it through the day. Late that afternoon, he got in touch with the Brown County Sheriff's office and told the story of Cheryl's leaving.

"Nothing much we can do, Lester, sorry," Sheriff Jim Wolney said.

"But I think she's being held against her will," Lester insisted.

"Yeah, but there's no real proof that she's in danger. We've got to show cause to go in. It really sounds like a domestic problem."

Lester wished it was that simple.

CHAPTER **30**

The following week, Cheryl filed for divorce.

Lester, still confused by this turn of events, arrived at the Brown County courthouse for a ten o'clock appearance before the judge. Lester's attorney, Ted Collins, was an old high school friend; he knew just how distraught Lester was and had tried consoling him personally as well as advising him legally. Ted led the way down the cavernous hallway. Their footsteps echoed on the marble.

"Don't say anything to anyone, especially to Cheryl," Ted told Lester.

As they approached the courtroom, Lester spotted Cheryl in the hallway. She was with a woman Lester didn't recognize—probably one of the people she was staying with. He heard someone call the woman *Ruth.* She glanced over at Lester and whispered to Cheryl.

What's she telling her? Lester wondered. Who is this woman? Lester ignored Ted's advice, walked up to Cheryl, and looked her straight in the eye.

She looked away.

"How are you?" he asked.

"All right," she said coldly. Ruth Ryan pulled Cheryl away; they moved down the hall and into the courtroom.

Despite his attorney's protests, Lester fully intended to seat himself next to Cheryl, but Ruth beat him to it. Lester took his seat next to his attorney.

In filing for divorce, Cheryl was seeking a restraining order that would prevent Lester from coming around her—in this case, the Ryan house in Whiting. She also requested that visitation between Lester and the children take place at her parents' house, and that it be supervised.

"Why are you seeking this divorce, Mrs. Gibson?" the judge queried.

"My husband is beating me and the kids, and running around with other women."

Lester just shook his head.

Cheryl knew her charges weren't true, but Ryan had told her to say it. When she'd asked why they should lie, he'd told her Yahweh ordered it.

But when the hearing ended, Cheryl had the restraining order, and child visitations were to take place at Cheryl's parents' house.

Feeling helpless, Lester watched Ruth Ryan usher Cheryl from the courtroom.

The next weekend Cheryl returned home long enough to pack the things she wanted for her and the children. Brown County Sheriff Jim Wolney and one of his deputies were present—the court had ordered that they supervise the move.

Cheryl's parents and Jimmy arrived in a pickup to help. Mike Ryan and three other men arrived, too, though Lester didn't know the others. One drove a black Celica, the other a yellow Datsun—both with Nebraska tags, Lester noticed.

Cheryl, surrounded by the men, refused to acknowledge Lester's questions about why she was leaving.

Lester's temper flared. "Cheryl, for God's sake, why can't we talk about this? Why won't you even talk about this?"

"Just leave me alone. You never cared before. Why would you care now?"

"Goddamn it. Talk to me!"

The sheriff stepped between them. "Lester, let's not

cause a bigger problem here right now. Let Cheryl get her things like the court ordered.'' Later, the sheriff jotted down the tag numbers on the two Nebraska cars. He'd run a check to find out who these guys were.

As Cheryl and the others piled into their vehicles and pulled out of sight, Lester's anger turned to despair.

Three days later, Ted Stone told Lester that the Ryan bunch had cleared out of the house in Whiting. That evening, Lester drove by the house. Evidently, Stone was right. The run-down place was deserted. Lester had no idea where his wife and kids had gone. He filed missing person reports on Cheryl and his children with the Hiawatha police, Brown County sheriff, and the Kansas Bureau of Investigation.

But Lester couldn't make them understand it was more than a divorce. And even if Lester had known it, would the police, the sheriff, or the KBI agents have believed that Cheryl had become Mike Ryan's second wife? That Ryan had married them in a ceremony before Yahweh?

CHAPTER 31

Compelled by the impending glory of the battle, Yahweh's family had moved to Rick Stice's farm two miles north of Rulo, Nebraska. The secluded farm provided the perfect setting for the paramilitary base camp they needed. Further, Ryan said he needed a safe house; someone had a fifty thousand dollar contract out on his life. It had to do with his ongoing CIA connection, he told them. The farm would also provide a hideaway for Cheryl and her kids. They all knew that Lester would be looking for them.

The move occurred just as Ryan was ordering the family to break ties with the Posse Comitatus. He was increasingly disinterested in the Posse's political agenda, and didn't think the Posse gave enough attention to Yahweh. He figured he no longer needed the Posse, or anyone else, to guide his faith in Yahweh. Though his beliefs were rooted in Posse doctrine, he ordered the Wickstrom tapes destroyed. "I don't agree with Wickstrom on a lot of things," he told them. "Wickstrom's not accurate with all his opinions and he didn't go straight to God with his ideas before he made those tapes."

It was just as well, Ryan said, since the jailed Reverend

Wickstrom was no longer accessible to them as a spiritual or tactical adviser. Now, it was time to build on all they had learned from Wickstrom and take care of their own. "Gather with like minds," was the phrase that Wickstrom had repeated so often.

At first, Rick was hesitant about all of them moving onto his farm. But Ryan persuaded him it was what Yahweh wanted; once again, Ryan was right. Rick knew that they'd all be together eventually to fight in the battle. "Yeah, I figure it is the thing to do," he told Ryan.

Anyway, it was all to Rick's advantage. He was now enjoying favored status with Mike Ryan. Rick became Ryan's "right-arm" man—it was Rick's arm that Ryan used most often when he communicated with Yahweh. Protocol demanded that Mike speak with Yahweh on all important issues; however, the men could use the arm test among themselves to receive instructions about mundane issues or daily chores.

Shortly, the women also had permission to use the arm test among themselves for answers to questions on daily routines—cooking, cleaning, and laundry for a total now of eighteen.

Cheryl, using Ruth's arm, learned that she was to set up a classroom. She knew with her family and the Ryans in hiding most of the children could not return to the public schools in the fall; only Rick's two oldest children would be going to school. Using old grade school texts, she tutored the children in math and spelling every morning. The arm test even determined lesson plans.

Sometimes the arm test got confusing, though. The men and woman couldn't always make sense of the answers they'd get; sometimes in the course of completing a task, they'd get all yes answers or all nos. They'd go to Ryan and he'd say that they'd angered Yahweh, or one of them was in trouble. Still, the arm test governed.

With spirits high, everyone pitched in to prepare the encampment. The priorities were: make the two trailers livable, stockpile food and weapons, and then wait for the battle.

The men toiled through the June heat, jubilantly following Yahweh's orders to fix up the north house, a trailer with an addition built on. First they repaired the plumbing. Running water was a welcome improvement for Ruth Ryan. Using cheap lumber, they fashioned one of the bedrooms into a barracks. They built two sets of bunk beds, three levels high, into the wall. At the end of the bunks, military style, they put footlockers for their field gear and combat clothing.

One morning in the midst of the construction, Ryan considered with consternation an east entrance to the house. Then, he issued the order. "I want this east door blocked. This is Satan's door." His tone was foreboding. "Blocking this door will keep Satan from entering someday."

By day's end, the windowed door had been replaced by a solid wooden door and was painted white, pure white—to fend off the darkness of Satan. Inside, a two-by-four-inch plank was placed across the door as extra reinforcement.

Once the north house construction work was near completion, the Ryans and their three children, along with Cheryl and her five children, moved in. Mike determined the sleeping arrangements. The men and boys slept in the barracks. The girls doubled up in a small bedroom. Ruth and Cheryl shared a bedroom. Most nights Ryan fell asleep in his orange recliner.

Now that they lived under the same roof, Mike began focusing a lot of attention on Cheryl. Ruth tried to swallow her jealousy; she believed Mike when he told her it angered Yahweh. "We've got to do Yahweh's will," he'd told her.

According to Mike, Yahweh had ordered another marriage. Rick and young Lisa Haverkamp were now married before Yahweh. Although Lisa liked Rick, privately she cried about the marriage. She had wanted to return home to finish her senior year in high school. But she surrendered to Yahweh and now made her home in the south trailer with Rick and his three children.

The new living arrangement was stressful for Rick's children. Still recovering from the loss of their mother, they resented having their farm invaded by eight other children. Little Luke was the most demonstrative about it, and his fussing had angered Ryan. Still, Ryan let it be known that he considered all the children, eleven total, his children; he took on the role of a stern disciplinarian.

The encampment was taking shape.

Ruth and Cheryl slid an old brown and navy striped sofa against the far wall of the living room. The console television set was placed against the opposite wall. Above the TV, they tacked up the red, white, and blue of a Confederate flag.

At the end of the living room, next to the window, they placed a worn and faded orange brushed velvet chair— Ryan's chair. It clashed with the green and white curtains at the window, Ruth thought, but the battle was coming—what did it matter? The room would serve as Ryan's command post.

From the orange chair, Ryan had a full view of the lane leading up to the main house. He put a two-way radio on a bookcase next to his chair; with the two-way he could communicate with Rick in the south trailer. To the right of the orange chair, Ryan bolted two wooden holsters to the side of a gray metal desk. Each holster held a gun—a .45 and a .38. Loaded assault rifles hung above the doorways.

A basement under the addition to the trailer became the pantry. They carried box after box of food down the narrow stairway off the kitchen. They lined shelves, extending to the ceiling, with gallons of canned goods—green beans, peas, peaches, corn, mixed vegetables, instant mashed potatoes, dehydrated potatoes, and vegetables; five-gallon buckets of dried beans, oatmeal, and powdered milk.

To make the base camp complete, Mike and Yahweh wanted other members of "the family" to move to the farm. James moved in next; he gathered the few belongings he'd taken with him to David Andreas's farm, where he'd stayed the past few months. James didn't tell his parents he was moving to Rulo.

Jimmy had given up on his hog business in Mercier; he had filed bankruptcy and had no job. The farm was his best hope.

Now, James and Jimmy joined the other men, filling their morning with chores Yahweh assigned—helping Rick in the hog shed, chopping wood, cutting weeds, and doing odd jobs around the two dwellings.

In the afternoons, the men often outfitted themselves in camouflage and took to the woods for target practice. As they crawled through the field grass, the spray of automatic gunfire echoed through the timber. Now, Mike was more willing to share war stories from his Green Beret days in Vietnam.

"What did you do with the Green Berets?" David asked.

"I blew away all those fucking gooks—even women and children—I didn't give a shit." Ryan's eyes were hard and cold. "They pulled me out to join an intelligence unit, the CIA. I was in charge of putting together torture devices. I had devices for taking their fingers apart and skinning them alive!"

"How'd you take their fingers apart?" David asked, astonished.

"I made this clamp," he said, pinching his knuckles with two fingers to show how it worked. "Then I'd put the hand in a press and pull on the clamp until the joints pulled apart."

"You actually did that?" Jimmy asked.

"Hey, Nam was a nasty place. We had to do all sorts of things. One time, I had to go in to take intelligence photos of Ho Chi Minh. When I left North Vietnam to go back down south, I had to hide up under a train to get back."

David shook his head in disbelief. Ryan's wealth of experience never ceased to amaze him and the other men.

In the evenings, they smoked marijuana and watched movies. Ryan, who earlier had sworn off dope, was now smoking it daily. And he convinced the others to use it, too. Rick bought the grass from a buddy of his in Falls City.

"I've done my share of drinking," Jimmy said, "but I've never gotten into marijuana . . . until now."

"I've tried it a couple of times," David said, "but it never did anything for me."

"It's a reward from Yahweh. He wants us to relax with it," Ryan insisted.

The movies they watched were on videocassette; *Red Dawn* and *The Ten Commandments* were their favorites.

Ryan also liked *Star Wars* and *The Empire Strikes Back.* He identified with Luke Skywalker—the small-time country boy who became a hero when he led the rebel forces to victory in the battle against Darth Vader of the Evil Empire. Just as Luke Skywalker had mastered "the Force" to fight evil, Ryan was tapping into greater powers to lead his people here at the farm.

And they trusted his word. Obedient to Ryan as their leader, the eccentric family was grateful for the safe haven. They felt sure they'd found deliverance on this farm outside the small town of Rulo.

CHAPTER 32

Rulo was a dying town, and had been for years. At the turn of the century, it had been a bustling river town—it was the first major white man's settlement west of the Mississippi River. Originally named after Charles Rouleau, a member of the Fremont expedition, the spelling was later changed to Rulo by postal authorities. The rugged topography lent a peculiar beauty to the town nestled in the hills along the mighty Missouri. The once rough river town quickly grew to its peak population of 877 in 1900.

A prospering community, Rulo competed with Falls City, Nebraska, nine miles away, to become the county seat of Richardson County, but the advent of the Nebraska–Atchison Railroad changed Rulo's fate. The expansion overland, by rail, meant decline for the river town.

Now, in 1984, a green sign at the edge of the city limits listed a population of 260. The only things reminiscent of days long gone by were tugboats still churning down the river, the melancholy wail of their foghorns floating on the air.

Rulo's main street had little life left in it. Most storefronts were boarded along the block of red-brick, two-story buildings. It was easy to miss the pale white letters on one window with white, lacy curtains: U.S. Post Office, Rulo, Neb. 68431.

Just down the street, at the end of the block, a black and white sign, Rulo Library, hung over the door of a forlorn building. But from the looks of the dirty plate-glass windows and vacant interior, the library had died long ago.

Across the street, the only sign of life was an orange neon Budweiser sign blinking from the window of Ye Old Tyme Saloon. A pair of wooden, swinging doors hung in the tavern's recessed entryway. Inside, a dark mahogany bar with matching cabinets behind stretched half the length of the tavern. Mirrors, extending to the ceiling, reflected a single row of liquor bottles. The bar served food, too; barbecued pork ribs were listed on the menu as the house specialty.

But the town's hottest spot was Camp Rulo—a restaurant and honky-tonk bar—standing on the banks of the Missouri River. A sign at the edge of the gravel parking lot welcomed diners: Fish–Steaks–Dining–Dancing.

With its sloped roof and picture windows, the restaurant resembled a scaled-down version of a mountain lodge. The view, aside from the rickety fishermen's shacks nearby, was spectacular. From their tablesides, diners gazed at the cutting waters of the muddy Missouri.

Fried catfish and carp, plucked fresh from the river, were the fare that had drawn patrons for years. And the onion rings. Crispy, golden onion rings piled high on platters the waitresses cradled in their arms.

Rulo's houses were tucked into a cluster of hills, some of which offered a view of three states—south to the hills of northern Kansas, east to the spreading flats of Missouri, and, of course, Nebraska.

The residents in and around Rulo were typically midwestern, small-town folks. They were easygoing and accustomed to knowing just about everything about everybody. Now the rumor mill began grinding out weird tales of gunfire ringing through the pastures at the Stice farm and men darting through the woods in camouflage.

Not all of it was rumor.

MID-JUNE

Ryan, with his .45 holstered at his side, stepped into the middle of the gravel road that ran past Stice's farm and confronted neighboring farmers Virgil Martin and his son, Bob. They were heading into one of their fields to check fences. "You guys are trespassing," Ryan said gruffly. "You've got no business being here."

Virgil Martin wasn't intimidated by this bearded man strutting before him. "I've been around here for seventy years," Martin said, "and I'm telling you that I do have business being here. And I'm going in there to check my fences."

Ryan, unaccustomed to direct challenges, was at a loss for words. Without speaking, he stepped aside and Martins passed.

Virgil Martin shook his head as he drove on into the bottom land. That guy thinks he's in charge of some little kingdom out here, Martin thought. What are these fools up to, he wondered. Martin wasn't the only area resident that Ryan had tried to run off.

Earlier, Ryan put the run on Ralph Steinbrink, the former mayor of Falls City. Steinbrink liked to fish on the Martin pond. But after Ryan ran him off, he was leery of going back. Virgil Martin had offered to escort him back to the pond personally, but Steinbrink declined his offer. "I don't want to stir up any trouble," he told Martin.

Virgil Martin began keeping an eye on Ryan and his bunch, while putting up hay right across the road from them. He saw them coming and going, and compared notes with a neighboring farmer. "I've seen Big Daddy Ryan strutting around with his gun on his side. I've heard automatic gunfire coming out of the woods on weekends; you'd think the National Guard was on duty," he told his neighbor.

Martin's neighbor had heard the gunfire, too. "Yeah, I've heard what sounds like an M-16 going off in the middle of the night. I know what an M-16 sounds like. I carried one in Vietnam."

"They're up to no good, that's for sure," Martin said.

Garneta Butrick had heard the rumors, too, and they frightened her. She had more than a passing interest—her grandchildren, the Stice kids, lived on the farm. She hurried to her car when she got off work at the Falls City nursing home where she was a nurse's aide. Garneta, fifty-one, was short and plump, with a gentle round face. She drove straight to the modest dwelling on Lane Street where she lived with her husband, Tom. It was a few minutes after seven o'clock in the morning—she worked the night shift—and she was usually ready to go to bed by this time. But today, she was determined to see their grandchildren at the farm.

"I'm going out there this morning, Tom, and I'm going to see my grandchildren," she said emphatically. She hadn't seen the kids in a month. Rick never brought them by the house anymore, and the last time she'd gone to the farm, she hadn't been allowed past the gate. "Some teenage boy told me the kids weren't home," she'd told Tom. "If I have to, I'll wait until school starts in September and go visit the two oldest kids at school during their lunch period." But Luke wasn't in school yet. She worried about him—he was the baby. He had been only three when his mother, Sondra, had died, and he still didn't understand her death. It broke Garneta's heart every time they drove past the mortuary and Luke asked, "Can we go see Mommy?" She'd tell him, "No, Luke, Mommy's in heaven."

Tom Butrick, in his fifties, was tall and lanky with wiry white hair and a throaty voice. Easygoing, he never met a stranger and loved talking to folks; he usually followed his departing visitors to the curb, talking all the way. Tom worked in a meat locker in town and tinkered with cars on the side.

Today, Tom couldn't get off work to go out to Rick's farm with Garneta. "I want you to be careful about going out there," he said. He didn't think she'd be in real danger, but he felt better warning her. They knew Rick had those Posse guys living there and that they had a lot of guns. "Keep plenty of gas in your car in case they chase you out of there,'' Tom said. ''And back into the drive so you can drive out of there quick if you have to.''

But Garneta wasn't the least bit afraid for herself. She just wanted to see her grandchildren. She'd pledged to her dying daughter, Sondra, that she'd keep watch over them.

Shortly after eight o'clock, she pulled up to the farm gate. Dennis Ryan came outside. ''What do you want?''

''I want to see Dawn, Barry, and Luke,'' she said resolutely. ''My grandkids.''

''They're not here.''

That had been what he'd said the last time. ''Where are they, then?''

''Don't know,'' Dennis said.

''Do you know when they'll be here?'' she asked impatiently.

''Nope.''

''Is Rick here?''

''No.''

Realizing the futility of her effort, Garneta climbed slowly into the car and drove home. She went to bed, but she didn't sleep.

CHAPTER 33

MID-JULY 1984

Clanging pots and pans and the aroma of frying eggs and pancakes signaled that Yahweh had ordered the women to prepare a hearty breakfast on this early summer morning.

"Yahweh, do you want us to serve juice with breakfast?" Ruth asked through Cheryl's arm. Their heads were bowed.

Yes.

"Yahweh, do you want us to ask about our noon meal at this time?"

Yes.

"Wolverines!" two of the little boys yelled, darting through the kitchen, ducking behind chairs. In their game of make-believe war, they referred to the enemy, Wolverines, in *Red Dawn*. The children frequently played war games; they also spent a lot of time outside or in the barracks, where they played with toys.

In the barracks, Jimmy was pulling on his jeans when he heard Ryan, coming out of a stoned stupor, rising from his reclining chair. Jimmy had noticed dramatic changes in Ryan in the past two or three weeks. He was cocky and self-righteous, and he acted like he was better than the other men. Jimmy felt a widening gap in their friendship, but he quickly minimized the changes in his own mind. Mike was still his leader.

Jimmy looked out into the living room. There, Ryan was putting his daughter Mandy's dress on her; each morning she'd carry her dress to him, insisting that only he dress her.

"There you go," he said, pulling her little arm through the sleeve. "Now you're looking good." Ryan kissed the toddler as she slid off his lap.

"Mornin', Mike," Jimmy said.

"Uh, mornin'," Mike grumbled as he lit a joint.

Ryan was ready to begin his morning ritual. Using Rick's arm, he asked what chores the men were to do today. That done, he went down the list of names of everyone on the farm, asking if anyone had angered Yahweh by being weak in faith. Punishment usually meant fasting and repentance, but Ryan often meted out stiffer penalties to the men than to the women.

Ryan learned that James and Jimmy had angered Yahweh with their actions the day before. Yahweh had instructed them to find more cattle. Late in the afternoon, they had returned triumphant, having found just the place.

But they had returned fifteen minutes late. Yahweh had specifically stated that they should leave at noon and return at four o'clock. Now, James and Jimmy would have to be punished for disobeying. They were ordered to sleep outside the next two nights and be limited to only four hours of sleep each night, and they were to clean the hog shed.

About two dozen dead baby pigs had been rotting for weeks in the manure pit of the hog shed. The piglets had died after falling through the floor grates. Rick had given up on the hog business, and had never gotten around to cleaning the shed.

Now, Jimmy and James, nearly gagging from the stench, scooped shovel after shovel of the rotting mess from the bottom of the shed. Once done, they washed down the cement until the shed was clean.

That night, Jimmy and James, without blankets or pillows, stretched out on a grassy spot not far from the south trailer. Jimmy felt a little silly, if not hurt, about sleeping on

the ground. He considered protesting, but his better judgment told him not to argue. Ryan was dead serious about
them being punished. But why? Jimmy wondered. Being
ordered to sleep outside on the ground seemed excessive for
being a few minutes late. Jimmy felt uneasy. He was seeing
a side of Ryan that he'd never seen before.

CHAPTER 34

Rick was beginning to dread the morning ritual. It seemed he was continually aggravating Yahweh.

Ryan studied Rick. "You're having doubts. Doubts about all of us being here at the farm," Ryan said, his stare cold and vacant.

Rick swallowed hard. Shit. Ryan could tell. The look in Ryan's eyes scared him. What had happened to Mike? Rick wondered. The farm was bringing out the worst in him. Rick had known that Mike had a lot of anger toward other people, but he'd never known him to direct it at his friends—especially those who shared his beliefs. But now, his anger was coming out more and more. The slightest issues enraged him.

"You just better stay straight with Yahweh, bud," Ryan said.

The morning ritual also included going down the list of children's names to see if any of them had angered Yahweh. Rick's arm stayed extended when Ryan called out the name of one of Cheryl's little boys. According to Yahweh, it was that child who had broken the band on a watch that one of the men had left in the bathroom. The boy would have to be spanked.

Mike Ryan and son Dennis, spring 1984, while still living at their Whiting, Kansas, farmhouse.
© *World Herald Photos*

Lester Gibson, pictured the day after his family was
located on the Rulo farm, holds a flier that he
circulated during a yearlong search for his wife and
five children. © *The Kansas City Star*

James Thimm, 26, was a victim of a torture slaying at the farm. Ryan said he'd angered Yahweh.

Five-year-old Luke Stice was beaten and abused for months prior to his death. © *Falls City Journal*

Private investigator Dennis Whalen, who helped
Lester Gibson in his yearlong search for his family.
Photo by Anne Johnson Steinhoff

Cult member Tim Haverkamp, 23, is led into the
Richardson County Courthouse in Falls City,
Nebraska. Photo taken shortly after his arrest.
© *Falls City Journal*

Cult leader Mike Ryan is led into the Richardson
County Courthouse shortly after his arrest.
Richardson County Sheriff Cory McNabb is at
right. © *Falls City Journal*

Nebraska State Patrol Investigator Terry Becker, right, talks to reporters amidst stolen equipment recovered at the Rulo farm. Cult members said Yahweh directed them to steal in preparation for the approaching Battle of Armageddon.
© *Falls City Journal*

Several hundred bags of charcoal were discovered at the Rulo farm; plans were to use the charcoal to make bombs for the Battle of Armageddon.
© *Falls City Journal*

October 16, 1986: Mike Ryan is sentenced to die in Nebraska's electric chair. Here he's led away from the Richardson County courtroom where he was sentenced. At right, Sheriff Cory McNabb.
© *Falls City Journal*

*   *   *

Ruth had just come in from picking vegetables in the garden and was grinding goat meat for stew. She hoped Mike would ignore her this morning, but she felt him come up behind her in the kitchen. He took her by the shoulders and turned her toward him. She locked eyes with him and then turned away.

"You've angered Yahweh," Ryan said gruffly. "I can tell what you're thinking, Ruth. I can see right through you."

"Mike, everything is fine."

"Yahweh is angry at you for being jealous about the other women here on the farm."

"Mike, I'm sorry. I'll do my best . . ."

"Yahweh wants you to do a day of fasting and repentance. Got it?"

"Yes, Mike." Ruth lowered her head, submitting one more time.

This morning, Ryan stood before the group. "We're going to get organized around here. Yahweh has let us know what we need to do and we will obey." Ryan assigned rankings to the family of Yahweh.

The men accepted their assigned ranks as privates, with the understanding that they would be able to advance to the position of general if they proved themselves worthy. Young Dennis Ryan was to be a prince, a title that flattered the fifteen-year-old. Mike Ryan was, of course, the king of Israel.

Rick accepted his title as the high priest, but he tingled with jealousy when Mike named Lisa the queen of Israel. He'd seen Ryan coming on to her. Now, Ryan seemed to pair himself with her. And Ryan's constant talk about sex when he was around the men was getting old, Rick thought. Rick was no prude, but he was beginning to think Ryan was some kind of sex pervert, always talking about sex and how women loved him.

"When you boys get married, come talk to me about how to please a woman," Ryan said. "I turn women into love machines."

*   *   *

Life on the farm had become radically different in the first month. The euphoria, the honeymoon phase, of the banding together at Rulo was over.

Some tension was natural. Under the best of circumstances, communal living was stressful. But with each passing week Ryan had imposed more rules; he'd become stricter, more militant.

He wanted the men and women separated. They were no longer allowed to communicate—only small talk was permitted when the men picked up their plates at mealtime. The women, with the exception of Lisa, weren't allowed to use the phone. And the women could wear only dresses—Yahweh told them which ones.

It was as though something had snapped inside Mike Ryan's mind. The man who'd been their understanding friend was becoming a tyrant. His unspoken rule was: don't think, don't question . . . just believe.

They quickly learned that to anger Ryan was to anger Yahweh. And Ryan constantly reminded them that he was not a man to cross. He'd bolstered his killer image with tales of his latest CIA assignment—taking out an FBI man during a recent visit to Kansas City. "Yeah, the guy was tracking me, getting too close to finding out about my past," Ryan told the family. "I ended up shooting him in the back of the neck with my.45."

According to Ryan, his CIA experience, which mostly involved assassinations, had been so secret that his military records, back at Fort Bragg, had been destroyed, and his age had been set back four years to cover up his involvement in the military. "But because of my past, some other agents are still out to get me." He was still on the CIA payroll, he said, and received his assignments through a secret post office box.

He had Mafia contacts, too. Clayburn was his man. Clayburn, a top hit man, could rub out anybody. All it would take was a phone call.

The children also grew increasingly fearful of Ryan. They whispered about "Mean Mike" as they witnessed Ryan's abusive treatment of Rick's youngest son, Luke.

Simply put, Ryan and Luke despised each other. Still missing his mother, Luke's sense of safety was further threatened by Ryan. The boy often cried when Rick left to spend time with Ryan.

Ryan, irritated by the child's dislike for him, was further aggravated over Luke's squabbles with his daughter Mandy. The two children had fought over toys and coloring books; finally, Luke's fussing had sent Ryan into a rage. "He's of Satan!" Ryan proclaimed. Other times Ryan knocked the boy out of his path, shouting in his face, calling him a mongrel, a dog. The defenseless five-year-old boy became a scapegoat for Ryan's pent-up frustrations.

Rick, feeling totally powerless, looked on and prayed that the abuse would stop.

Cheryl feared for her children, too. Ryan seemed to have little patience with them. Although he rarely mistreated her kids, he had raised welts on her two-year-old daughter when she wouldn't eat her vegetables. He whipped the toddler and demanded that she sit in a corner in the next room. Her crying made him angrier. "Stop your crying, you little bitch!" Ryan had screamed in the terrified child's face. The more she cried, the louder Ryan screamed at her. "I'll train her not to cry, dammit!" he'd said.

Cheryl prayed that her children wouldn't do anything to anger Yahweh.

CHAPTER 35

Lester awoke in the middle of the night, thinking about his children. He rubbed his eyes and looked at the digital clock next to his bed. It was 1:30. Too wound up to sleep, he lit a cigarette, pulled on his jeans and his red Converse tennis shoes. He trudged outside and began pacing up and down the country road like he'd done countless nights before. Some nights he'd walk miles.

In the weeks since Cheryl's disappearance, Lester had kept a fighting attitude, despite his depression. He was going to find his wife and kids. He learned from Sheriff Wolney the names of the three strange men who had helped move Cheryl's things from the house. A check of the license plates showed the cars belonged to Rick Stice of Rulo and James Thimm of Beatrice, Nebraska. The third man was David Andreas, also of Beatrice.

It was a good lead. He traveled to Nebraska to see Richardson County Sheriff Gene Ramer. Maybe he could help.

Ramer was a tall man of medium build, balding on top. At age forty-eight, he'd been battling colon cancer for the past year and a half. In December of 1982, his doctors had given him six months to live. But Gene was a fighter and had beaten back the disease a couple of times before. Now he listened patiently to what Lester had to say.

"Yeah, we know Rick Stice," Ramer told Lester. "We also know the name Mike Ryan; these guys have been known to attend these Posse meetings. So far, though, we don't know of anyone breaking the law."

"Well, I know that my wife did not leave of her own will," Lester insisted. "Something's wrong. She's been sucked into this and I think she and my kids are in danger. Maybe she's out there at Stice's farm in Rulo. Is there anything you can do to help me?" Lester's voice quivered.

Ramer pondered Lester's predicament. "The hell of it is, we don't have any right to go onto that farm to look for her. It puts us in a bind, it being a Kansas case and all," Ramer said.

"But she's broken the law," Lester protested. "She's left with the kids and that's in violation of the court order. The court was in charge of the kids. She wasn't supposed to leave without the court's permission." Lester's tone was urgent.

"Yeah, but have any charges been filed against her? Is there a warrant out for her arrest?"

"No," Lester admitted. "But I'm working on that. If we can file charges, then you can go after her, right?"

"We'll try to get in there and see if your family's at the farm, but that's about all we can do right now. Even if she is there, we can't do anything about it. We can't just snatch her, unless we've got charges against her. And even then, with Kansas charges, she'd have to be extradited."

Lester drew in a deep breath and rubbed his chin; his eyes filled with tears. He opened a large brown envelope containing pictures of Cheryl and the children; he spread the photos across Ramer's desk, pointing at the pictures as he named each child.

Sheriff Ramer said he'd do what he could.

On July 14, 1984, Ramer sent two undercover men from the state patrol in Lincoln to the Rulo farm. Ramer briefed the men and showed them pictures of Cheryl and each of her five children, as well as pictures of Cheryl's brother and parents.

In the early afternoon, the undercover men, carrying clipboards, were met by Rick as they stepped up to the gate of the Rulo farm. They introduced themselves as workers for the Army Corps of Engineers.

"What can I do for you?"

"We'd like to look at the levees down by the river to see how they took that flooding a few months ago," one of them said.

Rick shrugged. "Guess so," he said.

"Thanks, we'll just look around. It won't take us long."

As they headed for the bottom land, the agents observed two little boys playing in the front yard and three cars parked at the side of the north house. Both men believed the boys were sons of Lester Gibson.

They positively identified Jimmy Havercamp. And a check of the tags on the cars in the drive showed them belonging to Stice, Thimm, and Norbert Havercamp. There was no sign of Cheryl, though.

Ramer shared the details of his preliminary probe with Lester the next evening at Ramer's farm home outside of Rulo. He'd given Lester permission to call on him there.

"What can we do about it?" Lester asked.

"Like I said before, at the moment, there's not much we can do. We can try to keep an eye on the place, but so far, no warrants have been issued."

Lester reluctantly said he understood.

Ramer mentioned the calls from farmers in the area, complaining about hearing gunfire, perhaps machine gun fire. "We need to check out those reports. Maybe we can try again to find out if your wife and kids are out there."

"Thanks," Lester said.

"I'm going to talk to Terry Becker about it, too," Ramer said.

Terry Becker, an investigator with the Nebraska State Patrol, had worked a lot of cases with Gene Ramer. Becker, too, had heard the town rumors about gunfire at the Stice farm. He had people question him at ball games and in restaurants. "What's going on up north of Rulo?" they'd asked. Becker agreed with Ramer that the rumors should be checked out. In fact, Becker offered to pay a visit to the farm. "I'll take one of our men from the headquarters in Lincoln with me," he told Ramer.

Becker, at thirty-five, had been with the Nebraska State Patrol for six years. Blond and blue-eyed, with rugged good looks, the former marine was in the prime of his career and the prime of his life. He was active both on and off the job. When he wasn't working, he fished with his boys or got involved in civic activities and sports. He liked to pump iron and had biceps to prove it.

"The thing about the rumor mill," Becker told Ramer, "is that it can get out of hand so fast. You can have a firecracker go off on one side of town and by the time the rumor spreads to the other side of town, you've got a double homicide."

Sure, maybe there was some kind of paramilitary activity going on at the farm. That stuff alone was not illegal, but law enforcement agencies, like the patrol, county sheriff, and local police, had been developing intelligence about paramilitary groups and right-wing extremists—just in case.

Becker himself had attended a seminar on paramilitary groups a couple of years earlier. So far, there hadn't been any problems with these groups in southeast Nebraska.

The rollers on his wooden office chair clicked across the seams of the tile floor as Terry Becker reached for the telephone to call Rick Stice.

A woman answered.

"Is Rick there?" Becker asked.

"Just a minute. Ree-uck . . . tella-phone . . ." the woman yelled.

A few moments later, Rick answered the phone.

"Hi, Rick. This is Terry Becker with the state patrol office here in Falls City."

There was a pause at the other end of the line. "Yeah?" Rick responded cautiously.

"Rick, I'd like to visit with you. We've got some rumors floating around town about some of the folks who live near your farm hearing a lot of gunfire—some say automatic gunfire. I just wanted to check that out, see if there are any problems down your way."

"Well, we're not having any problems here," Rick replied.

"We'd still like to talk with you . . . maybe put an end to the rumors, at least."

"Okay," was Rick's reply.

"Why don't you just come by my office here at the courthouse, say, early this afternoon, and we can talk. Would that work?"

"Yeah, that'll be okay," Rick said.

"How about one thirty?"

"That's fine."

"See you then," Becker said, dropping the phone in its cradle. Becker, like Ramer, had a list of area people who were believed to be connected with the Posse Comitatus, Rick's name included. But none of them had been known to be lawbreakers.

At 1:30 sharp, Rick, wearing a white T-shirt and faded blue jeans, appeared in the doorway of Becker's office. He carried a rifle case.

"Come on in, Rick. Have a seat."

Rick accepted and pulled a rifle out of the case. "Well . . . here's the gun you're talking about. I use it for target practice," Rick explained before Becker had a chance to ask anything.

"What have you got there, Rick?"

"It's just a .22. I put this crank on it, this attachment, so that when I turn it, it does sound like an automatic," Rick said. He handed the gun to Becker.

Becker looked down the barrel of the gun, then turned it over, examining it. "Well, Rick, I don't see any problem with this rifle, but I can't imagine this gun would make that much noise—the kind we've been hearing rumors about."

"Well, that's what it is!" Rick interrupted.

"You don't have any other, bigger weapons out there?"

"Nope."

"By the way, Rick, who's living at your farm? Is there anyone living there besides you?"

"Nope. Just me and the kids and my wife, Lisa."

Becker nodded. He didn't know Rick had remarried since his wife's death. "Rick, would you mind if my sergeant and I come out and take a look around later this afternoon?"

"There ain't much to see, but you can come out—see for yourself."

"Okay, then, we'll drop out later this afternoon. Thanks for coming in, Rick."

The two men shook hands; Rick picked up his rifle and left.

Becker and his boss, State Patrol Sergeant Jim Snyder, arrived at the farm about three forty-five. As they stepped into the sweltering August heat, Snyder, a man in his early fifties, loosened his tie.

As Rick hurried to the gate, Becker noticed a young woman in the doorway, but she quickly stepped out of sight.

Neither Becker nor Snyder noticed the movement at the curtains in the window. Neither did they see the tip of the gun barrel trained on them as they walked along the drive.

"Who's the girl?" Becker asked Rick.

"That's Lisa, my wife. We got married a while back."

"Congratulations," Snyder offered politely.

"Can we come in and talk?" Becker asked, knowing that the straightforward question would be their only chance for getting inside the house. They had no search warrant.

"No, you can't come in," Rick answered decisively. "A man's home is his castle and I won't allow you to come in. But you can look around the farm." Rick certainly didn't want them to know about Cheryl and her kids being there, or even the Ryans, for that matter. Not much of the world understood their mission here at the farm. The less the law knew, the better.

Rick was well within his rights in not allowing them into the house, Becker and Snyder knew, but it made them wonder if he was hiding something. Did he, in fact, have other guns in there? Becker wondered if there were children inside—children belonging to Lester Gibson.

"Why don't we just have a look around the property, then," Snyder said.

"Fine, I'll show you around," Rick offered.

The entire farm was quiet, Becker observed. Totally quiet. There were no kids around, not even any toys in the yard.

Rick led them down past his hog shed to a field where he said he held target practice. He pointed at a piece of plywood tacked between two posts. The plywood was full of bullet holes, but not from large-caliber weapons.

"This is it," Rick said. "Not much to it. We just come down and shoot targets."

"Who's we?" Snyder wanted to know.

"Oh, just some buddies of mine who come out once in a while."

"Well, Rick, like I said in my office, that .22 of yours just wouldn't make the kind of sounds that we've been hearing about. You're sure none of your buddies have any automatic weapons down here?"

"Nope, none that I know of . . ." Rick said.

"There's no law against target practice, but there would be a problem if people were using automatic weapons," Becker said.

Rick nodded. "Yeah, I know."

Becker and Snyder weren't sure Rick was telling them the whole story, but they had no evidence to the contrary, either.

"I think we've had a pretty good look around," Becker said.

The three men walked back to the entrance gate.

"Say, Rick, you know that Cheryl Gibson and her children from Kansas are missing? Rumor has it they've been up around here. Have you seen anything of them?" Becker asked.

"Nope. Sure haven't," Rick said.

"Okay, then, Rick. Thanks for letting us look around. Let's keep the lines of communication open. Give us a call if you have any problems," were Becker's departing words.

Becker and Snyder hopped into their car. Becker made a three-point turn in the drive and headed down the lane.

Inside the house, Ryan lowered the rifle he had trained on the lawmen as they walked the property. He pulled back the curtain and watched the car disappear in the gravel dust.

CHAPTER 36

Ryan was furious over Becker and Snyder showing up at the farm. "Someone around here is having doubts. Yahweh is mad at someone. That's why these cops are coming around."

Ryan became paranoid about Cheryl being discovered at the farm. "I've had special instructions from Yahweh about Cheryl and her kids. They'll be hidden until after the Battle of Armageddon. No lawman's going to find them." As a precaution against unexpected visitors crossing the gate, Ryan ordered the posting of guards. "I want someone on guard duty at all times, from six o'clock in the morning until ten at night," Ryan said, slamming his fist on the table beside him. "I don't want anyone coming near this place that doesn't have any business coming up here."

James Thimm was to take the first night shift. Dennis Ryan, glad to see his dad kick ass, was to take the day shift.

"You men make sure you carry a loaded pistol at all times," Ryan ordered.

Ryan also wanted a sign posted. Immediately, the sign was painted and hung: NO TRESPASSING. VIOLATORS WILL BE PROSECUTED.

"I've got more faith than any of you here," Ryan yelled. "I do everything I'm told by Yahweh, no questions asked!"

Ryan turned to James Thimm. "You get a message to David Andreas to get his ass up here. He's in big trouble with Yahweh. He could burn in hell."

The next day, James found David in the barn milking cows. "Mike wants to see you up at the farm. He says you're in trouble."

David took the message from Ryan seriously, but it was hard for him to get away. He was a hard worker—couldn't find enough hours in the day. "Tell Mike I'll come up there as soon as I get my work finished on Saturday," he told James.

David had thrown himself into the upkeep of the family's farm; he kept hoping he could get the place into the black. If that weren't a big enough task, he held a full-time factory job at Store Kraft—a company that manufactured fixtures for stores—in Beatrice. He'd worked there for twelve years, since 1972, and was earning around twenty thousand dollars a year. He was also a reservist in the National Guard, a job that paid him around fifteen hundred dollars a year.

On Saturday, David saw the stern look on Ryan's face when he walked into the north house.

"David, Yahweh says you're in danger of eternal damnation. You could burn in hell if you don't do what he wants."

"What . . . what . . . what have I done? What does he want?" David asked, stuttering nervously.

"Well, all I know is we're supposed to ask Yahweh about you moving up here, so let's get it done."

"Okay," David agreed, as Rick looked on.

Ryan first positioned Rick in front of him for the arm test. Using Rick's arm he asked, "Yahweh, Heavenly Father, is David Andreas supposed to move here to the farm with us?"

Rick's arm stiffened. The answer was yes.

"Okay, let's ask again, see if we get the same answer," Ryan instructed. Only this time he would use David's arm.

David moved over in front of Ryan.

"Heavenly Father, is David Andreas supposed to move up here to the farm?"

Again, the answer was yes.

David slowly lowered his arm. What about my job and the farm? he thought to himself.

"It makes sense to me," Ryan added, reflecting on Yahweh's instruction. "Other people have already moved up here . . . we're all getting ready. Makes sense that you should come, too."

"I . . . I . . . I just have a lot of responsibilities right now," David said.

"David, you're too worried about your farm and your job. Too worried about material things. You aren't concerned enough about Yahweh, and something real bad can happen because of that. You can burn in hell for that!"

True, David was exhausted. Despite his hard work, the farm wasn't making it. He owed money on equipment, and to add to his stress, he hadn't filed income tax returns for several years. Even though he knew he didn't owe the IRS much money, to him it was a bookkeeping nightmare. And there were family squabbles over the farm. David's father was trustee of the farm, and several relatives disliked that. They also disliked David's being there. David was tired of the bickering. Yes, maybe it was time to go to Rulo.

David called his boss at the factory and asked for a couple of days off, knowing that, in reality, he would not return at all.

"Of course, Yahweh wants you to clear out your checking account, too," Ryan ordered.

David complied, closing out his checking account, which included a thousand dollars he'd just borrowed from the bank to pay bills at his farm, and turned it over to Ryan.

On Sunday evening, when Ryan, Dennis, and Rick arrived to move his things, David felt pulled. He didn't want to leave. But he gave in to the pressure of Mike Ryan, shutting out the voice inside of him that coaxed him to stay. He scribbled a note and tossed it on the kitchen table:

To my relatives who want me off the farm, I hope you are happy.

To my parents, I would advise selling everything you can of mine to satisfy the creditors because I am not coming back again. Anything left behind I don't want anyway. I am through living under this system.

David

P.S. Don't look for me!

As they loaded David's things, Ryan spotted several head of cattle in the adjacent pasture. "We should ask Yahweh if he wants us to take the cattle." The herd included a heifer, two steers, and three bull calves, each weighing between six and seven hundred pounds. A separate Holstein belonged to David.

"Those belong to my neighbor lady. She's paid me to take care of them," David said. He didn't feel right about taking them.

But the answer from Yahweh was immediate—take them.

The cattle were sold the next morning. Ryan ordered Norbert Haverkamp to be at the stockyards in St. Joseph, Missouri, the next morning to sell the cattle in his name. Asking no questions, Norbert complied.

The summer of 1984 had become a season of fear for the Haverkamps.

CHAPTER 37

Maxine's chest tightened with tension as she parked in the driveway of the Rulo farm. She was afraid of Ryan. She tried to hide her anxiety from her fourteen-year-old son, Danny, in the seat beside her. Ryan's demands for cash and supplies at the farm were starting to overwhelm her family.

As Maxine had done in past weeks, she came to the farm at the order of Mike Ryan. He'd usually send Jimmy or Rick as a messenger or have them call her and tell her to come up. Each time she was ordered to bring a specific amount of cash. Ryan would take it and decide how to spend it.

Today, along with cash, Maxine brought bags of groceries, more items to be placed in storage.

Ryan was sprawled out in his orange recliner in the living room, drinking 7UP and leafing through a copy of *Gun World* magazine. He looked up from the magazine. "You bring the supplies?" he asked Maxine.

"The groceries are in the kitchen, Mike," she said. "I'm going to help Ruth carry some of them to the basement."

Young Danny came in and took a seat on the couch next to Big Mike, as he had come to call him.

"What's up, bud?" Ryan asked, not looking up from the magazine.

"Oh, not much," Danny replied.

"What's your dad doing?"

"Dad just got back from another road trip."

"Oh, yeah, where?"

"Colorado, mostly, I think," the boy said. "But he was happy about it. I think he made good sales."

"Oh. What else did your dad say?" Ryan asked, suddenly interested.

"Nothing much, really," Danny said.

Ryan smiled, ignoring the boy now. He knew all he needed to know. Norbert had cash.

Shortly, Maxine entered the room and handed Ryan an envelope with the money he'd asked for.

As Ryan took the envelope, he studied Maxine's face. "Maxine, you're having doubts, I can tell." It wasn't the first time Ryan had accused her of doubting Yahweh's word. In fact, he refused to use her arm for the arm test, claiming that her faith was too weak. "If you doubt Yahweh, don't forget that all kinds of shit can happen. If you don't obey him, you can bet something bad is going to happen to your children, or maybe your grandkids."

Maxine hadn't forgotten Ryan whipping her two-year-old granddaughter. Ryan had gone into a rage, screaming into the little girl's face. The more she had tried not to cry, the louder he had screamed. Maxine had been too terrified of Ryan to pick up her granddaughter.

Maxine had heard Ryan talk about killing women and children in Vietnam without batting an eye. And he'd told her before that as part of the CIA network, he knew hit men across the country who owed him favors. He could have anybody bumped off, he said.

Maxine worried about her brother Dennis, in Denver. Ryan might have someone kill him out there. When she'd confided in Dennis some of the things that were going on between her family and Mike Ryan, Dennis had expressed concern and wanted to come visit. Ryan had threatened to shoot him if he crossed the gate.

Maxine believed it when Ryan told her that he'd killed a

former Brown County sheriff in Kansas; the sheriff had been found dead a few months earlier alongside his motorcycle on a country road. The sheriff had actually died accidentally when his cycle had crashed.

"It would be a shame if something happened to Norbert," Ryan said, his eyes narrowing to a squint.

"Mike, I'm doing everything that is asked of me. Please."

True . . . Maxine had done everything Mike Ryan had asked of her. Just about everything. She was not prepared for what would happen a few nights later when she followed his order to come to the farm late one night.

"Yahweh wants you and me to be man and wife," he told her once she arrived.

Maxine, in a state of shock, tried to go along with it.

As everyone gathered for the ceremony outside, Rick could see that Maxine was distraught. Rick didn't think this marriage was right, even though Ryan had gotten Yahweh's approval through his arm. But Rick's charge was not to understand the arm test, but rather obey it. He performed a short, impromptu wedding.

Shortly after the ceremony, Yahweh ordered that Ryan and his new wife leave for Omaha. Maxine had an idea of what was in store, and had she felt she had a choice, she'd not have gone.

"All I know is Yahweh wants us to go to Omaha," Ryan told her. But, in reality, Ryan knew more than that—the trip was to be their honeymoon.

Halfway to Omaha, he told her, "You know, Maxine, I am directly descended from God—like Moses. So are you. We are separate from any mortals on this earth, and someday, after the Battle of Armageddon, you will be my wife. In fact, you are one of my wives now, according to the eyes of Yahweh, but in name only right now." Ryan called up a Bible Scripture that said one man could have seven wives.

"Mike, that can't be," Maxine said. "I've been married to Norbert for thirty years."

"Maxine, why are you fighting it?" Mike was getting agitated.

Maxine froze.

"Doubts, Maxine. You're having too damn many doubts. What a pity it would be if something happened to Norbert out on the road. I'd hate to see him get killed in an accident just because you had weak faith and did not believe in Yahweh. It could be a violent death."

Yes, she was having doubts and she was afraid not to believe Ryan's claim that he could read her mind. He'd tell her things Norbert was saying about her, then she'd find he'd told Norbert something different. She was always confused, off center, around Mike Ryan.

"Maxine, you probably know that Norbert is running around on you. You oughta hear the tales he tells about other women he's met out on the road. Shit, you ain't even married to him in Yahweh's eyes. Maxine, don't you see, Yahweh wants you and me to be man and wife now."

Maxine wept.

"If you don't do what Yahweh wants, you're calling him a liar. Something could happen to your children."

Maxine could not begin to know how to challenge the mind of Mike Ryan. Silence was her best defense.

On to Omaha they drove, where Ryan checked them into a motel. They would stay until Yahweh wanted them to leave, he told her.

Maxine was cornered, helpless. She couldn't escape.

"Maxine, Yahweh wants you to be my wife in every way! How can you go against what he wants?" he shouted in her face. "Can't you understand the will of God? I can talk to God. My way is the right way!" His harangue continued for two days until finally, on the third day, Maxine was too tired to resist. She gave in.

When they checked out of the motel, Ryan handed Maxine the bill. She paid for what he considered their honeymoon and she considered an act of rape.

As they drove home later that day, Ryan gave her strict instructions. "Do not tell Norbert about this and do not have any sexual relations with him."

Ryan was right about one thing—she was too afraid for her family to tell anyone about it.

Ryan's parting words to Maxine were more instructions,

"Tell Norbert to get his ass up to the farm. I need to talk to him. Yahweh is really pissed at him."

The next afternoon, Norbert drove up to the farm in his Jeep Wagoneer. He delivered another twenty bags of charcoal, just as Ryan had ordered.

Ryan had close to a thousand bags of charcoal, to be used for making bombs and cooking, stacked in one end of the hog shed. The weight of the charcoal had caved in the grates covering the shed floor.

Norbert had been hauling supplies to the farm, on Ryan's orders, for weeks. Again, Ryan would send his messages through Jimmy or Rick. Typically they'd ask for between five hundred and twenty-five hundred dollars' worth of supplies. Then, Ryan would call him on the phone to see if he'd bought the supplies. Ryan would scream at him, telling him he'd angered Yahweh if he'd not made the purchases.

When Jimmy had carried these messages to him, Norbert had tried to question Jimmy about the wisdom of Ryan's demands. But Jimmy was always under strict orders to return to the Rulo farm by a specific time. And he always brought one of the other men, usually Rick or James, along with him. It seemed impossible for Norbert to discuss things with Jimmy.

The requests for cash had started coming in around June 1984. Ryan would tell Norbert that if he didn't provide a certain sum of money, Yahweh would cause something bad to happen to one of his children. Norbert knew he didn't dare refuse. Ryan said the requests came from Yahweh, but Norbert knew they came from Ryan.

Months earlier, Norbert had agreed with the rest of the family that perhaps Mike Ryan did have a direct link to God, but now, Norbert was learning the sad truth. He'd first sensed something was wrong when Ryan talked on and on about all the women he'd had on the road. Norbert had thought men of God did not brag so. At first, Norbert had even believed Ryan could read his mind and predict the future. "You're going to get a big feed order next week, Norbert," Ryan had told him. When the order didn't come through, Ryan explained that Yahweh had decided it wasn't the right time. Whatever happened, Ryan always attributed things to his ability to talk to Yahweh.

Now, Ryan met Norbert at the door. Ryan was holding an interdynamic KG 99 with a fifty-round clip. "Norbert," Ryan said, his tone cocky, "Yahweh wants me to show you my new gun."

"Oh . . ."

With that, Ryan stepped forward and sprayed bullets at Norbert's feet.

Rat-a-tat-tat-tat! Shell casings flew up into the grinning face of Mike Ryan.

Norbert jumped back, his face ashen.

"If you ever get in my way or you don't do what I want done, I'll just cut you apart. This gun can take care of anyone that gets in my way or Yahweh's way.

"Or," Ryan continued, "you could have another heart attack, Norbert. And if you did, we'd take over your feed business and we'd do just fine without you."

Ryan knew that Norbert had had open-heart surgery years earlier and that now, at age fifty-four, he had experienced a flare up with his heart just six months earlier. "You know that heart attack you had last December was a warning from Yahweh. He's trying to tell you, point-blank, not to fuck up!"

Speechless, Norbert hurried to his car.

"Don't you forget what I'm telling you, Mr. Haverkamp," Ryan yelled, waving the gun at the Jeep.

Norbert slammed the car door and sped off. *I oughta go back there with a shotgun and do away with that son of a bitch*, Norbert thought.

Once home, Norbert told Maxine, "I'm a dead man if I ever cross that gate again." He felt he was over a barrel. He knew there'd be more demands for cash. "With five men up there, why can't they hold jobs? Here I am with a heart condition and they're bleedin' me for money!" Norbert had already given Ryan close to ten thousand dollars. "Where will we get more money?" he asked Maxine. "I'll have to cash in insurance policies."

Like the other members of the cult, the Haverkamps' fear served to ensure their obedience to Ryan.

CHAPTER **38**

$\mathbf{T}$he front door to the Rulo farmhouse blurred and then came into focus as Lester adjusted the lenses of his binoculars. Out of breath, he settled into a thicket of weeds. Sweat trickled down his face as he alternately crouched, then lay in the weeds that had become his watch post.

Lester had hidden his car next to an abandoned barn about a quarter mile away and had sneaked across a pasture to this ridge overlooking the farm. He was determined to get as close as he could, to find out for himself if Cheryl or the children were there.

The front door swung open. Lester jerked his binoculars into position. It was a boy—a teenager—coming out, holding a rifle. The boy looked down the road and went back inside.

The farm was quiet, no children to be seen. Certainly, there was no sign of Cheryl. An hour passed, then two hours, then three. Disappointed, Lester decided he'd seen all he would see today.

But, he would be back again . . . to watch and wait. No one had as much interest in his case as he did. With his persistence and the help of his attorney, Ted Collins, a special prosecutor had been assigned to the case and criminal charges had been filed against Cheryl. Lester had been reluctant to have criminal charges filed, but realized it could mean help from the law in finding his family. "The authorities are treating this as a domestic case," Ted had told Lester. "We need to consider criminal charges."

When Cheryl had filed for divorce, a Brown County judge had ordered the five children to be placed in joint custody; Lester had visitation rights. By law, Cheryl was not to remove the children from the state without Lester's and the court's permission.

Now, the special prosecutor, Pam Fahey, had filed two counts of interference with parental custody against Cheryl. Both counts were Class E felonies. A warrant was issued for Cheryl's arrest; pickup orders were issued for the five children.

When the charges were filed, the local paper, the *Hiawatha Daily World*, ran a big, front-page story with pictures of Cheryl and her children—the missing Gibson family. The article quoted Fahey as saying that she believed Cheryl was tied in with a splinter group of the ultraconservative group Posse Comitatus, operating out of Nebraska, and that the group was assisting Cheryl in evading authorities.

The same article quoted Ted Collins: "My client has gained information which has made him extremely concerned as to the health and welfare of his children in relation to the activities of this group. We have reason to believe that religious fanaticism is heavily tied to the beliefs of this group."

Though Lester welcomed the efforts of the special prosecutor, he didn't like the pace of law enforcement. It had taken four months to get this far. He pressed on with his own agenda.

Unfortunately, support from his family and friends was beginning to dwindle.

"Lester, you've got to snap out of this," his father told him. "This cult stuff doesn't happen in small towns. Cheryl left and there's nothing you can do. You've got to move on with your life."

But Lester had learned that there was something he could

do. He'd begun attending meetings of the Cult Awareness Network in Hutchinson, Kansas. He was attending a meeting tonight.

Here, Lester found the support that he'd longed for the past three months. Three young women who had once been members of cults spoke. "Anyone of those women could be Cheryl," Lester whispered to the woman seated beside him.

"There's always hope, Lester. Don't give up. There's always something you can do," she assured him.

When Lester was invited to address the group, he was nervous but eager. He pulled back his shoulders, drew in a deep breath, and took the podium. Once he got started, he couldn't speak fast enough. And, as he spoke, he saw expressions of concern on every face in the audience. Yes, he thought, there is hope.

After Lester spoke, the group formed a semicircle and began an open discussion. One member of the group had a suggestion for Lester.

"If you need help in finding Cheryl and your kids, you might want to contact a private detective in Omaha— Dennis Whalen. He's worked on a lot of cases . . . has rescued a lot of people from cults."

Lester jotted down the name. Before leaving, he picked up a packet of literature.

Two nights later, as he thumbed through the articles he had picked up, he read about Ted Patrick, a nationally known deprogrammer in California. He dialed directory assistance in San Diego.

"I've two Ted Patricks listed," the operator said. "Would you like the number for the deprogrammer?"

Lester grinned. "Yes, I sure would."

Lester dialed the number.

Patrick answered on the second ring. "Patrick here."

Lester launched into an awkward introduction of himself and began rambling about his wife, his kids, and the Posse Comitatus.

Patrick had taken calls like Lester's before. "Now, Lester, you're going to hear a lot of things about what is or what might be going on with your wife . . . but pay no attention to them. Anything that you hear about her or anything that she does—remember, it's not your wife talking. It's somebody else. It's not her mind. She's doing what somebody else wants her to.''

"Well, how can I get her away from these people?''

"That depends on what the situation is. It can be very frustrating because she may be doing what she thinks is right. That's the hell of it. Even if you can find her, she may not listen to you. Sometimes these people in cults are even abused and they still won't leave. They can't tell right from wrong.''

Lester asked Patrick if he knew about the Posse Comitatus.

He did. "Some of these people are crazy, Lester. They've killed people in California and Texas. Don't go taking these guys on by yourself. Don't get caught out someplace where you shouldn't be. And when you're out looking for your family, never go alone. Always take someone with you. If you need some help, contact Dennis Whalen in Omaha. You need someone who knows what he's doing. Whalen can help you.''

No one answered at Dennis Whalen's residence. Then an answering machine clicked on.

Lester began his message after the beep. "Uh, yes, uh, my name is Lester Gibson . . . I'm calling . . . Ted Patrick said I should call you.'' Lester paused. His voice quivered; he cleared his throat. "And, uh, my wife and kids are missing in a cult, and I was hoping you could help me.'' He left his number for Whalen to call.

About midnight, Lester's phone rang. It was Dennis Whalen.

They set up a meeting for the next evening at seven o'clock at a truck stop restaurant in Mound City, Missouri.

"How will I recognize you?'' Lester asked.

"Don't worry,'' Whalen told him. "I'll know who you are.''

CHAPTER 39

Lester arrived at the truck stop forty-five minutes early. At the entrance, he stopped to read a missing children's poster—two Des Moines paperboys who had been missing since 1982. Johnny Gosch and Eugene Martin. Both cases had gotten national publicity. Lester studied the smiling faces of the little boys. What a tragedy. He had an idea now of what their families had gone through.

Lester chugged down coffee and smoked cigarettes impatiently as he waited for Whalen. He made a trip to the rest room, and had just settled back into his booth when a black van pulled up in front of the restaurant. A small man slid out of the van and came inside. He looked at Lester and pointed.

I must stand out like a neon sign, Lester thought to himself.

Dennis Whalen removed a dangling cigarette from the corner of his mouth, introduced himself, and joined Lester in the booth.

Whalen appeared to be about fifty. His wavy hair and mustache had silvered. He was small and wiry—five six, one hundred forty pounds. He looked comfortable wearing jeans, pointed-toe cowboy boots, and a gray corduroy jacket with an open-collared western shirt. Lester felt immediately comfortable with the private investigator.

"Tell me the story, Lester, give me some background," the soft-spoken Whalen said, stirring his coffee.

Lester had the story down pat by now. He took Whalen back to the beginning, explaining how Cheryl's brother had been the first to go to Posse meetings. He told how Cheryl had started going to Bible studies on Saturdays without his being aware of it. He told Whalen about the restraining order and the arrest warrant. He also told him of his forays onto the edge of the Rulo farm to watch the house.

Whalen took notes in a small spiral notepad he pulled from his shirt pocket.

"Posse Comitatus, huh?" Whalen had heard of them but had never come across the group in his work. He'd mostly pulled people out of the Unification Church—the Moonies and The Way International, cults like that. "I'll have to do some digging into what this Posse is all about."

Lester filled him in as best as he could. He explained that Mike Ryan was the known leader of a group in Nebraska and that Cheryl might be involved with them.

"The thing to remember," Whalen said, "is that you can't pay any attention to anything Cheryl has said or done. Remember, she's not operating of her own free will, if mind control is involved here."

"Yeah, I realize that now," Lester said, once again feeling tremendous relief that he'd met someone who understood his frustration. "So what can we do?"

Whalen had several ideas. "We can get her out," he told Lester, "but you have to realize it could take a while. These things aren't always easy."

Lester said he understood.

"I'll need some things for starters," Whalen said, sipping his coffee.

Lester pulled out his notebook. "Whatever it takes."

"First, I'd like pictures of your wife and all five kids, with their full names. If they have social security numbers, I'll need those so we can trace any welfare payments. And I'll want names and phone numbers of any friends or relatives you think might know something about Cheryl."

"Okay, no problem," Lester said.

"And I'd like names of all the people you think she's associating with in this Posse Comitatus." Whalen paused, sipped his coffee. "Lester, do you think Cheryl and your kids are still in the area?"

"I don't think so. I think she may be on the move—possibly between the Rulo farm and Colorado or Arkansas." Lester explained that Cheryl's father did business in Colorado and Arkansas and that Cheryl had an uncle in Denver.

"Okay, we've got a lot to start with. Let me think about it and I'll give you a call tomorrow night," Whalen said, starting to get up from the booth.

"But wait a minute," Lester said. "I need to talk to you more. What can we do? What will this cost? My finances are in a bad way."

Whalen sat back down and lit a cigarette, an unfiltered Pall Mall. "Can you come up with fifteen hundred dollars?"

"Yeah, I think I can do that."

"Well, we'll worry about the rest later. Right now, we can start doing several things. But you've got to be patient, Lester. It may seem like nothing's happening, but it will be. We'll start cracking on this."

Whalen talked about circulating flyers about the missing family to states in the region, working with the Missing Children Project out of Omaha and getting media attention—maybe even national attention.

"Let's check out as much as we can on this Ryan character."

The next Saturday Lester and Whalen drove to the Whiting house where Ryan had lived. The place was deserted. Just as before, the house was run down, the yard littered.

Whalen's boots made a knocking sound as they crossed the front porch. The front door was unlocked. They went inside. The rooms were empty except for boxes of trash strewn about, but Whalen liked people's trash.

"You know, Lester, the things people throw away say an

awful lot about them. If you want to learn something about somebody, just go through their trash. You'd be surprised.'' Whalen stopped when he came across a wooden case—an ammo crate the Ryans had left behind. He pulled a bill of lading from inside the crate. "Look at this.'' He was holding up a bill of sale for fifty thousand rounds of ammunition. "It's .223 ammo somebody's ordered here. Over seven thousand dollars' worth! Why would anyone have all this ammo?''

Lester peered over his shoulder.

"The shipment looks like it came from a gun supply company out of Massachusetts, but it was shipped to a gun shop over in Seneca, Kansas. This Ryan sure as hell must be well-armed.''

They poked through the rest of the house, but found only an empty knife case and an old crossbow case. The rest was junk—bottles and rags.

Before they drove off, they walked around the yard. Lester kicked at a rusty tin can, full of bullet holes. An old truck body sunk into the lawn at the side of the house was full of bullet holes. And the side of an old barn had been riddled with bullets.

"Well, we know they like guns,'' Whalen said.

"I want to do some surveillance on the Rulo farm,'' Whalen told Lester during the drive back to Hiawatha. "I want to find out who's coming and going. We'll try to develop other intelligence there, too. We'll find out all we can from others in the area.''

"Great,'' Lester said.

"And, I want to get started on publicity. We'll circulate fliers around the Midwest. We'll go with about three thousand per state . . .''

CHAPTER **40**

Late Monday morning, Ryan and Rick returned from their weekend in St. Joseph, Missouri. The story was, according to Ryan, that Rick had dropped him off at the airport in St. Joseph and he had flown to Oklahoma City on a CIA mission, and had blown up a government computer center. Mike told everyone he had killed two FBI agents and, in the process, had suffered a gash on his arm. He peeled back the bandage to show the wound.

"Looks like you should have had stitches in that," Jimmy said. "That's a pretty good cut."

"Nah, it's my own fault. I was getting too self-confident—I let one of 'em get me with his knife," Ryan said, pressing the bandage back in place.

Rick, saying nothing, turned away and walked into the next room as Ryan bragged of his latest conquest. Only Rick knew that the wound was self-inflicted. Ryan had cut himself with his boot knife. The weekend had just been one of the getaways that Ryan liked when he was feeling shut in at the farm. He and Rick had hung out in a motel and smoked dope.

Rick accepted the lie only because Yahweh had told

them, through Rick's arm, that Mike should cut himself to make his story real and to instill fear in the others. Ryan's lying like this rubbed Rick the wrong way, but he kept his doubts to himself.

And now, with the weekend behind them, another matter required attention. Ryan, who was agitated by the increasing media attention Lester was getting on his missing family, had a plan. "We'll take pictures here of all of us and mail 'em from Colorado. Send 'em back to our relatives. The postmark will make everyone think we're living out there!"

Ryan and Rick would drive to Denver to mail the letters.

The Ryan family huddled before Rick as he aimed the Polaroid camera and snapped photos. In the Ryan family photo, Dennis and Mike wore matching black and brown checkered shirts and caps. Dennis beamed with pride. The picture would go to Mike's folks in southwest Kansas and to Ruth's sister, also in Kansas.

Rick even took a photo of David Andreas, so that he could send it to his parents in Beatrice. David wrote a note saying, "I just wanted to let you know that I'm all right . . . I'm more relaxed than I have ever been. With winter coming on, I'll be able to go skiing again. Someday I would like to visit when I'm ready. Until then, don't worry about it . . . Love, David."

"I'll take care of the photo of Cheryl and her kids," Ryan said. And he did.

Cheryl's letter, written at Mike's direction, was to the editor of the Hiawatha newspaper, in response to the article that had run about them. Cheryl wrote, "I've heard all about your article on me and your accusations. This is to let you know that I am fine and well."

The editor of the paper printed Cheryl's letter and his response under the heading, "Publisher Answers Letter from Fugitive." The editor, who knew Cheryl and Lester personally, wrote for Cheryl to "be careful . . . if you've joined this cult . . . and come back to us and live in the sunshine again."

During the ten-hour drive to Colorado, Rick became more aware of the increasing tension between him and Ryan. Not only was he nursing doubts about Ryan, he was jealous. Just when he had begun to dream of building a new life, Ryan was butting in, trying to take his new wife away from him—his pregnant wife.

Once inside the Denver city limits, the two men mailed the letters and returned home.

Mike paid no attention to Rick's jealousy and continued spending time with Lisa, using her arm to talk with Yahweh, watching TV, playing cards. Yahweh always ordered it. But about a week after they'd returned from the Colorado trip, the rivalry over Lisa exploded in violence. Mike found out that she was pregnant with Rick's child. The marriage had been consummated, contrary to Yahweh's instruction.

Ryan bristled with rage and waited for Rick to return from the grocery store.

Lisa told Mike that she hadn't wanted to have sex with Rick, but Rick had insisted.

Lisa's explanation was good enough for Ryan.

Rick was caught off guard when he entered the trailer. Ryan came storming at him with his fists flying. "You filthy, rotten, motherfuckin' son of a bitch! Who do you think you are?"

Rick tried to shield his face as Ryan swung at him.

"Mike, what's wrong . . . what's going on?" Rick tried.

Ryan slugged him in the stomach. Rick dropped to his knees and Ryan caught him again with a slap across the face, knocking his head against the wall.

"You raped Lisa, didn't you? You raped her! You weren't even supposed to have sex with her until Yahweh told you so."

"I didn't rape nobody," Rick said, cowering.

"Then, how come she's pregnant?"

"Well, because I love her, she's my wife. It didn't have anything to do with rape."

"All I can tell you is, you're in big trouble in the eyes of Yahweh! You'll burn in eternal hell for this, boy!"

Rick crouched on the floor, holding his stomach.

"If you ever lay another hand on her, I'll kill you!"

*   *   *

That afternoon, Ryan smoked a joint as he laid out the Monopoly board for him and Lisa. "I'll be the banker," Ryan said, as he counted out the pink and blue dollar bills. In the course of the afternoon, Ryan instructed Lisa to call her mother. "There's a sewing machine for sale at an auction in Falls City on Saturday and Yahweh wants your folks to go get it." He handed her the sale bill he'd torn from the newspaper.

Lisa made the call.

Maxine pledged to follow through.

His plan was working.

That evening, Ryan called Jimmy in to the south trailer. "Yahweh's got a job for you."

"Yeah, what is it?"

"Well, I'll just tell you point-blank. Yahweh told me that your dad has a lot of cash in his house right now, and Yahweh wants us to have it."

Jimmy's eyebrows darted up. "Mike, are you sure about that? How do you know there's money in the house?"

"Yahweh just told me. He just came to me and told me," Ryan said.

"So, you've double-checked with Yahweh and you're positive . . ."

"Yeah, I asked several times because, you know, I couldn't understand it myself. But the only thing I could find out was that Yahweh is mad at Norbert."

Jimmy swallowed hard. "But, Mike, how can we do this to my folks? The Bible says we shouldn't lie or steal, except from our enemies—those people who are not true Israelites, Satan's people. Every time we've taken something, we've always asked to make sure if we were taking things from people who were not Israelites. Are you sure this is what God wants?"

"I know. I know. I questioned it, too, at first. I didn't get it. But now I know it's what Yahweh wants."

"Mom and Dad aren't our enemies. I just don't get it." A sinking feeling came over him.

"Yahweh told us point-blank that things would never be

easy. And it isn't easy. Doing His will can be very hard. We'll talk about it again in the morning," Ryan said.

Jimmy knew now that the matter was non-negotiable. Heartsick, he went to bed with a knot in his stomach.

The next morning, Ryan checked again with Yahweh. The message was the same: take the money from Norbert. Only this time, Ryan had received more instructions on how to carry out the mission. "The money is hidden in the house," Ryan informed Jimmy. "You'll have to look for it. Take Rick with you."

Finding the money wouldn't be difficult, Jimmy knew. His father often hid money in a gun case under his bed.

"Yahweh wants you to break into the house . . . don't use a key or anything," Ryan ordered. "Make it look like you broke in so it will look like a real robbery and they won't suspect you or think it was someone they knew."

Jimmy listened, realizing he must go through with it.

"Don't forget, Norbert has some guns there at the house. You're supposed to get those, too. Norbert could hurt himself with those guns."

"When?" Jimmy asked.

"This Saturday afternoon," Ryan said. "Your folks will be gone. They'll be at a sale in Falls City, buying a sewing machine."

The assignment from Yahweh challenged every facet of Jimmy's faith. But in the end, he knew he could not be a true believer if he was a doubter.

When Norbert and Maxine returned from Falls City with the sewing machine, they discovered the break-in. Frantic, Norbert made a dash for his gun case under the bed. He knew before looking that it would be empty. It was. Ten thousand dollars—gone!

Trembling with anger, Norbert called the Rulo farm. "You took my money," Norbert said, nearly shouting.

Ryan said he was surprised to hear of the break-in and assured Norbert that none of them had taken his money. Still, Ryan had instructions: Norbert was not to report the theft to the police.

He didn't.

CHAPTER **41**

CHAPTER **41**

"**S**on of a bitch!" Ryan exclaimed, hollering
for everyone to gather around the radio in the living room.
This was the biggest thing to happen since the Gordon Kahl
shootout. "Listen!"

The evening news was reporting that a farmer in the little
town of Cairo, Nebraska, had been killed in a shootout with
the state patrol SWAT team.

"Geez!" Jimmy said, coming into the room from the
barracks.

According to the broadcast, a bank had been serving legal
papers against forty-nine-year-old Arthur L. Kirk. Because
Kirk had known ties to the right-wing groups Posse Comitatus and National Agricultural Press Association, the bank
asked three Hall County, Nebraska, sheriff's deputies to
serve the papers. When the deputies arrived in the afternoon, Kirk had pointed a .41-caliber Magnum handgun at a
deputy's head and ordered them off his property. Then, Kirk
had run into the house and returned with a shotgun. The
deputies had retreated. The sheriff had called the Nebraska
State Patrol SWAT team, which had surrounded Kirk's farm
around seven thirty that evening.

Kirk had told negotiators on the phone, ''I am ready to die, but I'm going to take a lot of them with me.'' Shortly before ten o'clock that evening Kirk had run from his house carrying an AR-15 rifle that had been converted to automatic with an M-16 firing mechanism. He wore a gas mask and camouflage helmet and had blackened his face.

He ran toward a bunker near a windmill that was stocked with other guns and ammunition. Two members of the SWAT team yelled for him to freeze.

Kirk fired shots in their direction. The two officers returned the fire, dropping him dead in his tracks.

For days to come, the family huddled anxiously around the radio, following the Arthur Kirk incident. For Tim Haverkamp, the farm's newest recruit, the story underscored everything Mike Ryan had been telling him. The Battle of Armageddon was very, very near.

CHAPTER **42**

Twenty-two-year-old Tim Haverkamp, a cousin to the other Haverkamps, had dropped by the farm two months earlier, in October 1984, while working a construction job near Rulo. Tall and lanky, Tim parted his short brown hair in the middle and wore wire-rimmed glasses. When Ryan had asked to borrow Tim's car, Tim had thought he meant for the evening, but Ryan didn't return for three days. That was long enough for the others to talk Tim into staying.

He'd been adrift—feeling like the black sheep of his family. His six brothers and sisters had either finished college or were college-bound. His mother was working on her education degree at nearby Kansas State University in Manhattan; his father was a successful farmer in northeast Kansas.

Tim had tried college at Kansas State—ag studies. "I went to college for a year, but that wasn't what I wanted. My parents wanted it," he'd told Jimmy. Tim had returned to the farm to help his father. He didn't like farming, though, and he and his father didn't get along, so he had moved out and gotten a job. Now employed by Hall Brothers Construction, a company that built forms for bridges and concrete culverts, Tim did mostly carpentry work. He liked it and took pride in his craft.

Now, in December, the weather had brought about a slowdown in construction work for Tim. He spent more time around the farm and fell deeper under the influences of Mike Ryan.

"You need to get out of that job, anyway," Ryan told him. "You're too concerned about material things."

"Yeah, I guess you're right," Tim said. He didn't question Mike. Mike had given him a position of authority.

"I'm putting you in training for being the high priest here on the farm," Ryan had told him. He had inherited the high priest's job from Rick, who up until recently, had been the number-two man at the farm. But now, Rick had fallen into disfavor with Yahweh as a result of his rivalry with Mike over Lisa.

For the first time in a long time, Tim felt very good about himself. He was important. Trusting Mike Ryan, he'd become a soldier of Yahweh and taken his place alongside the others.

Ryan had convinced Tim to give him the five hundred dollars out of his savings account and had persuaded Tim to hand over most of his paychecks. Now he wanted more.

"How many head of cattle do you have, Tim?"

"Four."

"You need to sell 'em."

Tim, taking James Thimm along with him, showed up at his parents' farm for the cattle. Tim's mother was thrilled to see him. "I've got a big chocolate cake in the kitchen. It's your dad's birthday, you know. Come on and have some."

Tim gobbled down three huge pieces of cake as Janet looked on, delighted at seeing him in the kitchen, enjoying her cooking. "How about another piece?" she coaxed.

Tim shook his head. When he saw his father coming toward the house, he and James went out the back door to meet him. "Dad, we've come to get my cattle," Tim said.

"Which cattle?" Al asked.

"The four head I've got here with yours."

"What do you want to take them for?"

"Just want to sell 'em, get the money."

"No," Al said firmly. "You're not taking those calves off this farm."

"They're my cattle. I'm taking them!" Tim yelled in his father's face.

"I said you're not and that's what I mean." Al was more worried than angry.

"Hey, come on, old man, they're his cattle," James snapped.

"Don't be smartin' off to me, boy!" Al said, removing his cap. "I'll clean you right here and now. Don't think I won't!"

The following morning, when Al went to his barn lot, the four calves were missing. Shoulders sagging, he went back into the house. "Tim's calves are gone, Janet. They must've come and taken them during the night. This just isn't like Tim."

Al and Janet Haverkamp continued to worry about their son. They'd heard about the Posse Comitatus, and had known of Jimmy's link to it over the past couple of years. Now they wondered what influence the Posse and Mike Ryan were having on Tim. The latest incident involved Tim showing up at the hometown bank in Baileyville, Kansas, trying to pick up a ten thousand dollar federal crop insurance check. The check had been issued to Al and Tim after their milo had been hit by an early frost.

The banker had called Al to tell him that Tim had come in for the check. Al had arrived at the bank just in time to stop him from picking it up. Mike Ryan had been waiting for Tim in the car.

"Now I know what's going on at that farm," Al told Janet. "It just adds up to no good. All those men there, nobody holding down a job."

In their attempts to reason with Tim, their words had been lost on him. Maybe his younger brother Brian could talk some sense to him. The boys were close; they'd worked side by side on the farm for years. It was worth a try.

*   *   *

On Sunday, Al and Brian, armed with a plate of fresh cookies, drove to the Rulo farm.

Jimmy eyed them suspiciously as he came to meet them at the gate. "Yeah? What do you need?"

"We want to see Tim," Al said.

"Just a minute," Jimmy said, returning to the house.

"Hi, Dad, Brian," Tim said, surprised to see them. "What are you doing here?"

"Tim, we want to talk to you," Brian said. "Please sit down with us."

"Okay," Tim said. He crawled over the gate and came to the car.

"Get in," Brian said. As Tim got in the car, Brian considered hitting the gas, kidnapping his brother.

"Your mom sent some cookies for you," Al said, handing him the paper plate covered with tinfoil.

"Tell Mom thanks," he said, pulling the foil off.

Al let Brian do the talking. He didn't want to spark an argument.

"Tim, we're really worried about you," Brian said. "We don't know what's going on up here, but you're not yourself. We're afraid of whatever it is you might be getting into here. We all want you to come home."

"But I'm fine here. I'm happy."

"Yeah, but something just ain't right," Al said. "I got a bad feeling about it. All those guns I've heard about. All these people up here, none of 'em holding jobs . . . something's wrong."

Al and Brian bombarded Tim with every argument they could think of: the entire family was worried about him; his work on the farm was waiting for him; there was money to be made.

"Even if you don't want to stay on the farm, you can come home for now. We'll help you get back on track, then you can go do whatever it is you want. Honest, Son. We'll help you."

Finally, Tim blurted out, "Okay. Okay. If it means that much to you, I'll go. Jesus. Let me run and get my coat."

"Shit," Brian said to his father, "we shouldn't have let him out of the car."

Brian was right.

Tim had just gone into the house when Jimmy came out. "What do you think you're doing?" he yelled across the gate.

"We're taking Tim out of here," Al answered.

"No, you're not. He's staying where he is."

Al Haverkamp bolted out of the car and started for his nephew. "I'll whip your ass, boy, if you keep smartin' off to me."

Jimmy jumped back from the gate and turned to run. But Al stopped just short of crawling over the gate.

Still, it was too late. Inside, Ryan reminded Tim of the horrors he faced by abandoning Yahweh. Within minutes, Ryan had enticed him to stay.

Tim came to the door. "I'm not leaving," he yelled.

Al stood at the gate, letting the words sink in.

"I'm just not . . . I've got things to do here. I'm not leaving," he said, his voice softening.

Al heard sadness in Tim's voice.

He glanced at Brian. They knew it was no use. They'd been so close. . . . Wearily they climbed back into the car and drove home, the plate of chocolate chip cookies between them on the seat.

CHAPTER 43

Lester fumbled with his notes and watched as television cameramen strung light cords across the room and reporters aimed microphones at him and Dennis Whalen, seated at a table beside him. Lester recognized the faces of an anchorwoman and other reporters he'd seen on television.

Whalen, unaffected by the bright lights and famous faces, had been around the block many times with the media. He had chosen the afternoon of Christmas Eve in Omaha to enlist public help in finding the Gibson family.

Fortunately, their news conference was not overtaken by other, fast-breaking news events, and they had a good turnout—all three Omaha television stations, two radio stations, and the *Omaha World Herald* sent reporters.

To the right of their table, Dennis had placed a poster headed "The Gibson Family." He'd attached fliers picturing Cheryl and each of the five children.

"Missing" topped the flier that pictured the five children; under black and white snapshots of each child, pertinent information was listed—full name, age, date of birth, color of hair and eyes, and a computer number—for the National Crime Information Center. Their names had been registered with the system on October 16, and had also been entered in the computers of the National Center for Missing and Exploited Children in Washington, D.C. According to the center, the Gibson family, with five kids, had more children missing than any other family in the country.

A second flier showed two photos of Cheryl and said that she was linked to the Posse Comitatus.

Dennis opened the news conference with an overview of the case and introduced Lester.

Reporters peppered him with questions. "Why did she leave?" "What charges does she face?" "Where do you think she is?"

"We think we know where's she been, at least some of the time," Lester said, "but we can't prove it." He didn't want to mention Rulo; if she was there, she'd be moved.

"What do you do next?" asked one reporter.

"We want to do a mass mailing of fliers," Whalen answered. "We are now receiving donations of paper and printing for a mass distribution that will saturate a seventeen-state area—approximately three thousand fliers per state. We'll be mailing to law enforcement agencies, county social service agencies, and truck stops."

Lester breathed a sigh of relief as the room cleared. He helped take down the posters and carry them out to Dennis's van.

"Thanks, Denny," Lester said, extending his hand.

"You bet, Lester. This will help get the word out. Couldn't have gone any better."

"Merry Christmas, Dennis," Lester said, then ducked his head and went off to his car.

"Merry Christmas . . . " Dennis watched Lester cross the parking lot. He looked lost and lonely.

Lester was heartened by the media response. But alone in the car, he couldn't escape the loneliness, especially on Christmas Eve. Still, he had to focus on the positive. He and Denny had accomplished a lot in the past six months.

One of the first things Dennis had done was put the Rulo farm under surveillance—four people, watching the farm at various times from the road or from the field. He had made some deals, too, with other people who would fly over and do air surveillance, take pictures.

The reports flowed in. They'd monitored a lot of activity at the farm. They saw Jimmy and Rick coming and going a lot. They watched Ryan, who didn't leave the farm much, going in between the two trailers. They followed Maxine as she transported huge amounts of food she got at a Hiawatha food co-op.

But they didn't see Cheryl or the kids.

"With all her relatives around, you'd think Cheryl would be close by," Whalen told Lester. At one point, Whalen had wanted to raid the farm—take some of his men and go in. "All this information isn't getting your kids back," Whalen had told Lester. "Let's storm the place."

"No! It's too risky," Lester had insisted. "Someone could get hurt."

Lester had spent every spare moment trying to get help. He spoke often with Sheriff Ramer, usually at Ramer's house. The sheriff had tried to help with the surveillance. He still wanted to get an ID on Cheryl before trying to go in. He'd had the National Guard fly over and take photos of the farm. He had the mailman watching the farm for Cheryl and the children; he'd asked the school bus driver who picked up two of the Stice children for school to keep an eye out.

Lester circulated family photos to neighbors around the Rulo farm, asking them to report any sign of the Gibson family. Still, there had been no sightings since July 14, when Ramer's undercover men thought they'd spotted two of the Gibson boys.

Through his connection with a computer networking service, Whalen obtained copies of Norbert and Maxine Haverkamp's phone bills. He wanted to find out who and where they were calling.

After tracing the calls, Whalen and Lester traveled to the towns to which the calls had been made. They'd talked to law enforcement officers and checked out the area's Posse meetings. They took down tag numbers and came up with an exhaustive list of Posse members.

By late fall, they'd covered much of the states of Kansas and Nebraska. They had even traveled to Anthony, Kansas, and tried to find Mike Ryan's parents, but the Ryans had been out of town. Whalen and Lester did locate Ryan's brother, but he said he didn't know what his brother Mike was up to.

Whalen also had traveled to Arkansas, where a neo-Nazi splinter group, the Covenant, the Sword, the Arm of the Lord, had a training camp of sorts near Oakland, Arkansas, just across the Missouri border. A few miles to the south, the group had a much larger encampment—a haven for the Battle of Armageddon.

From his investigation, Whalen knew that this group was one of the most militant ones within the movement; he'd also heard reports of this group hiding fugitives from justice—members of other groups, such as the Klan, the Order, and Aryan Nations.

Whalen had gained entrance to the encampment by telling an armed guard that he was interested in learning more about their group, that he might be interested in joining them. Whalen was led to a big man with red hair, clean shaven, wearing blue jeans and a plaid shirt. He was second in command.

"What's your name?" the leader asked.

"Dennis Whalen," he said, thinking it was okay to use his real name here in the Ozark mountains.

The man wrote the name down on a piece of paper and handed it to one of his men standing by.

"You know, I'm looking for a woman by the name of Cheryl Gibson," Whalen went on. "Cheryl and her children, actually. I'm really worried about them. Have you seen or heard anything of them?"

"We heard of 'em," the man said, still studying Whalen carefully.

Within minutes, the assistant had returned. They'd run a computer check on Whalen. They had his date of birth and his social security number.

"You're a private detective!" the commander said angrily, looking up from the printout. "Mister, you better leave here now and never come back."

Two men armed with Uzis had escorted Dennis to the gate.

The Arkansas trip turned up nothing, but Whalen's networking turned up a good lead in Hutchinson, Kansas, where Whalen attended a court hearing for a Posse member from south-central Kansas.

There, Whalen met Bob Lang, a producer for ABC's *20/20*, who was working on a program segment about survivalist groups in the Midwest. Lang told Whalen about a man by the name of Donald Zabawa, a twenty-six-year-old Posse member from Minnesota, who had gotten into trouble in Franklin County, Kansas. Zabawa had been arrested for threatening local law enforcement officers for not releasing his comrades from jail and for subsequently shooting up a sheriff's car. After a conviction on charges of making terroristic threats and criminal damage to property, Zabawa was sentenced to a term in the state prison in Lansing, Kansas.

In going through Franklin County court documents, Lang had been surprised to find a statement Zabawa had given to two Kansas Bureau of Investigation special agents. In his statement, Zabawa provided information about Posse activity throughout the region, including Rulo.

"I'm pretty sure Zabawa mentioned the name Mike Ryan, too," Lang told Whalen. Lang copied the transcript and shared it with Whalen.

Whalen had struck pay dirt. At the bottom of page five of the statement, taken on May 23, 1984, he read with interest: "Michael Ryan is Jim Wickstrom's main man in Kansas. I first met Ryan at James Haverkamp's house three or four months ago. A week later, I went to Ryan's house once. He wanted to know if I could get any weapons. He showed me two AR-15s that had been converted to fully automatic. He pointed out the piece he said he altered. He said he had some M-60 machine guns. He said he had some C-4 grenades."

Whalen flipped the page. "Ryan's group has vowed not to be taken alive. They don't believe in a lot of paperwork. They just want to kill Jews, people against the movement."

Whalen's interest grew as he read on· "Steve Patterson has told me Ryan's group steals machinery and cattle from farmers and sells them. I don't know who or where. Rick

Stice and James Haverkamp and one or two more guys in Nebraska are in Ryan's group.''

Several days later, Whalen and Lester were on their way to the prison in Lansing; Whalen wanted to hear from the horse's mouth what Zabawa had told the two agents. ''Plus, if he's got that kind of information,'' Whalen told Lester, ''he might know a lot more.''

Zabawa seemed pleased to see them, like he was glad someone had taken an interest in what he had to say, Whalen thought. However, Zabawa had little other information to add to what he'd told the agents. And he knew nothing of Cheryl Gibson, he told Whalen and Lester.

''I will say one thing though,'' Zabawa said,''anybody mixed up with that Ryan's group is in danger.''

Whalen pressed his lips together and nodded. ''Thanks for your help,'' he said.

''Yeah, thanks a lot,'' Lester said, shaking Zabawa's hand as he and Whalen left the prison visitation room.

At last, Whalen thought, they'd hit upon something that the law could use as probable cause to go to the farm with a search warrant and in the process find out if Cheryl was there.

Whalen delivered copies of the Zabawa statement to the sheriff's offices in Brown County, Kansas, and Richardson County, Nebraska. He also gave copies to the Nebraska state patrol in Lincoln and to an assistant to the attorney general in Kansas.

But there was no search. The Zabawa statement was several months old.

Whalen was frustrated. ''Maybe the state patrol doesn't want to get involved for political reasons,'' Whalen told Lester. ''The patrol took a lot of heat when its SWAT team killed that Posse guy, Arthur Kirk, out in Cairo, Nebraska, a few months ago.''

Whalen and Lester pressed on.

CHAPTER 44

Dennis Whalen and Lester had been right. Cheryl was at the Rulo farm. She had been all along. There had been no sightings of her or the children because they hadn't been allowed outside the farmhouse since August. Fearing that they'd be spotted, Ryan had ordered the women and children not to go outside until after the Battle of Armageddon.

Now, on Christmas Eve, Cheryl closed the book she'd just finished reading to her two youngest children; they crawled off her lap and scampered off to the bedroom. She was glad they didn't understand it was Christmas. There was no Christmas tree or gift exchange at the Rulo farm.

"To decorate a man's house with silver and gold is the way of the heathen," Ryan told the clan. "Hell, Christmas didn't have anything to do with Yeshua's birthday. I think he was born sometime in September. December 25 is a pagan holiday. People should not get gifts. Yeshua deserves the gifts!"

Still, Cheryl yearned for a touch of Christmas for her children. But she quickly suppressed the thought. Cheryl glanced in the mirror. Six months of staying indoors had made her complexion pasty white. Her fingers were pale and slender. The indentation her wedding band had made on her ring finger had disappeared. Ryan had hocked her ring. Brushing her hair, she reflected on the last six months of her life. At times, it seemed like she'd left home yesterday, and other times, it seemed like she'd been on the farm for years. Once in a while, she resented the confinement; only occasionally had she been allowed to go outside. Then it was only on dark, moonless nights. The main thing, though, was that her faith had never waned and had, in fact, grown stronger. She accepted Yahweh's will without question.

She even accepted Ryan's taking a fourth wife—her sister Lisa, two weeks earlier.

"Yahweh wants you and me to go to Kansas City," Ryan had told Lisa. Once there, he informed her that Yahweh had divorced her from Rick and they they should marry. "The baby isn't Rick's," he said. "It was an immaculate conception."

Ryan, like kings mentioned in the Bible, thought he should have more than one wife, he told Lisa. "It tells you right there in the Bible how Saul, David, and Solomon all had more than one wife."

Trained to obey, Lisa became his wife.

Ryan and Lisa managed to keep their marriage secret from the rest of the family for the first week, although everyone suspected Mike had taken another wife. Rick's relationship with Ryan was deteriorating more each day.

Ruth reacted to the marriage with indifference. "If Yahweh tells you to do it, fine," she told Mike. At first she had been jealous over the other women, but now she'd gotten to the point where nothing surprised her.

"You know I never make love to them unless Yahweh tells me to," he'd told her.

"Yeah, I guess," Ruth said, still feeling some pangs of hurt. She'd watched him give them attention she'd always wanted. He'd never let Cheryl or Lisa see his violent temper. He'd never beaten them.

In late December, Ryan had another of his prophetic dreams. Some of the family at the farm were going to end up in jail. Ryan feared that he, like Moses, would be singled out. Moses had been isolated, had had to hide in the desert, after he had killed the Egyptian who had struggled with the Hebrew.

The idea weighed on Ryan. Then finally, in the long afternoons he spent with Lisa, he learned through her arm that things would change dramatically on the farm after the new year began. The tensions would ease, or else. Yahweh had instructed him to make a speech at midnight on New Year's Eve. Ryan spent hours alone in the dark at night contemplating ''it.'' He planned for it and waited.

CHAPTER **45**

A nasty, wet sleet slapped against the windows of the farmhouse on New Year's Eve. A fire crackled in the belly of the wood stove. The family gathered.

Ryan gulped his 7UP and checked the clock on the wall—11:45 P.M. He pulled a bag of marijuana from his top desk drawer. He rolled a joint, licked the seam, lit it, and passed it around.

At midnight, Ryan stood up. "There are some things Yahweh wants said here tonight. And some things He wants done different from now on.

"Yahweh has showed us and told us what is in the Bible for many months now. These are the things we've all talked about. We've sat down so many times together and discussed the Bible . . . all these things that we live by here on the farm.

"But some people here are having doubts. They're causing problems, mostly by not doing what Yahweh wants them to. You have to let Yahweh rule you. He's like a dictator, but he's doing the right thing. Even a jerk like Hitler did some good things. He got Germany back on its feet, brought their economy around.''

Ryan's voice was calm—no anger.

Rick found that unsettling. He was used to seeing Ryan work himself into a rage.

"The Bible says the people who die in Armageddon will be judged. That's their privilege, but the rest of the people are going to burn in hell. Like it says in Revelation, Yahweh is going to ask Yeshua, 'Do you know this man?' And if Yeshua says no, he's going to burn in hell for a long time. Eternity is a long time.''

Ryan took a hit off the joint and tapped ashes into a white porcelain Coors ashtray on the table next to his orange chair.

"Now, what it boils down to is that Yahweh wants everyone to think about whether or not you want to stay on the farm. He wants you to think about this for two weeks. After two weeks, if you want to stay, it means that you accept Him and will live here on the farm under the laws that Yahweh has told us. If you break your word, it's treason against the rest of us, pure and simple.

"So, you've got two weeks to decide. If you want to leave, you can, but know that you will burn in hell.

"Yahweh is telling me that the first half of the new year could go along okay, but if he keeps having problems—if there's things he wants done that are not getting done—then there could be serious trouble. If the turmoil goes on inside the group, then before six months is out, we will lose some of the stuff we've worked for, like our food and weapons.

"And then, if Yahweh still isn't happy, we could lose everything. And Yahweh is flat out telling us that if someone breaks their word to Yahweh, they could end up dead. I'm worried about that.''

A few days later, Ryan decided the men should sit around the table and talk about Yahweh and their commitment. As a routine part of the ritual, a joint was lit and passed around. Ryan was smoking more and more dope these days. "It's okay. Herbs heal. The Bible says so,'' he'd say.

"I think everybody should just relax and say what's on their minds,'' Ryan said. He went first, warning that the battle was near, that the Antichrist was a sign. "He's already here, you know, here on earth. The Bible says just before he comes there will be trouble with the economy. There'll be wars and rumors of wars and great turmoil. And, the Antichrist will appear and will imitate Christ. He's got every hair on your head numbered and knows just what you're thinking!"

Jimmy jumped in. "Well, you know, I just believe in Yahweh. I know he's real. I know he's leading us. He has chosen to speak to us. I've just seen too many things happen that I know wouldn't have, if I didn't have faith in him. I just know it in my heart."

Rick nodded. "I do believe Yahweh is directing us. I just believe it."

James was next. It was difficult for the others to know what James was thinking or feeling. He was quiet. "I've been thinking a lot about it," he said. "I don't know about some of the things Yahweh is telling us. And, I'm not always sure it's possible to talk to God through the arm."

Ryan grew red in the face. He rose to his feet. "How can you say that? After all the time we've lived here, following Yahweh. After you've been around Wickstrom and all his teachings." Ryan's voice grew louder and angrier. "The time you spent with the Posse! How can you say you've understood all this stuff and say you did believe in Yahweh and then turn around and say you're not sure?"

Now James slunk in his chair. He was frightened. So were the others.

Ryan was out of control. "You blasphemed Yahweh when you said that!

"You don't deserve to be on this farm," Ryan yelled. "You need to get the fuck out of here if you're talkin' like that! Yahweh doesn't want Satan's people on this farm, bud. You're a proselyte! There's only one place for you . . . that's in hell. You better think about leaving!"

"I do want to get straight with Yahweh," James said, sitting up straight. "Really, I do."

Fed up, Ryan announced that he was deeming James, Rick, and Luke slaves—given to him by Yahweh. James's doubts about Yahweh, the rift between Rick and Mike over Lisa, Luke's fussing and defiance, were too much trouble.

The three of them were of Satan and didn't deserve to live with the rest of the family, Ryan said. They were to be isolated in the south trailer and never allowed to enter the north house.

Lisa, along with Rick's two oldest children, moved into the north house.

No one questioned the punishment of James, Rick, and Luke. It was an order from Yahweh. In fact, the action served to cement the group's loyalty to Ryan. Such demotion and separation was shaming; it reminded them that to stay in good graces they should do as they were told. Everyone knew if he screwed up with Yahweh, he could end up in the south trailer, too.

As part of their punishment, Rick and James were assigned menial chores. During the day, they took care of the goats and chickens and did other odd jobs, such as fixing fence and cutting wood. At all other times, they were confined to the trailer, where Rick or James covered guard duty—watching the road for visitors to the farm.

At mealtime, the women fixed three plates, one of the men delivered them to the south trailer. After each meal, dirty dishes from the north house were stacked in a box and taken to the south trailer. Rick and James washed and dried the dishes and returned the box to the door of the north house.

But the chores were the least of their worries. It was Ryan the three of them feared. Regardless of how well they obeyed or how much they prayed to Yahweh, they could not please Ryan. He was quick to anger and quick to throw punches. The assaults on Luke were becoming brutal, too. Here, isolated from the others, Ryan could punish them as he saw fit.

Rick considered picking up the phone and calling for help, but fear prevented him from doing so. If he called someone, Ryan would find out and things would get worse.

CHAPTER 46

In the beginning, Mike Ryan was a disciple of Yahweh. Now, Yahweh was working for him. Ryan kicked back in his orange recliner and flipped on the cable television by remote.

"Hey, Cheryl, let's play a game of cards," he said. Today he'd learned that Yahweh wanted him to do what he did most days—relax, smoke dope, watch TV, and play cards.

"Okay," Cheryl said, laying her embroidery aside. She pulled a deck of cards from the desk drawer.

As Cheryl shuffled the cards, Ryan watched her. "You are one of the most beautiful women I have ever known," he said tenderly. "You are put on this earth for a special purpose. Yahweh loves us," he said.

Cheryl smiled.

A gentle Ryan charmed his women in the north house, but his trips to the south trailer had become his retreat into perversion.

Ryan stalked into the south trailer, carrying a Polaroid camera. "Luke's a mongrel. A dog!" Ryan shouted.

Luke, startled, jumped to his feet and backed away from Ryan.

"A dog doesn't wear clothes," Ryan said to Luke. "Take your clothes off, now!"

Luke stood there, looking at Ryan with questioning eyes.

"I said, take off your clothes!"

As quickly as he could, Luke stripped to his underwear, revealing the bruises of earlier punishments. In recent days, Ryan's spankings had turned into beatings.

"Here, doggy . . ." Ryan said, opening the trailer door. "Come on, mongrel!" He shoved the boy out the door and into a snowdrift. "Roll around like a dog!" Ryan ordered.

Luke, shivering, rolled in the February snow. He was too frightened to cry.

From the corner of his eye, Ryan saw Rick coming at him. Then Rick stopped. Ryan knew Rick wouldn't try anything.

Rick knew it, too. His stomach in knots, he prayed— prayed to Yahweh to make Ryan stop.

Ryan stepped farther onto the porch and snapped a Polaroid picture of Luke in the snowbank. Ryan laughed. He set the camera down and grabbed his bullwhip. "Hey, dog!" Ryan yelled. He wrapped the end of the whip around Luke's neck and picked up the child.

Luke, gasping for air, kicking his feet in the air, pulled at the strap around his neck.

Cheryl and Ruth watched in horror from the window of the north trailer.

When Ryan saw them watching, he dropped the whimpering child on the porch of the trailer. "Time to go in, mongrel!"

Luke crawled back inside.

"Get your ass out of here," Ryan said, kicking at him as he scurried to get away. "You're just one of my toys!"

Rick grabbed a blanket and wrapped Luke up in it. Rick had never felt so weak.

Just before bedtime, Ryan was in the doorway, staring at Rick. He took a deep drag off his cigarette and studied Rick long and hard. ''You're thinking about leaving, aren't you?''

''No,'' Rick said, trying to maintain eye contact.

''If you leave this farm, Stice,'' Ryan said through clenched teeth, ''I will hunt you down and kill you and you'll burn in eternal hell.'' Ryan flicked his cigarette ashes on Luke, turned, and walked out the door.

Back at the north house, Ryan announced prophetically to the others, ''Rick Stice will leave the farm. But he will return in seven days.''

Garneta Butrick clocked out of the nursing home at 7:00 A.M. She'd been thinking about her grandchildren all night.

Once home, she stared sadly at the children's Christmas gifts, yet to be opened. Here it was January. It distressed her so that Rick had not brought the children by the house in Falls City over Christmas. She guessed she'd have to take the presents to them at school.

Garneta boxed the Christmas gifts—clothes and toys, including the road grader for Luke, and carted them off to the school.

"Sorry Christmas is late this year," Garneta said, her voice trailing off at the sight of their pale, thin faces. Both had lost so much weight, they were skin and bones, she thought. And Barry wore overalls that hit him way above the ankles. She tried to keep her spirits up for their sake. "Santa Claus didn't forget you! Merry Christmas, sweethearts," she said, handing gifts to each.

"Thank you, Grandma," they said, almost in unison.

As they ripped into the presents, Garneta studied their thin little bodies. Children don't lose weight like this unless they're being abused or malnourished, she thought. What was going on out there at the farm? Rick had always been a good father to his children until after Sondra died and he had gotten involved with that Posse and started buying all those guns. What's got into him?

Now, she was really concerned about Luke. "How's that little brother of yours?" Garneta asked.

"He's fine," Ora said, beaming over the sweater her grandma had given her.

"Are you sure he's doing okay?"

"Yeah. He's okay," Barry said. "Thanks for the truck, Grandma!"

"I got Luke his road grader. Will you be sure to see that he gets it?"

"Yeah." Both children nodded, accepting the gift for Luke.

Garneta missed Luke terribly. She agonized at the thought of the children being mistreated.

That evening, she told Tom, "I'm reporting this to the authorities. I think the children are being abused. They're skin and bones." She'd considered making a call earlier, when she'd not been allowed to see the kids at the farm. But she was afraid that if Rick traced the report to her, he would never allow her to see the children.

Even now, she made the call to a statewide child abuse hotline without giving her name.

"Are the children in immediate danger—is this an emergency?" the hotline operator asked. The state social services department had two types of responses to reports of child abuse—an emergency response and a planned response. In case of an emergency, they reported the case immediately to the sheriff. In a planned response, the call was reported to the local social service office for follow-up.

Garneta didn't think the children were in immediate danger. "They just look malnourished and I know both kids have missed a lot of school," she explained. "I just feel like they're being neglected." Garneta gave the hotline the children's names and told where they were living. "I can't tell about Luke, he's not in school yet. I haven't seen him in months.''

The hotline volunteer assured her that the case would be turned over to the local social services for follow-up.

Thank God, she said to herself. I should never have waited so long.

CHAPTER **48**

"Hey, mongrel! Ever wonder what would happen if I shot you with my 30.06?"

Luke, pushing his Tonka truck aside, shook his head vigorously.

"It would be a sight, I'll tell you that." Ryan turned to the two-way radio. "Hey, Tim. Come over here."

Tim came to the door. "Yeah."

"Go out to the shed and bring me a chicken. I gotta show Luke here something."

In a couple of minutes Tim was back with a live chicken.

"Aw, Mike, come on now," Rick said. "Leave the boy alone, please."

"Shut up or I'll blow your head off."

Cowering, Rick fell into a chair, shaking his head in disgust.

Ryan took Luke out behind the south trailer and ordered Tim to place the chicken about five feet from the child.

Luke stood helpless, wincing at what was about to happen.

The squawking chicken flapped its wings as if preparing to fly off just as Ryan took aim with the rifle.

The chicken exploded, splattering blood all over Luke's legs. Afraid to run, Luke shook with fear as he stared at the blood on his legs.

Ryan laughed and ordered Tim to bring two more chickens. Again, he shot the chickens at Luke's feet, blood exploding onto him.

"Now get your ass inside and clean yourself off!"

Luke ran for the trailer, Ryan following him.

"Hey, mongrel. Do you think I would shoot you?" Ryan asked.

"No!" Luke said.

Ryan whipped out his .25-caliber pistol, spinning the chamber. "Well, I'm not going to shoot you. I'm going to make you shoot yourself!"

Luke didn't know that Ryan had removed the bullets.

"Here. Take the gun and hold it," Ryan said. He cocked the gun and handed it to Luke.

Luke slowly reached up and took the pistol.

"Now, stick the barrel in your mouth."

Luke put the gun barrel to his lips.

"Now, pull the trigger. Pull it!"

Luke trembled. Urine ran down his leg and into a puddle at his feet. He fell to the floor, sobbing.

"You fuckin' little jerk. Look at the mess you made. Get to the bathroom."

Luke ran to the bathroom, Ryan on his heels.

"You don't think I would shoot you, do you?" Ryan yelled at Luke. Ryan quickly reloaded the pistol and fired a bullet into the wall.

Luke jumped at the shot.

"Get your ass back out here. I'm not finished with you!"

Luke crept back into the living room, pulling on clean underwear.

Ryan pointed the gun at him and pulled the trigger. "Click!"

Luke jerked.

"You don't think I'd shoot you, do you, mongrel?"

"No." Luke said, trying to conceal his fear.

Ryan took aim again, shutting one eye and looking down the nose of the pistol.

Bang! The shot rang out.

Luke lurched forward, moaning and grabbing his upper arm. He fell to the floor, blood gushing from the bullet wound.

Rick, stunned at what Ryan had done, ran over to Luke. "Oh my God! Luke, let me see your arm."

Luke, dry-eyed, moved his bloody fingers off the wound. The bullet had missed the bone, and ripped through the fleshy part of the boy's upper arm.

"Oh, Luke! It'll be okay," Rick said, quaking with anger. He glared at Ryan.

Ryan looked shocked. "I didn't even pull the trigger on the pistol," Ryan said to Rick. "Yahweh made that gun go off." He ran out the door. In a few moments, Ryan was back with a first aid kit. Obviously rattled, he packed cayenne pepper in the wound to stop the bleeding and then wrapped it in gauze.

"It's your fault, Rick. Yahweh made Luke get shot just to show you that you and James better come to your senses or you'll be in more trouble. This was a warning."

"I don't believe that!" Rick snapped.

"Fuck you!" Ryan threw a heavy punch into Rick's stomach. As Rick doubled over, Ryan brought his knee up under Rick's chin, knocking him back against the wall. Rick crumpled on the floor, gasping for breath.

"You guys are in trouble!" Ryan said as he slammed out the door.

Rick got to his feet and took Luke on his lap. The boy clutched his bandaged arm and buried his face in Rick's chest.

Rick thought he'd just seen through Mike Ryan. Here was the Mike Ryan who had never flinched when he'd killed women and children in Vietnam, but had been rattled when the gun went off and struck Luke. Now Rick knew, without a doubt, that Ryan was lying about a lot of things.

"It'll be okay, Luke. It'll be okay."

Rick would have to make it okay. He had to get them out of this insanity. In spite of Ryan's hold over him, somewhere deep inside, Rick believed that it was not God, but Ryan, who was angry. Rick had to get away.

CHAPTER 49

Rick waited until nearly midnight. He peeked out the window. The north house was dark. He'd decide later how to come back for the kids.

He stuffed some cash he'd been hiding deep into his pocket and crept quietly onto the wooden deck. He stopped abruptly when a door opened at the north house.

"What's going on?" It was Tim.

Rick felt himself stiffen with tension. "Nothing," he said. "I thought I heard some commotion down in the hog shed. I was going to check on the chickens."

Tim shrugged and walked back inside.

Rick hurried to the hog shed, circled it, and kept walking. I've got to get the hell out of here, he said to himself. I've got to get out of here.

Within an hour he was in Rulo. Tonight, the town was alive. A freight train had derailed by the grain elevator the night before. Clean-up crews and inspectors were still working around the clock to clean it up.

Rick hung around the elevator, hoping that he could catch a ride. When he saw one of the inspectors heading for his pickup, he approached him. "Excuse me, sir. Are you going into Falls City?"

"Yep, sure am," the inspector said. He tossed his clipboard onto the seat of the pickup.

"Do you think I could catch a ride with you?"

"Sure, hop in."

Rick hustled around to the other side of the truck and slid into the seat. "Thanks a lot, mister."

Rick wondered if he'd been missed yet. He was worried about his kids, especially Luke. What might Ryan do to Luke? Rick glanced out the rear window of the truck to see if anyone was following them. "You can drop me off right here," Rick said as they neared the Stephenson Motel on the edge of Falls City. "Thanks," Rick said, stepping out of the truck.

He got a room and crawled into bed. Finally, he felt safe. He'd feel even safer when he got out of town.

Early the next morning, he caught the bus to Omaha. Once there, he took a cab to a Motel 6.

Inside his motel room, Rick lay down on the bed and buried his head in the pillows. He felt lost, confused, like he was coming out of a daze. And he felt deeply ashamed, especially about the abuse of Luke.

What can I do? he kept asking himself. He needed to get a job, maybe here in Omaha, make a totally new start. He called an old high school friend who was living in Omaha. He hoped that the plant where his friend worked might be hiring. But the plant wasn't hiring, and in fact was laying off workers, his friend told him.

Maybe I could go to truck driving school, Rick thought. Driving an eighteen-wheeler, he could make a decent living for himself and the three children. He called one of the truck driving schools he'd found listed in the phone directory. He'd have to come up with two thousand dollars for tuition, which was out of the question.

He stayed at the Motel 6 another night. He splurged and bought himself a couple of shirts the next morning, then took the bus back to Falls City.

He spent the next four days at his sister's house in Falls City. During that time, he talked to another friend and his dad about borrowing the money for truck driving school. Neither had the money to lend.

By the week's end, Rick was growing more and more anxious over what might be happening to his kids. Finally, he picked up the phone and called.

Jimmy agreed to pick him up at the Lil' Duffer Restaurant on the main highway through town.

"Am I going to get the shit beat out of me if I come back?" Rick asked Jimmy.

"Mike says no. But he said if you don't come back your kids will burn in hell."

"I'll come back if I'm not going to catch hell for it," Rick said.

"It's okay. You can come back. Mike says it's okay. Think of Lisa. She's about to have her baby."

Rick agreed that he should return.

Back at the south trailer, Ryan, with Dennis at his side, seethed with anger as he waited for Rick.

Luke huddled in the corner of his bedroom. James had sunk back into a chair in the corner of the room, sensing what was going to happen when Rick got there. He heard the car pull up and doors slam.

Ryan bolted out the door. "Hey, bud, welcome back," he said, walking up to Rick. "You did the right thing by coming back."

But as Rick stepped inside the trailer, Ryan punched him in the stomach. Rick doubled over; the sack he carried dropped to the floor. He tried to duck.

"You son of a bitch!" Ryan screamed.

"You said you wouldn't do this if I came back," Rick said, moaning. He tried to back away.

Ryan threw himself onto Rick and the two of them toppled onto a chair and fell to the floor.

Ryan scrambled to his feet. "What's in the sack?" Ryan demanded.

"A couple of shirts."

"Let me see. I don't know what you brought in here." Ryan yanked the shirts from the sack. "Oh, these will fit Dennis just fine."

"Yeah," Dennis replied, taking the shirts and holding them up to his chest.

"What else you got on ya?" Ryan asked.

"What do you mean, what else?" Rick said.

"How do I know you're not wired or something, coming in here after a week?"

Ryan's playing the secret agent game, Rick thought. "Well, I'm not. I don't have anything . . ."

"Strip," Ryan said. It was an order. "I want you strip searched, now."

Rick slowly took off his clothes.

"You're really going to pay for this. You're really going to have to prove yourself now, asshole. Bend over, spread 'em," Ryan ordered.

Rick hesitated.

"I said, bend over!"

Rick bent over, pulling his buttocks apart.

Ryan half glanced at Rick's rectum. "Just wanted to make sure you're not sneaking anything in on me now, bud."

Rick straightened.

"I should've shot you back there when you and Jimmy were at Lil' Duffer. I was hiding outside, had a rifle on you the whole time. I should've blowed your head off!"

Dennis took his lead from his dad. "Yeah, Rick. You're in trouble with Yahweh. Big trouble." A goat was bleating in the pen behind the trailer. "At least the goat is glad to see you're back," Dennis said with a laugh.

Ryan looked at Dennis and smiled. He went over to the two-way radio and called the north house. "Tell Jimmy and David to get over here now. We've got something to do."

Seconds later, Jimmy and David were at the door of the south trailer.

"Go bring one of those female goats around here to the side of the trailer," Ryan told Jimmy and David. "Rick here's going to prove just how far he'll go to show Yahweh that he's sorry."

Rick cringed.

"Get outside, Stice," Ryan ordered.

Rick walked naked out into the backyard. Ryan and Dennis followed behind him.

"Now, Rick is going to show us just how much he

believes in Yahweh, how much he'll do for him. Jimmy and David, you hold the front of the goat. Hold it tight now.''

They grabbed the squirming goat by the head.

Ryan turned to Rick. "Fuck it!"

Rick stared at Ryan.

Ryan put his face into Rick's. "I said, fuck the goat. Get down there and fuck the goat!"

His face red, Rick positioned himself behind the goat. He fumbled as he tried to insert himself into the goat. Finally, he barely managed to cram the tip of his limp penis inside it. He thrust himself against the goat several times before pulling away in complete disgust.

Ryan threw back his head and laughed a wheezing laugh.

As Jimmy led the goat back to the pen, he prayed to God this would never happen to him. He had to stay in good with Yahweh.

To prevent his leaving again, Rick was to be guarded by Dennis or Tim during the day and chained up at night. That night, Rick was stripped naked and a three-quarter-inch log chain was wrapped around his ankle and fastened to the porch railing. As temperatures dropped, he curled up in a ball on a piece of cardboard and shivered against the cold. "Yahweh, please help us get out of this," he prayed.

Over at the north house, Ryan gloated over the accuracy of his prediction. Rick had returned in seven days.

CHAPTER 50

Ryan knelt in his white room—his private sanctuary for communing with Yahweh. He'd had the men build the room onto the northwest corner of the house. The white, he said, would fend off the darkness of Satan. Ryan slept here now, usually with daughter Mandy beside him on a small bunk; and he prayed here, always with the lights off, always facing the north.

Now, he prayed for Rick's ailing seventy-year-old father, Otho Stice, to die. He prayed hard. Otho still held the deed to the farm, and if he died, the farm would go to Rick. Ryan knew he'd have his hands—or name—on the deed in no time.

But Otho Stice didn't die. And he wanted to get out from under the farm. Rick had given up on the hog business and the crops. The place was going under. Otho avoided bankruptcy by signing over the farm to the Richardson County Bank. The bank agreed to wipe out the debt in exchange for the deed to the eighty-acre farm and the eighty acres of bottom land across the river.

Ryan's prayers weren't answered, but Yahweh had another plan for them to stay on the farm. Yahweh demanded that they stay, Ryan told everyone. The battle was very, very close. They had to buy time.

"Jimmy, Yahweh wants you to drive to western Kansas and tell your brother-in-law, Lynn Theile, that you and him should buy this farm. If he doesn't, something will happen to one of his kids."

Jimmy took off on the six-hour drive to Norton, in western Kansas.

Jimmy was dead serious when he looked Lynn Theile in the eye and delivered the message.

Lynn and Deb, a sister to Jimmy, were God-fearing, hardworking farm people. They'd been too far away from Rulo to take an active role in Ryan's scheme, but they'd been around Ryan enough to be sucked in. They were afraid to believe him and afraid not to.

Lynn had never forgotten the chilling effect Ryan had had on him during one of Ryan's trips to his farm. Ryan, stoned and sipping his 7UP, had told Lynn, "I could be crying my eyes out over you and inside be thinking about how I was going to kill you."

Fear, in part, had pulled the Theiles into Ryan's aura. But they had gradually come to believe that he had supernatural powers. Months earlier, when Jimmy had paid them a visit, they had questioned Mike and his powers.

It was at that moment that Ryan had called on the phone. "You guys are having doubts about Yahweh, aren't you?" Ryan had asked.

"That guy is unreal," Lynn said with a nervous chuckle.

Finally, it was the arm test that had convinced the Theiles that Ryan was on to something. Using the arm test as their guide, Lynn and Deb had picked the best days in December of 1984 to sell their wheat. They'd gone down the days of the month, and their arms told them which days to sell. Those days had turned out to be the highest market days that month. "It's funny how it works," Lynn told his wife. "It's like there's no mind involved in it . . . something else is moving my arm."

In spite of the arm test now, Lynn had mixed feelings about making a down payment—ten thousand dollars—on the Rulo farm. He thought the asking price of eighty-six thousand was too high. But he took seriously the threat from God. He wasn't willing to risk one of his children being harmed. And, he told his wife, "Maybe that's a pretty cheap price to pay to keep Ryan and all the rest of them in Nebraska and away from here." Lynn knew they'd all come piling in on him if they ever left Rulo.

In the end, he and Jimmy borrowed the money and made the down payment to the Richardson County Bank. The family would stay put.

CHAPTER 51

Ryan had drilled into the other men, including Rick, that Luke was of Satan. As their emotions became more and more blunted, none of them openly questioned Ryan's treatment of the little boy. As the abuse directed at Luke escalated, Rick prayed even harder that it would stop.

Alone in the south trailer, Luke played with his road grader and toy Tonka truck. He never questioned his confinement, his separation from the other children, or even the abuse. Ryan had thrown him against walls, forced him to run up and down the hall until he collapsed, and made him eat off the floor like a dog. Ryan had spit in Luke's mouth and would also flick his cigarette ashes in the child's mouth.

Luke rarely cried now when he was the target of Ryan's sadistic acts. Luke was weaker, more withdrawn.

Ryan lumbered up to the porch of the south trailer and unlocked the chain around Rick's ankle. "Is the mongrel still having doubts about Yahweh?" Ryan asked, motioning Rick inside.

Rick could see that Ryan was stoned.

Ryan grabbed Luke by the arm and dragged him back to the bathroom.

Rick followed helplessly.

Ryan turned the cold water on full blast in the bathtub. When the tub was half full, he grabbed Luke and dunked him in the water.

The boy choked and sputtered as Ryan pulled him up.

"Do you believe in Yahweh?" Ryan shouted in Luke's face.

"No!" Luke said defiantly.

Again, Ryan plunged him beneath the water. Seconds passed.

Rick panicked. "Let him up, Mike!"

Ryan jerked the boy's head from the tub. "Tell me, mongrel, now do you believe in Yahweh?"

Luke, choking, couldn't answer.

Ryan's voice grew louder. "Do you believe in Yahweh?"

"Yes," Luke said. "Daddy, make him stop," Luke pleaded.

"Now, Rick, you ask him if he believes in Yahweh. Ask him!" Ryan flipped on his tape recorder.

Hovering over Luke, Rick asked, "Son, do you believe in Yahweh?"

"Yes, Daddy. Yes!"

Ryan held up the camera and snapped a picture of Rick bending over Luke. "There now. I got a picture of how you treat that boy bad. I got a picture and a tape recording of you doing it."

Rick pulled Luke away from the tub and dried him off.

Ryan pulled a red Magic Marker from his pocket. He grabbed Luke and wrote the numerals *666* across the boy's forehead. "That's the mark of the devil." Then, Ryan spun the boy around and wrote the word *DOG* in red letters across his back. "Now, let's hear you bark like a dog."

Again, Ryan turned on the tape recorder.

Luke managed a weak barking sound.

In the days ahead, Ryan grew bored with the day-to-day punishment he doled out. He found new titillation in sexual perversion.

"I said fuck him in the ass, dammit," Ryan shouted at James. "Do it or get your heads blowed off!"

Rick was on his hands and knees in the middle bedroom. James, totally subservient now, pushed himself up against Rick. "I can't," he said, exasperated. "I can't get it in." He pressed his flaccid penis against Rick.

"Come on, you queers. I said, fuck him. You do what Yahweh says or it'll get worse."

James futilely pushed himself up against Rick.

Ryan ran down the hall and came back with a plastic syringe, the kind used by veterinarians. "Here, stick this tube in his ass. That'll stretch him out."

Rick threw back his head, groaning in pain as James pushed the syringe into his rectum.

"Now pull it out of there and fuck him!" Ryan yelled, his excitement building.

Then, angry at James's fumbling, Ryan kicked him in the buttocks. Rick's head slammed into the wall.

"Go on, shove it up his ass!" Ryan jeered.

Still, James couldn't.

Ryan kicked James again and marched out of the trailer. "Fuckin' queers," he said.

CHAPTER **52**

Dennis Ryan was impressed with his father's most recent act of courage. Mike Ryan, after ramming a nine-inch hunting knife deep into his thigh while cleaning a deer, had sewn the wound shut himself with a needle and sutures from the first aid kit. Ryan had blamed the incident on Maxine. She'd been having bad thoughts and Yahweh had punished him for it, Ryan said. Young Dennis agreed.

Dennis believed whatever his father believed, even when it came to violence and killing. A recent conversation between the two of them had been a turning point for Dennis when it came to Yahweh's mandate to slay their enemies.

Dennis had cried as Ryan explained that they'd have to do a lot of killing during the Battle of Armageddon. "I just don't know if I can do it," Dennis said, his lip quivering. "I'm afraid. . . ."

The boy's attitude angered Ryan. "Dammit, you've got to be willing to kill for God if that's what God wants," Ryan yelled. He threw his 30.06 at Dennis in disgust.

Dennis caught the gun and looked down at it.

"We've got to get this through your head. You'll have to do it one day! You may even have to kill friends!"

Dennis wiped the tears from his eyes; he knew his dad didn't like it when he cried.

Then, Ryan calmed down; his voice took on a gentle tone. "Listen, Son, just remember that killing is okay as long as you're doing it for God. I remember my first time. But believe me, after the first time, it's easy."

Dennis had stopped crying now. He looked up at his dad and listened to his soothing words. It never dawned on Dennis that his father was lying.

Indeed, it was another of Ryan's stellar performances.

"Son, one day when all this is all over, when Armageddon is over and I'm dead and gone, then you can sit under an oak tree and cry over having to kill so many people. Until then, I don't want you to ever cry again."

The message had sunk in. And that was the last time that Dennis worried about killing.

As Ryan had demoted others on the farm, he had accorded Dennis more power. Ryan had learned, he told them, that he would be killed during the Battle of Armageddon and that Dennis would take his place. As Dennis became a psychological clone of his father, he too was learning the art of sadistic amusement.

Dennis opened the window and propped his rifle on the window casing, taking aim at a sparrow. He fired but missed. Irritated, he turned to James. "Boy, you better stop having bad thoughts. You're really in trouble. You're going to burn in hell if you don't straighten out."

"Oh, I thought I was doing pretty good," James said, attempting to humor Dennis.

Dennis interpreted the remark as sarcastic. He'd repeatedly told his father that James didn't respect him. "I know better," Dennis said, his anger rising. "You're still having doubts and you know you're in deep shit."

"Whatever you say . . ."

"I mean it. Maybe I should just shoot you!" Dennis said, jerking his rifle in James's direction. The gun went off. The bullet struck James in the left cheek.

James fell to his knees, grabbing the side of his face. "Oh

my God, he shot me! He shot me!'' Blood poured from his mouth and both sides of his face.

Dennis blanched, flung the rifle onto the couch, and ran out the door. ''I shot Jim Thimm in the head!'' he yelled to his father, who was out on the porch. ''I didn't mean to. I shot him in the head!''

Ryan ran for the first aid kit and came to the trailer. Rick and Tim were huddled around James, propping him up on a chair, trying to stop the bleeding. Ryan brushed them aside and took command.

The bullet had entered James's left cheek and exited the right side of his face, tearing through flesh and bone.

''You didn't do it, Dennis. Yahweh made it happen,'' Ryan assured Dennis. ''This is how Yahweh punishes.''

''Get David over here!'' Ryan hollered. David had been a medic in the National Guard. ''Maybe he can do something.''

Dennis dashed out the door to call for David.

David and Jimmy came running into the trailer, shocked at the sight of James; his face and the front of his shirt were covered with blood.

David examined the wound. ''I don't really know what to do for a head wound like that. Just put pressure on it and put a clean bandage on it,'' he said.

''Are you in pain?'' Jimmy asked.

James shook his head. ''Not too bad.''

Ryan packed cayenne pepper into the wounds to stop the bleeding and taped gauze bandages over them.

''I'll keep an eye on him,'' Rick said.

Ryan and Dennis left the trailer, but not before Ryan warned James, ''You better listen to what Yahweh is saying. Next time He might decide to kill you.''

CHAPTER 53

Rick could see the progressive deterioration in James's condition—mentally and physically. He had grown thinner and weaker. His injury and the beatings had taken their toll. James looked like a feeble old man—run down, pale, and emaciated. He lived in a narrow world of fear and shame. His sense of self destroyed, he did the only thing his dependency allowed: he focused on the external authority of Mike Ryan, his leader, to supply his reality. Yahweh was his only hope for lasting happiness.

When they were alone, Rick asked, "Don't you think you should get the hell out of here?"

"No," James replied. "I want to do right by Yahweh." He was steadfast in his belief. "Besides, Mike would know where I am and come find me," James said, looking out the window. James had spent many long hours at the window, on guard duty. His feet swelled after he stood guard for nearly two days straight.

Later that afternoon, as James stood on guard duty and Rick washed dishes, Rick watched from the kitchen window as Ryan headed toward the trailer.

Once inside, Ryan's target was James.

God, James is so beaten down, Rick thought, how can Ryan keep browbeating him? Rick had watched Ryan chewing James out before. The more he'd chew, the madder he would get. He'd just work himself up until he was furious.

Now, Ryan was in James's face. "You are just jealous because I have the spirit of the archangel. You just can't stand it, can you? That's why that gun went off at you!" James hung his head and didn't answer.

Starting for the door, Ryan said, "I'm just real sick and tired of you two. Things are going to get rougher around here if you don't get it right!"

Little Luke stood in the hall, trying to avoid Ryan.

As Ryan stormed out the door, he shoved Luke out of his path. The boy went flying backward, striking his head on a bookcase.

Stunned by the blow, Luke slowly picked himself up. His eyes rolled back, he started shaking, and his knees buckled. He collapsed and began gasping for air.

Rick ran over to Luke and raised his head off the floor. The child was unconscious. "Oh my God!" Rick said, holding Luke's head.

Dennis ran out the door, hollering for Ryan.

Rick and Tim kneeled over Luke.

"Is he breathing?" Tim asked, worried.

Luke's breathing was shallow. Rick tried massaging the boy's chest.

In a few minutes, Ryan was back inside the trailer, standing over Luke. "Shit. I wasn't even mad at him. I just gave him a little shove. Let me see him." Ryan pushed the others out of the way. "I can fix him." As Ryan straddled Luke, he glared down at him, intimating that his stare had the power to heal.

Just then, the boy started breathing normally, although he did not regain consciousness.

"I'll go over to the other house and ask Yahweh what to do," Ryan said.

Rick massaged his son's chest and checked his throat to see if he'd swallowed his tongue.

When Ryan returned he told Rick, "Yahweh does not

want us to take Luke to a hospital. I fried his brain with my mind. Wrap him in a blanket and put him in the bedroom. We'll just have to wait and see what happens.''

Again, Rick was chained to the porch that night. He prayed for Luke.

CHAPTER **54**

The next morning, Rick pulled at the chain around his ankle and scooted closer to the door of the trailer. He could hear the voices of Ryan and the others inside. What were they saying? He strained to hear. Then, he heard them say it. Luke was dead. He'd died during the night.

"Oh, my God," Rick moaned. His head throbbed as the wave of grief overtook him. Then, in a split second, he numbed out, refusing to feel the pain. To survive now, he had to silence the voices screaming inside of him, blaming him.

Ryan came out onto the porch. He said nothing to Rick to acknowledge Luke's death. He wanted the boy buried, now. "Wrap the boy in a blanket and carry him outside. Put him in the galvanized tub in the back of the pickup," he told Rick. "Yahweh wants the boy buried down south of the hog shed, in the fields down there." Ryan had used Dennis's arm to learn where Yahweh wanted the grave.

Despondent, Rick went to the bedroom and slowly pushed the door open. There lay Luke, his face blue. His body was stiff. He'd been dead for several hours; rigor mortis had set in. Rick wrapped his son in a yellow blanket and carried him to the pickup. As he lifted the little boy's body into the waiting tub, the blanket fell away from his face. Rick tried not to look at him.

Ryan sent James for shovels, and ordered Jimmy up to the south trailer to stand guard. The rest of them jumped in the back of the pickup and rode down into the bottom of the field, just below the hog shed.

It should have been me, Rick thought. I failed my son.

As Rick and James lifted the body from the truck bed, Dennis poked Rick in the hip with the butt of his rifle. "You're in trouble," Dennis told him. "Watch out or I'll shoot you!" Then Dennis spat at him.

Rick ignored Dennis.

Ryan picked out the spot for the grave and instructed Rick and James to dig. Three feet by six feet—Yahweh had been explicit in detailing the measurements for the grave.

Rick and James dug. The other men looked on, their hands in their pockets.

"Look at that," Ryan remarked, pointing at Rick and James, who were now shoulder deep in the grave. "It's the dead burying the dead."

Rick kept on digging. Out of the corner of his eye, he scanned the horizon. He wanted to find a landmark he could refer to in relocating the grave. The day would come, he told himself, that he would come back for his son. He would tell his story. He spotted a clump of dead trees and burned a picture of it in his memory.

"Put him in the grave facing west," Ryan said.

Rick and James lifted the boy from the tub and laid him in the grave. Rick looked down at the lifeless body of his little boy. As his emotions rose again, he shut them off like a spigot. He slammed his shovel into the dirt and began filling in the grave.

"Shit. That boy was just a gook, a mongrel," Ryan snarled at Rick. "He wasn't a true Israelite. You better wake up. Yahweh is trying to tell you something, bud." Then, Ryan walked about thirty yards from the grave and knelt, looking to the heavens.

In a few minutes, Ryan returned to the grave. "Just as I thought. Yahweh told me Luke's death was all Rick's fault.

Rick's headed for eternal hell. I ain't going to say no prayer . . . so if you are, you better go ahead," Ryan said.

Rick, leaning on his shovel handle, bowed his head and prayed, his voice in a monotone. "I ask that Yahweh be with Luke's spirit and that He take it back and strengthen it. Be with him, watch over him, and protect him. Amen." Then, Rick turned and walked away from the grave with the others.

They crawled into the back of the pickup and returned to the house.

Ryan told the men not to tell the women and children of Luke's death. "Come back and disk over the field here," Ryan instructed David. "Nobody will know there's a grave."

Days later, Luke's grandma, Garneta Butrick, was distressed to learn that local authorities apparently had not been out to see the children at the farm as a result of her call to the child abuse hotline.

A social worker told her she'd been afraid to go to the farm alone; she'd heard the rumors about a paramilitary group with guns. And, according to the school principal, school secretary, and the teachers, no one had come to the school to check on the two older kids.

Once at the school, Garneta again asked the two older children about Luke.

"Luke is safe," they told her. "Daddy says Luke is safe."

Why haven't the kids seen Luke? she wondered. What do they mean, safe? Later she told her husband Tom, "The kids just keep saying Luke is safe when I ask about him," she said.

"Hell," Tom said. "Safe could mean six feet under, for all we know."

CHAPTER 55

The women weren't supposed to know about Luke's death, but they soon did. Ryan told Ruth.

"What happened?" Ruth wanted to know, horrified.

"We might not ever know. He just died in his sleep over in the little bedroom. But it had to be what Yahweh wanted because . . ."

"Mike," Ruth snapped, "if that's what Yahweh wanted, then okay, but I just don't want to hear anything about it." Ruth didn't believe that Luke had died in his sleep. She knew Luke was being mistreated. She had overheard Mike playing a tape recording of Luke crying, being held under water in the bathtub. She remembered hearing the little boy pleading, "No. Don't! Please!" Soon after the incident, Mike had burned the tape. Now, she figured something dreadful must have happened.

He was just a little boy. I can't believe that was the will of God, she thought. Something besides God was controlling their arms—maybe it was Satan. She knew Mike was capable of hurting an adult, but never imagined he'd seriously hurt a child. She tried to put it out of her mind, but couldn't. Too much was going haywire—Mike having all these wives, little Luke now dead. Something unearthly was occurring here.

Yet Ruth faced her horror alone. She feared for her own life and for everyone at the farm. But as in the past, she didn't know how to get away. She thought about confiding in Jimmy but didn't, for fear Mike would find out. He always did. He had people spying on each other, reporting back to him what everyone was saying. He always had a way of finding out things.

With increasing frequency, Mike had threatened to move her to the south trailer, for doubting Yahweh and for having feelings of jealousy about the other wives. "I've asked Yahweh about it. It could happen," he told her. "He's not saying it will happen, but it could." Although she'd had little contact with James since he'd been confined to the south trailer, she knew he'd been abused.

The children remained unaware of Luke's death. Rick's two older children had no idea that their little brother had been killed.

Cheryl was sorting laundry when she got the news of Luke's death. It was God's will—she forced herself to believe it. Now her denial was her only defense against the truth. Still, deep inside, she worried about her own children more than ever. Ryan had not seriously abused the other children. But it seemed so easy to anger Yahweh. Would one of her children be next? Resolutely, she prayed to Yahweh to strengthen her faith, to forgive her for doubting.

CHAPTER 56

Rick didn't sleep that Monday night. He knew if he didn't get off the farm, he would be the next to die. Rick confided in James that he was leaving and pleaded with him, "Come on, man. Come with me!"

"No. I want to make it right with Yahweh," he said with a sigh. "Besides, Mike would come find me anyway."

Rick just shook his head. He could see that there was no reaching James. He remembered back to the time the men had sat around the table and James had angered Ryan when he had expressed doubts about Yahweh and the arm test. It was almost like James had written his own death warrant with those remarks, Rick thought.

On Tuesday afternoon, Rick was to go into town and cash his social security check. He'd drawn the social security funds for his children. He had routinely cashed the check in town and turned it over to Ryan. Today Tim would take him to Falls City.

Rick had not had an opportunity to escape. He and James had been chained to the porch at night and were under guard during the day. But today had to be his best chance, he knew. He needed money, though, to live on until he got to wherever he was going.

Rick spotted his checkbook in a sack of his clothes on the back porch of the trailer. Boxes of things belonging to him, Sondra, and Luke had been sitting on the porch. Ryan had ordered that their things be thrown away after Rick had left the first time. Rick's things were evil, he'd said.

Rick tore a check out of the checkbook and stuffed it in his shoe. He figured Ryan might do a strip search of him before he let Tim take him into town.

As Rick and Tim started for the car, Ryan looked Rick in the eye. "If you take off, you'll be back in three days. Then, I'm going to tie you down, stretch your arms out, and take my machete and chop off your arms. After that I'm going to chop off your goddamned legs and your head, too. You'll bleed to death. But I'm going to make sure you suffer before you die. Yahweh will make sure of that. I might even skin you alive!"

"I'll be back," Rick said grimly, trying to remain calm. He and Tim walked out the door.

In town, Tim dropped Rick off to go into the bank to cash his check. "You ain't going to try to make an escape, are you?" Tim asked anxiously. Ryan had told Tim to shoot Rick if he tried to escape.

"Why would I? I got my kids out there at the farm. I don't want to leave my kids."

"Man, I think if I was you, I'd be runnin'. I'd be runnin' because, man, you're going to die!" Tim said.

Rick hopped out of the car, cashed his check, and returned. "I need to stop at my attorney's office and sign a tax form," he told Tim.

Tim pulled the car around the corner to the attorney's office. "Go ahead, try it. Try to make a run for it," Tim said. "Remember, I'm watching you."

Rick didn't respond. He entered the attorney's office, signed the tax form, and returned.

The last errand was to pick up some movie videos at Jack's TV in Falls City. They were also to see about getting a new VCR. Tim parallel-parked along the brick-paved street in front of the TV and video store.

"You ain't going to try anything, are you?" Tim asked one more time, as they got out of the car.

"Nope," Rick said. He slammed the car door behind him.

The moment they walked inside the store, Rick began scanning the store for an exit. How could he sneak out the back door? Rick pretended to be paying attention to the video selections as he and Tim browsed through the racks of videotapes.

"Afternoon, fellas," Jack, the owner, said as he approached them. "Anything I can help you with?"

"Well, we need to pick up a couple of movies and, uh, we're interested in a new VCR," Rick said.

"We can handle that," Jack said.

"Talk to Tim here about that," Rick replied. "He's the one with the money. I'll look at videos."

"Here's a VCR over here you might like," Jack said, leading Tim to the next aisle. "Has remote control and everything."

"Yeah, that might work."

As Tim examined the VCR, Rick spotted the rear exit. He looked at the door, then over at Tim. This was his chance. He kept his eyes on the videotapes as he edged down the aisle. At the exit, he glanced toward the front of the store. Tim had his back to Rick now and was still talking to Jack.

Rick's heart pounded. His throat was dry. "Now! Go! Run! Do it!" a voice inside his head shouted. The next moment he found himself in the alley. He made it about five steps down the alley before he stopped. He couldn't run and leave his kids out there. No way. Resolutely, he returned to the store. Tim and Jack were still dealing on a VCR. But Rick knew, no question about it, that if he went back to the farm he'd be a dead man. Tim still paid him no attention. Rick turned back toward the exit and made his second getaway, running down the alley as fast as he could.

By the time he reached James Oil Company, several blocks away, he was panting and out of breath. He ducked inside the filling station office. "I need some cash. Can I cash a check here?"

"Yeah, sure," the attendant said. He knew Rick; Rick's former brother-in-law, Sondra's brother, also worked there.

Rick looked through the plate-glass window, watching

for Tim. "Uh, I need about four hundred dollars. Can I cash it for that much?" His tone was urgent.

The attendant checked the cash drawer. "Yeah, I think that'll be all right." He took Rick's check and counted back the cash.

Rick folded the wad of twenty-dollar bills, stuck them in his pocket, and slipped out the door. From there, he ran across the street to Markee Video, the store where his sister Patty worked. "I'm going to Omaha to look for a job," he told her.

"What are you so flustered about?" she asked.

"Nothing," Rick insisted. "I just wanted you to know in case anyone comes looking for me. You can tell them that's where I went." Rick had no intention of going to Omaha, but he figured he could throw Tim or Ryan off the track if they questioned her. "I need a favor, sis. Can I borrow your car for a few days?"

Rick sounded desperate. "What's wrong, Rick?"

"Nothing, I just need the car for a few days, please?"

"Well, sure . . ." she said.

Minutes later, Rick was speeding toward southern Missouri, just south of Fort Leonard Wood, where his brother lived. He rolled down the window and drank in the fresh air. He was free. As he drove, though, he had to constantly reassure himself that Ryan hadn't abused his other kids. He hoped they would be okay.

When Tim returned to the farm without Rick, Ryan seemed to take the news in stride.

"He'll be back," Ryan said, sure of himself. "I was right the first time he left, wasn't I? Yeah, he'll be back."

CHAPTER 57

A truck driver from Hiawatha eyed the woman outside the Texas truck stop. She had several children with her. "That's Cheryl Gibson," he said to his buddy. He thought he recognized her from the posters he'd seen. He hurried to a pay phone and called Texas authorities.

Minutes later, two deputies arrived. As they approached the woman, two men fired shots at them. The deputies called for backup and the two men surrendered. They were taken into custody, along with the woman.

About an hour later, an FBI security patrol clerk called the Brown County sheriff in Hiawatha to see if the woman they'd just picked up was Cheryl Gibson. A quick comparison of social security numbers told them they weren't holding Cheryl Gibson from Kansas.

A number of sighting reports had come in to Dennis Whalen's office since he'd circulated the thousands of fliers, but none had led them to Cheryl.

However, today—April 25, Lester's birthday—they had the hottest incoming report they'd received. "This one's worth checking," Dennis told Lester over the phone. "A

guy at a truck stop out in Denver saw one of the posters and
called with a description of a woman and four kids he saw
out there. Sounds like Cheryl.''

"Okay. I'll get in the car, go out there, and talk to this
guy,'' Lester said.

"He's waiting at a pay phone at the truck stop on the west
edge of Denver now. Here's the number . . . you can call
him and make arrangements to meet him.''

Lester jotted down the number. "Thanks, Denny. I'll let
you know what happens.''

Lester dialed the number.

Bob Kelley was the man's name. He explained that the
day before he'd seen a woman and four kids who looked
like the ones in the poster. His descriptions were accurate
enough that Lester wanted to talk to him. If he had seen
Cheryl, maybe she was still in the area. They set up a
meeting at the truck stop the next day at eleven o'clock.

Lester and his brother Miles drove west across Kansas.
Miles was home on leave from the navy in San Diego; he
had offered to ride to Denver with Lester.

They arrived at the truck stop about thirty minutes early;
a man in camouflage clothing and black boots approached
them.

"Are you Lester?'' he asked.

"Yes, I am. Lester Gibson.'' They shook hands. He
introduced his brother.

"I'm Bob Kelley. I got a table there in the corner.''

Kelley looked like he was in his midthirties, about six feet
tall, with dark hair. Actually, he was sort of scummy looking,
Lester thought. "Tell me everything you saw,'' he said.

"It was right here yesterday, about this time. I'd seen the
poster of your wife and kids there in the doorway of the
truck stop. And as I was sittin' here having lunch, I saw this
woman and four little kids here in the restaurant, a couple of
booths away. They were with three men. I'd just seen the
poster and got to thinking it sort of looked like them.''

"Did they look okay? Did any of them look like they
weren't well or like they were being abused, treated bad?''

"No. They all looked okay. They looked healthy to me.''

"What did the woman look like?'' Lester asked.

"Oh, I'd say she was not very tall, maybe five four, or five five. Dark brown hair with a reddish color to it. She had freckles. Attractive young woman, about thirty, I'd guess."

"Yeah, that does sound like Cheryl," Lester said, scooting up on the edge of his seat. "But what about the kids?"

"Well, there were four of them. Three little boys and a girl. The girl was the oldest, around nine or ten. She had red hair, too."

Lester felt a surge of adrenaline. The descriptions were on target. Other questions were spinning in his mind. "Well, what about these men that were with her—what did they look like?"

"One was a big guy, husky, flattop haircut. A beard, too. Then there was two younger guys—one blondish-haired guy, small, maybe five-eight or nine. The other one was dark-haired, a little taller."

"Jesus!" Lester said. "That's gotta be Mike Ryan and Jimmy Haverkamp and one of the other guys from up there in Rulo. What were they doing? What were they saying? Could you tell?"

"Not really. When they got up to leave, I watched them. I heard the little boys calling the girl by some name. What was it they were calling her?" he asked himself, scratching his temple.

"Was it Elizabeth? Could it have been Elizabeth? That's her name, Elizabeth."

"No. It wasn't that. It was sort of a funny name . . . different. Does your daughter have a nickname or anything like that?"

"No . . . not really," Lester said thoughtfully.

"I know now. Now I remember what it was. The little boys were calling her Mimi. That's it, Mimi."

Lester was stunned. "Oh my God, that's them. That's them!" Lester's eyes brimmed with tears. "That's them. They were here!" He'd forgotten that the little boys early on had trouble saying Elizabeth and sometimes called her Mimi.

Miles reached back and rubbed his hand over Lester's shoulders.

"Did you see them leave? Did you notice what they were driving or what direction they headed?"

"Well, no. I did see them walk across the parking lot, but they turned the corner around the building and I didn't see what they were driving. I did notice that little girl, the one they were calling Mimi, sorta looked down at her feet when she walked across the parking lot. I wondered if she was real sad or something. She did sort of look beaten down, depressed."

Now Lester burst into tears. "That's Elizabeth," he sobbed. "That's her. She always did that when she walked, look down at her feet. That's her!"

After Lester regained his composure they ordered lunch, and Lester filled Kelley in on what had happened with Cheryl. Kelley was keenly interested, Lester noted. Lester told him about the Posse and how he'd been looking for his family for the past year.

"Well, I tell you what," Kelley said. "I might be able to help you get 'em back if we can locate 'em. If they're in with an armed group like that, you're going to need an army to get 'em out."

Lester studied the guy's face in silence, not knowing what was coming next.

"I'm a mercenary, Lester. I operate out of California. I've worked all over. And, if you want help and can come up with ten grand, we can get started on it."

Lester chewed his food slowly and swallowed hard. He appreciated the sighting report but was now offended by this macho mercenary trying to capitalize on his misfortune. "Nah, I don't want to do anything like that. I've had offers like that before. It's too dangerous. Cheryl and the kids could get hurt. No way I'd go for something like that."

"Well, it's just an offer, in case you're ever interested."

"Well, thanks but no thanks," Lester said. He asked for the check. "Hey, I appreciate what you've done, though."

"Any time, partner."

As Lester and Miles drove down an access road to return to the main interstate highway, Lester noticed a sign in front of an office: "Dennis Dick Insurance."

"That's Cheryl's uncle," Lester said, slamming on the

brakes. ''That's the name of Cheryl's uncle out here. He's in insurance. That's his office!''

''No shit.'' Miles was amazed that in a town the size of Denver, they'd happened to come across her uncle's office.

Lester couldn't believe their luck; and it even explained why Cheryl might be in the area. He couldn't wait to check out a little house that Cheryl's aunt and uncle owned in Evergreen, in the mountains west of Denver. But they found the house empty.

Lester talked to the local police to see if they knew of any activity—people from out of state coming and going from the house. The police hadn't seen a thing.

Next, Lester and Miles decided to pay a visit to Cheryl's aunt and uncle in Denver.

''Norbert was just here yesterday,'' the uncle told them. ''He was going on over to Alamosa on business.''

Lester knew the Alamosa area; he'd worked there one summer on a farm. By chance, they spotted Norbert's car as they cruised the town. They followed him out of the valley, onto Interstate 25, and into New Mexico. But there was no sign of his stopping to connect with Cheryl.

Lester and Miles followed Norbert into Texas, realizing at last that they were probably on a wild goose chase. Miles had to get back; his leave was about over and he had to fly back to San Diego.

At least they're okay, Lester thought.

Back in Rulo, Mike Ryan smiled when he got the phone call from Bob Kelley.

''Mission accomplished,'' Kelley told Ryan. ''He ate it up.''

Kelley's account of Cheryl and the children being in Denver was a hoax, set up by Ryan to lead Lester off the trail.

CHAPTER 58

"Something's wrong with this turkey," Ruth said, pulling it out of the oven. It had shriveled; the skin was crispy brown. Ryan looked over Ruth's shoulder as she settled the roasting pan on the stove. The nineteen-pound wild turkey had particular significance to him; he'd shot it for the feast to follow the upcoming birth of Lisa's baby—Yahweh's grandchild. They'd refrigerated the turkey in the south trailer. Finally, the women, fearing it would spoil, received instructions from Yahweh to cook it.

"The bones look bleached out," Ryan said, examining the two drumsticks. "All dried up." Mike thought a moment. "Wait a minute. Maybe James did something to the turkey out there in the south trailer."

Ruth didn't understand.

"Well, it smells sorta funny, if you ask me," Ryan said. He stuck his head over the steaming turkey and inhaled. "Yep, something's wrong. Something's been put on that bird. Smells like some kind of cleanser—like ammonia or something."

Mike whirled and headed out to the south trailer, collecting Tim along the way. "Don't say anything to Thimm right off about the ammonia in the turkey,'' Ryan warned. ''I just want to look around the trailer and see if we find any cleanser.''

Ryan and Tim entered the trailer, taking James by surprise. But they said nothing—just began looking around. In a small cabinet under the kitchen sink, Ryan found a bottle of Conklin cleanser. He held the bottle of liquid cleanser up to the light and read the contents—ammonia. Taking the bottle with him, he ran back over to the north house to his white room to ask Yahweh about it.

After asking questions through Lisa's arm, Ryan learned that yes, James had been pouring a capful of the cleanser on the turkey each day. Eventually, Yahweh even told them why: James knew that when the turkey was cooked, he wouldn't get any, so he decided to ruin it for everyone.

Ryan stormed back into the south trailer. ''Did you fuck with that turkey that was in the refrigerator out here?''

''Huh? No. What do you mean, Mike?''

''Somebody fucked with that turkey, put something on it—cleanser or something—and ruined it. We ain't never had any problems with any other turkeys out here. The women cooked it just the same as always.''

''I didn't do anything.''

''Bullshit. We found the bottle of Conklin cleanser. Don't lie to me, bud.''

''Honest, Mike . . .''

''You'll be punished tomorrow!'' Ryan slammed out of the trailer.

''Yahweh wants James Thimm off this farm,'' Ryan said to Lisa. ''Your baby cannot be born here until all of Satan's people are off the farm. But Thimm has to leave on his own. We've got to get both houses cleaned and ready for the birth.''

Lisa was now nine months' pregnant and miserable; she was having trouble sleeping and her back ached. ''I'm ready for this baby to get here,'' she said, pushing on her lower back with both hands. ''This is no fun.''

''That James Thimm . . . that cat's gotta go,'' Ryan insisted.

The plan was to humiliate James into leaving. So the next

day, David was instructed to take James down to the hog confinement shed and see that he fornicated with one of the goats.

David stayed in the distance as James tied the goat to a farrowing crate and put some hay down in front of it. Then he saw James thrusting himself at the goat. David was about thirty feet away—as close as he wanted to be—and his view was partially blocked, but that was okay with him, too.

In a few minutes, James said he was done.

David assumed that he'd faked it, but that was good enough for him. He reported back to Ryan then that the act had been completed. "Do you want him to go back to the south trailer now?"

"No. Chain him up in the hog shed. We can't have him in either house now with the baby due, and I don't think Yahweh is finished with him. Keep him out there overnight."

David led James to the hog shed, where James wrapped a log chain around his own waist and fastened it to a farrowing crate.

"See ya later," David said. His tone was apologetic.

"Okay," James said, resigned to taking his punishment.

Ryan stayed in his white room, asking question after question through Lisa's arm, about what else should be done to punish James. Humiliate him was the answer . . . Ryan knew just the trick.

David carried James his evening meal and took a sleeping bag and a thin foam mattress down to the shed for him to sleep on. "This will help a little," he said.

"Thanks," James said.

Around nine o'clock the next morning, David took a bowl of granola cereal to James. "Mike's coming back down here, James. He seems really pissed off."

"I guess I'll just have to trust in Yahweh," James replied calmly. "Whatever Yahweh God wants will happen."

About an hour later, Ryan told the other men—Tim, Dennis, Jimmy, and David—that it was time to go down to the shed. It was time to punish James for angering Yahweh.

James was sitting on his sleeping bag, the empty cereal bowl beside him, when they arrived.

"First thing is, Yahweh wants you to sign over the title to your Datsun," Ryan told James.

James didn't protest.

"Then, bud, you're going to get fucked in the ass with a shovel handle. That's what going to happen to you. Yahweh is really pissed off," Ryan said angrily.

Ryan unlocked the padlock on the chain around James's waist. "Now get over there and lean over that farrowing crate and drop your pants!" Ryan picked up a tube of grease and applied it to the end of a dirt shovel.

James, still silent, obeyed.

Ryan greased the tip of the handle and walked over to James, now bent over the crate. Ryan put the end of the shovel up to James's rectum and started turning it, pushing it in.

"Awh!" James moaned as the shovel handle slid into his rectum. He clinched the bars on the farrowing crate. His body tensed with pain.

"I said you were in trouble, goddamn it! Now, this is what you get!" Ryan yelled.

Ryan pushed the shovel handle four or five inches into James, causing him to yell out in pain.

Finally, Ryan pulled the shovel handle from his rectum. James stayed doubled over the crate, groaning, panting.

"Okay, guys. It's your turn. Yahweh wants us all to do it."

At that, James stood up and started to back away.

"Tie him up. Tie him to the farrowing crate!" Ryan roared.

Baling wire was used to tie James's hands and feet back into position over the farrowing crate.

"Come on, guys, go ahead and do it. He's evil! He's from Satan!"

"Mike, if I've offended Yahweh or anyone at the farm, I'm sorry. I am sorry," James offered, trying to reason with Ryan.

"Come on guys, do it!" Ryan ignored James's plea.

The men were hesitant, but Dennis was eager to impress

his father. He grabbed the shovel and pushed it into James's rectum.

Again, James yelled out in agony, louder this time.

"Dennis, go get some duct tape," Ryan ordered.

Ryan tore off a piece and stretched it across James's mouth.

With Ryan goading them, Tim, Jimmy, and David took their turns with the shovel handle, ignoring James's muffled groans. At last, it was done. The color had drained from James's face, but still he offered no resistance. This pissed Ryan off. He wanted more fight, more reaction—to see James begging for mercy.

"You know, Yahweh really wanted the shovel handle put up your ass about eight inches. I don't think we had it up there far enough. We'll have to go another round."

With that, Ryan applied more grease on the shovel and shoved it into James's rectum again, only this time he pushed harder.

James squirmed in agony, and the others could hear a deep moan coming from James's taped mouth.

Dennis took a second turn, and then Tim.

"Hey, wait a minute," Tim said. "It feels a lot different this time—looser or something. I think he's tore inside or is starting to tear." Tim withdrew the shovel handle and dropped it on the floor.

"Tim, did you break my toy?" Ryan asked, laughing.

Tim shook his head and backed away.

Then, Ryan got down in James's face. "Are you hurting?" His tone was sarcastic.

James, his eyes closed, nodded yes.

"Well, maybe you know now that Yahweh means business. We aren't going to fuck around with you anymore."

As Ryan lectured James, Dennis talked to Yahweh through Tim's arm. "Are his bowels busted?"

Yes, was Yahweh's answer.

Ryan ripped the tape off James's mouth and untied his hands. James fell to his knees, his ankle still chained to the farrowing crate.

Ryan ordered the men up to the north house with him. It

was lunchtime. They walked away from James, leaving him doubled up on the concrete floor.

When they returned at two that afternoon, James was almost too weak to walk.

"Yahweh is not finished with you yet. Take off your shirt!" Now, Ryan carried his leather bullwhip, which was about seven feet long. "You are to be whipped fifteen lashes by everyone!"

James was unchained and led to an open area in the shed. His hands were tied to an overhead pipe. Ryan drew back the whip and snapped it across the bare flesh of James's back.

James cried out. "Yahweh, forgive me for what I have done. Please stop this!"

Ryan drew back the whip and lashed him again. "You don't need to worry about that. Yahweh has given up on you!"

James's groans turned to silent sobs as each of the other men lashed him with the whip. His back was covered with red welts.

Then, his tormentors were gone. Gone for the night, leaving James in a heap, chained again to the farrowing crate.

That night, Ryan stayed up until midnight with Lisa in his white room, asking Yahweh questions about what had been done to James and what further punishment should be carried out.

"Are you happy, Yahweh, with the punishment we've done?"

Yes.

"Are James's Thimm's bowels busted from the probing?"

Yes.

"Should we take him to a hospital?"

Lisa's arm dropped. The answer was no.

They learned that Yahweh wanted James to leave the farm or die. And it seemed that James was unwilling to leave.

"It looks like I'm going to play Indiana Jones some more," Ryan said, snapping his bullwhip.

Ryan and the others returned to the hog shed late the next morning. Ryan was angrier than before. "Yahweh is madder than ever at you now. More things could happen to you today." Yahweh wanted more whippings, Ryan said. James was unchained and led to the south end of the hog shed.

A partition constructed of four-by-eight sheets of fiberboard separated the south end of the hog shed from the rest of the building. Ryan kicked down a three-foot section of the partition so they had a clear view of the main gate, in case anyone approached the farm.

James was weaker still, David could see. Maybe this has gone far enough, he thought. But not wanting to be a dissenter, he kept his mouth shut.

Eager to resume the punishment, Ryan ordered the others to use the baling wire to tie his hands to an overhead auger bar. James stood there, in a crucifix position.

"You still haven't had enough punishment," Ryan said, lighting a joint.

The lashing continued, this time across his chest. "Please, Yahweh! Forgive me and stop this!"

When it came his turn, Jimmy drew back the whip tentatively. He was afraid. But remembering what Ryan had said—James was of Satan, he deserved this—he managed to redirect his fear. Taking a deep breath, he snapped the whip across James's chest.

The men stood back and looked at James. His chest was covered with red welts.

"I'm going up to the house to bring some 7UP down," Dennis said. He ran to the house and returned with a six-pack of cold 7UP. He passed the cans of soda around.

Now Ryan, without the benefit of anyone's arm, mumbled to Yahweh. He was getting more instructions for what was to be done next. "Untie him. Yahweh wants the tips of his fingers shot off."

James dropped to the floor in a heap. His wrists were tied to the farrowing crate.

Ryan grabbed a block of wood and placed James's right hand on it, palm up.

"Let me use your gun," Ryan said to Jimmy.

Jimmy handed him his Ruger .22 pistol.

Ryan got down on his knees and held the gun barrel about an inch from James's index finger.

The gunfire made a loud, crackling sound inside the shed.

James shrieked in pain and his entire body jerked as the tip of his finger was blown off.

Ryan, now consumed by the sadistic frenzy, got down in James's face. "Don't be hollering and making a bunch of noise or I'll make it worse for you!" The veins bulged in Ryan's neck.

James looked up at his finger. His eyes began to roll back in his head.

Dennis shot James's middle finger. Tim shot off the tip of his ring finger. Jimmy shot his little finger, and David shot off the tip of his thumb.

James, not crying out now, looked at each finger as the men shot him. Then, he seemed to start losing consciousness.

Ryan got down in James's face again. Wild-eyed, he screamed, "We know you've got intelligence agents coming in here. How many? How many agents are you sending in?"

James shook his head from side to side.

"Don't want to fuckin' answer me, huh?" Ryan stood up. He raised his leg and kicked James as hard as he could in the left arm, breaking it.

James moaned in agony.

"Are you feeling hot, boy? You already feel the fire, don't you? Now you know what hell's going to be like— eternal hell!" Ryan stepped back, as if he was thinking, and stared at James. "Fuck. I'm going to come back down here and skin you alive," he threatened. With that, Ryan ordered the men back up to the house—for lunch.

No one talked about James during lunch, only, according to Ryan, "Yahweh wants James Thimm dead by six o'clock this evening."

"David, I want you to get on the tractor and go out and start disking the lower field down there," Ryan said. "Jimmy, I want you to keep an eye on the road. Make sure no one sneaks up on us."

After David had gotten the tractor started, he drove by the door of the hog shed and stopped. Ryan was already back inside with Tim and Dennis.

"You better come in and say good-bye to your friend," Ryan yelled to David. "Shit. James Thimm was a back stabber. He was a bad friend to you and you should tell him that!" Ryan told David as he approached the shed.

David, aghast now at what he saw, choked back sobs as he walked up to James, lying there beaten, covered with bruises and bleeding. David could hardly get the words out. "Good-bye," he said to James.

James barely opened his eyes. His voice was faint. "Good-bye. I'm sorry."

"You better get out there and disk the field, David," Ryan said.

David climbed up on the tractor and drove down into the field, to the place where Luke was buried. David knew he was preparing the field for another grave. This isn't real . . . this isn't real, he thought to himself over and over, tears rolling down his cheeks. But it's the afterlife that counts. It's where James is going that really matters.

The disk chewed into the weed cover, turning up chunks of black topsoil.

Ryan, Tim, and Dennis stood over James. "Yahweh wants me to show you how we skinned people in Vietnam. Dennis, go get me some razor blades and the rubber gloves."

Dennis ran for the house and returned with the blades and a pair of yellow rubber gloves.

Ryan stretched the gloves over his hands and squatted down by James. James hardly moved when Ryan sliced into the flesh of his calf and cut a strip about three inches wide and eight inches long. Ryan grunted as he jerked the pliers as hard as he could, stripping the skin away from muscle.

"Damn!" Dennis remarked.

Once Ryan had pulled the strip of skin off, he dangled the

piece of flesh in James's face. "You thought we didn't mean business." Ryan laughed.

James didn't respond; he was barely conscious now.

Dennis, like a kid eager to follow the leader, wanted to try skinning the leg. He cut a piece of flesh, but as he tried to pull the skin off, his sweaty hands slipped off the pliers. "Shit," he said.

Dennis and Tim wanted to break James's legs. They'd heard Ryan talk about torturing people, breaking every bone in their bodies while they were alive.

Ryan consulted Yahweh, again bowing his head and mumbling. "Yeah, do it!"

Dennis swung a lead pipe over his head and brought it down on James's leg . . . once, twice, three times.

"Hey, that ain't the way you do it," Ryan told his son. "Here, put this under his leg," Ryan said, moving the wooden block under James's leg. "Now hit it."

Dennis swung the pipe again and this time James's leg snapped.

Tim put the block under James's right leg and raised a rough-cut two by four over his head. The club struck James's leg with a thud, the force of the blow breaking the bone.

Ryan was down in James's face again. "Now do you think Yahweh means business? Answer me! Yes or no?"

James's lips barely formed the word yes.

Ryan stepped back and kicked James in the head, leaning into the kick with all his weight. "I'll cave his chest in. That's sure to kill him." Ryan jumped on James's chest, stomping the life out of him.

Finally, James was dead.

Later that evening, the men returned to the hog shed. They had to bury James.

James's body was lying on the sleeping bag near the south door of the shed.

David stared disbelievingly at James's mutilated body, noticing that his legs were broken and that a patch of skin was missing from one leg. "What do we say if anyone asks what happened to James?" David asked as if in a daze.

"Tell 'em he went south—just picked up and left," Ryan said. "And if anybody asks about Luke, tell 'em he went with his dad. Now, let's get on with it."

Dennis and Jimmy stuffed James's body in the sleeping bag and zipped it shut.

"Put his clothes in there, too," Ryan instructed.

Jimmy picked up James's shirt and jacket and stuffed them into the sleeping bag. They dragged the sleeping bag over to the door of the shed.

Ryan pulled the Jeep Wagoneer up to the door; the men loaded the body and drove down into the field.

"Yahweh wants the grave dug right here." Ryan pointed to a spot about thirty yards from where Luke was buried. "Three feet wide, six feet long, six feet deep."

Tim, David, and Dennis did the digging. It took about thirty minutes with the three of them at it. Then, they lifted the body and laid it next to the open grave. James's head was left uncovered.

"I want him facing east. That's the direction for Satan. That's the direction James Thimm needs to be," Ryan said. With that, he rolled James's body into the grave.

"Yahweh wants him shot between the eyes," Ryan said, handing his .45 pistol to Tim. "Make it look like an execution in case somebody finds the body a hundred years from now."

Tim took aim and fired one shot into the head of the lifeless body in the grave; the bullet pierced the left eye.

The men plunged their shovels into the mound of dirt beside the grave and began filling it in.

Suddenly, David began to cry, overwhelmed by what had happened.

"Don't feel bad about it. Don't let your emotions bother you," Ryan told him. "James deserved to die. Don't feel sorrow for his death. There will be other friends."

David bit his lip, trying to mask his emotion. He nodded that he understood.

"Hell, I'll have to kill you if you can't kill more freely once Armageddon gets here," Ryan said matter-of-factly. Then, Ryan turned from the grave diggers and looked westward.

It was dusk now. In the distance, lightning flashed through the summer sky. A light sprinkle of rain was falling.

"You can see Yahweh is trying to cleanse the earth . . . now that all of Satan's people are off the farm. Things will go better now for all of us. Lisa's baby, Yahweh's grandchild, can be born."

CHAPTER 59

The next morning Lisa gasped at the sharp, jabbing pain low in her abdomen. She rolled slowly out of bed and went to wake Ryan. "I've got pains; it's the baby," she said, holding her stomach.

Ryan jumped from his reclining chair. "It's time for the birth of Yahweh's grandson," Ryan told her. Not Yahweh's son, but his grandson, Ryan insisted. "Finally!"

He ushered Lisa into the birthing room, summoning Ruth and Cheryl. The moment they'd prepared for had arrived. Ryan had received thorough instructions from Yahweh. He was to deliver the child. It would be a boy and Ryan would do the circumcision. The birthing room, with a birthing chair they'd built, was stocked with sterile supplies— gowns, towels, scissors, and surgical gloves. The room had been washed down with Clorox twice each day.

Lisa groaned as they boosted her into the white pine high chair. She positioned her feet into the rounded footrests. Her labor pains grew intense.

Ryan blanched.

"Just keep breathing, Lisa. Nice and easy," Cheryl coached, her mouth dry with anxiety. God, she thought, what if something goes wrong? Lisa hadn't seen a doctor during her pregnancy. What if the baby needs help after it arrives? What if Lisa hemorrhages? Cheryl prayed to Yahweh. All they had to go on now was His blessing and what they'd read in books on natural childbirth.

"That's right, Lisa, you're doing fine. Just stay calm. You'll be fine," Ruth assured Lisa.

Ryan watched, open-mouthed.

Cheryl quickly assumed authority. Someone had to deliver this baby now. "Just stay calm, Lisa, breathe . . . thata girl . . . you're doing fine. Keep breathing."

"Ohhhh!" Lisa cried out. She blew short breaths and pushed.

Finally, in the afternoon, the baby was on its way.

Ruth stood at Lisa's head, wiping her forehead and holding her hand. "Squeeze my hand, Lisa. Squeeze my hand," Ruth told her.

"Push, Lisa. Push," Cheryl coached.

"I'm trying," Lisa panted.

"I can see the head. It's coming. The head is out. You're almost there," Cheryl said.

"Ahhh . . ." Lisa groaned, feeling the baby finally emerge from her.

"It's here!" Cheryl exclaimed. She lifted the new child from the table. "It's a boy, Lisa. It's a baby boy."

Lisa's eyes grew large as she looked down at the baby.

Ruth and Cheryl worked quickly to clean the baby. They suctioned its throat and nose and the baby drew its first breath.

Cheryl breathed a sigh of relief and placed the baby across Lisa's stomach.

Now, Ryan was ready to resume authority. With Cheryl's coaching, he cut the umbilical cord, then Cheryl tied it.

Yahweh had instructed that Ryan circumcise the baby, but now, Ryan waffled. "I'm afraid to," he said. No one encouraged him.

Ruth and Cheryl wiped the newborn, wrapped him in a blanket, and handed him to Lisa.

The young mother smiled and cradled the baby in her

arms. Then the baby started to fuss. His fussing turned to screaming.

"Yeah, he's a healthy baby boy," Cheryl laughed.

Ryan stood at Lisa's left shoulder. "He's squirming. I think he's trying to squirm his way over to me."

"Maybe you should hold him," Lisa said.

"No. He's too damned little."

"Go on, take him," Lisa said.

Ryan reached down and picked up the child. As he held him, the baby stopped crying. "This is Yahweh's grandson," Ryan said. He'd insisted all along that the baby was immaculately conceived. "People say this kind of thing doesn't happen . . . that only Yeshua was conceived through Mary who was a virgin. But I believe this baby was caused inside Lisa by the archangel Michiel, like Yahweh told us he was."

Ryan handed the baby to Cheryl. "It may not be over yet. Yahweh said Lisa might have twins. She should stay in the chair, in case another baby comes."

Skeptical but obedient, Cheryl fought to stay awake as she sat up all night at Lisa's side to keep the new mother from falling off the birthing chair in her sleep.

Maxine Haverkamp, eager to see her new grandson, had Jimmy drop her off at the farm the next day.

Maxine held the child and bragged on him. "I think he has your nose," she told Lisa.

The baby was a big hit on the farm. He was new, something clean, something good. Ryan held the baby by the hour, claiming, "That baby loves me and trusts me more than it does its own mother."

That afternoon, her visit at an end, Maxine kissed her daughters and new grandson good-bye; Tim offered her a ride. He led her to the yellow Datsun 210B that had belonged to James Thimm.

"This is James's car, isn't it?" Maxine asked as she slid into the passenger seat.

"Yeah, it was," Tim responded.

"Where is he, by the way? I haven't seen him for a while."

"Well, he just picked up and went to Texas. I'm not sure where."

"Oh."

"Yeah, I bought his car. He needed money to get to Texas so I helped him out and bought the car from him."

"Is James with Rick? Aren't he and Luke in Texas, too?"

"Uh, I don't know just where they are. All I know is that when Rick left he took Luke with him."

Tim made nervous small talk with Maxine during the rest of the forty-five-minute ride to her house.

Once there, Norbert came out to greet them. He too inquired about the car. "What are you doing with this?"

"I bought it from James Thimm. He went south—to Texas, you know."

"Oh, no . . . I didn't know that. Say, do you know where he is down there? I get down that way on business. I'd like to have his address. I'll look him up sometime."

"Uh, no, I don't know his address or just where he is right off."

"Well, can you get the address for me?"

"Yeah, sure. I can try to find out for you."

"Okay, I'd appreciate it," Norbert said. He wondered what had happened at the farm to make James leave so suddenly.

In Beatrice, Nebraska, Carl and Hilda Schmidt wanted an answer to that very question. Where was their son James?

The Schmidts were agonizing over him. It was May; they hadn't seen him since the preceding summer. He had come home for a family gathering on his birthday, but had been cool, aloof. He had insisted that his mother not bake a cake for him.

"That's okay, we don't have to have a cake," Hilda had told him. And although she didn't bake one, she worked a day in the kitchen, preparing fried chicken, potato salad, and homemade ice cream, one of James's favorites. She invited the Thimm family over; they too could see that James was merely accommodating them. That had been July 10.

The last time he'd come to the house was a couple of weeks later—July 24. Hilda peeked out the curtain as James came up to the door. Jimmy Haverkamp waited in the car outside. "They never let them travel alone or go anywhere by themselves," she told Carl, remembering her research on cults which stated just that—that most cult members are not allowed to leave the group alone.

"I need a dirt bike," James said. "I need five hundred dollars."

Hilda and Carl were surprised at his demand. He'd rarely, if ever, asked for money, especially for something as frivolous as a dirt bike.

"Why, James? Why do you need a dirt bike?" she'd asked.

"I just do. Do you want to give me the money or not?"

"I guess I just want to know it's worthwhile," Hilda said. "If I think something is worthwhile, I'll write you out a check for a thousand, but I'm just not so sure about this . . ."

"Just take it out of my inheritance," James interrupted. "You'll be leaving me money eventually anyway. Just take it out of that." His tone was curt.

"You know, James, we love you very much and we're worried about you. We don't know where you're living . . ." his father tried.

"Huh? You took me away from my real family. What do you mean you're worried about me?"

It pained Hilda and Carl to hear James talk like that, and afraid of losing all contact with him, Hilda agreed to give James half the money now; he could get the rest later. She wrote him a check for two hundred fifty dollars. And that was the last they'd seen of their son.

CHAPTER 60

 D ark, low-hanging clouds rolled across the southern skies.

David stood silent, gazing across the field—the place where James was buried. He hadn't been able to tell anyone of the grief he felt over the loss of his best friend. Maybe he'd never tell anyone. Maybe no one would ever understand. David himself couldn't understand how or why it had happened, but it had and now it was over. As a lump formed in his throat, he forced the memory of James from his mind. He had work to do. He and Jimmy had a big night ahead.

"It looks like rain. Maybe we better get an early start," Jimmy said, settling his camouflage booty hat on his head.

A few minutes after nine o'clock he and David jumped into Jimmy's truck and headed across the river into Missouri. Days before, Yahweh had directed them to a large fertilizer plant—the Cargill Company, on Highway 159, eight miles northwest of Oregon, Missouri, about three miles off Interstate 29. The plant's large, sliding garage doors opened into loading bins, so they could pull inside and go undetected while loading up.

Around nine thirty, Jimmy turned off 159 and into the drive leading up to the long, white Cargill building. The headlights off, he pulled the truck around to the back of the plant.

About four miles away, on Interstate 29, Cargill's plant manager, Wally Riebesell, was thinking of taking the turnoff and stopping by the plant.

"Honey, why don't we swing by and pick up my company car?" he asked his wife Kris. They were on their way home from a weekend with relatives in Spencer, Iowa. "Then you won't have to take me to work in the morning."

"Oh, I'm too tired," Kris said. "Why don't we just go on home? I don't mind bringing you over in the morning."

"Okay," Wally said, looking off to the south. "Boy, there's one hell of a storm rolling in. Look at those thunderheads."

The Riebesells drove on home.

It was starting to rain. Quickly, Jimmy used a crowbar to snap the lock on one of the sliding garage doors. He threw his weight into the door and slid it open. The rumbling sound echoed through the dark, cavernous plant.

David drove the truck inside and Jimmy slid the huge door shut.

"It's going to pour," David said.

"We're just in time, huh?"

Their flashlights guided them as they walked through the plant. The place was about half a block long. Offices filled one end. A big truck maintenance shop and fertilizer bins took up the rest of the building.

Breaking into the locked office, they spotted a Xerox copier. "We don't have one of them," Jimmy said. "Let's come back for it."

They moved on through the shop area.

"A lot of tools here," David said, aiming his flashlight across the room. "A lot of tools!" There were complete sets of tools in boxes stamped "Cargill."

They began loading—boxes of tool sets, sledgehammers, hand saws, chain saws, aluminum shovels, and drills.

* * *

Five miles southwest of the Cargill plant, Holt County Deputy Sheriff Melvin Hayzlett glanced at his kitchen clock. It was almost ten o'clock. He looked out the window. As lightning flashed through the sky, he could see a bank of black, low-hanging clouds in the southwest. A tornado watch had been issued several hours earlier.

"I think I better go out and get a look at the weather," he said softly to his wife. "It's getting pretty nasty-looking out there." As a deputy, Hayzlett was part of a spotter team that kept an eye on the clouds during tornado season.

Still in his tan uniform, Hayzlett put on his western style deputy's hat, his badge pinned in the middle. The hat added height to his five-foot-eight-inch frame. "I won't be gone long," he said as he patted his wife on the shoulder and walked out the front door of their country home. From the porch he scanned the skies, then climbed into his patrol car and drove off.

The fifty-eight-year-old deputy had lived in northwest Missouri all his life and took tornado watches in stride. Still, he knew Mother Nature was to be respected. He'd seen wall clouds spin into funnels and drop to earth, sucking up everything in their paths. He hoped this wouldn't be one of those nights.

Driving the back roads, he kept an eye on the clouds rolling overhead. Lightning shot across the sky and thunder rumbled across the pastureland, but there was no sign of funnel clouds. Large raindrops splattered on his windshield.

Hayzlett reached into his rear pocket and pulled out a round tin of Skoal chewing tobacco. He noticed he was about out as he pinched off a piece of the soft, moist tobacco and placed it behind his lower lip. He returned the tin to its home in his hip pocket, where the can had worn a ring in the fabric. He decided to drive over to the convenience shop on the edge of nearby Mound City and pick up some more. Then he would take a different route, Highway 159, back toward home.

Halfway to Mound City, it started to rain in sheets—the heaviest he'd seen in ages. His windshield wipers barely kept up; he couldn't see to drive. He slowed down and saw a driveway to his right. He pulled in. It was the driveway of the Cargill plant. Scanning the sky with each lightning flash, he still saw no sign of funnel clouds. Hayzlett radioed his base: "Deputy Sheriff Hayzlett here. I'm out here on 159, by the Cargill plant. A lot of rain out here . . . but no sign of any tornadoes. Thought I'd let you know, over."

The rain pounded the patrol car so hard he could barely hear the chatter on his police radio. He turned up the volume. "Ten-four. Thanks," the dispatcher radioed back. "The watch expires in fifteen minutes."

All in all, Hayzlett concluded, this was just another summer thunderstorm. And the farmers could sure use it.

As the rain let up, Hayzlett pulled out of the Cargill driveway and back onto the highway. He'd drive west a few more miles before heading home, he decided. Ten minutes later, he turned around at the Rulo Bridge, over the Missouri River, and headed back east toward Highway 159. He paid little attention to the dark-colored pickup he met heading toward Rulo, though he did wonder why anyone would be out on a night like this.

CHAPTER 61

Early Monday morning, Cargill Manager Wally Riebesell knew something was wrong when he saw the muddy tire tracks leading away from the building.

Inside, he quickly scanned the office; it hadn't been ransacked, thank God. They weren't after money, he thought. The safe was untouched. Moments later he discovered what it was the thieves had been after—tools. Virtually all the tools were gone from the maintenance shop. Damn! Immediately, he phoned the Holt County sheriff's office.

Deputy Sheriff Hayzlett was assigned to investigate.

Riebesell met Hayzlett at the main entrance and led him around to the rear. "Here's where they drove their truck in—you can see their tire tracks and some footprints," Riebesell explained, pointing to the fresh tire ruts. "Once they got inside, they had themselves a heyday. Even took our copier, a typewriter, and all the candy bars and cans of soda pop out of the machines."

"I'll want to get some pictures of those tire tracks and shoe prints after we look around," Hayzlett said, setting his briefcase on the floor and opening it. He pulled a notepad from the case and followed Riebesell into the plant.

"Did they make a mess of things for you?" Hayzlett asked.

"You know, that's what's strange about this whole thing. It's one of the cleanest thefts I've ever seen." Riebesell led him to the office. "They didn't destroy anything in here, really, or tear through office files—like I had done to me in another office one time. These guys didn't even try to get into the safe." He pointed to the safe in the corner. "They just took tools and equipment."

Hayzlett nodded. "Was the office locked?" he asked, examining the damaged office door handle.

"Yeah, they did jimmy that open, but the tools is where they really hit us," Riebesell said, leading the deputy sheriff back into the main shop. Riebesell scanned the area, rattling off the names of the various tools that had been taken. Then he looked over at Hayzlett, who was scribbling notes as fast as he could. "Oh, don't worry about making a list. I've got a good one I'll give you. We had a complete inventory, so it was pretty easy to tell what's missing."

"Okay, then, Wally, I want to go back and check those tracks."

They returned to the rear, sliding door where the thieves had entered.

Hayzlett pulled his 35-mm Yashica camera and a twelve-inch ruler from his briefcase. He positioned the ruler next to a section of tire track, focused, and snapped the photo; the ruler would provide a standard of measurement once the photos were developed. He took about a dozen pictures in all, carefully including the ruler in each. "These tracks aren't as clean as I'd like them, but they'll do," he said. He also took photos of shoe prints in the mud, again placing the ruler next to each print before taking the shot. It looked like two different sets of shoe prints. "I'll hang onto these photos in case we should come across the suspect vehicle or in case we want to compare these prints with anything we might get from other crime scenes."

Riebesell nodded that he understood.

"It must have been about a one-ton truck with dual wheels, from the looks of those tire tracks," Hayzlett said, slowly picking up his ruler and hanging the camera around his neck.

"Yeah, I'd say so," Riebesell said.

Hayzlett glanced back to the clean cement floor just inside the door. "Look. There's no mud tracked into the shop, but there are tracks in the mud leading away from the building. These guys were in the plant last night before it started raining, and they left after that downpour!"

"Yeah," Riebesell said tentatively, not understanding Hayzlett's point.

"For God's sake," Hayzlett said, putting his hands on his hips, "I was sitting out in your driveway last night, waiting for the rain to let up. I must've been sitting out here while these guys were in here loading up!"

He replayed the previous evening in his mind. He remembered passing that dark-colored pickup. Could that have been the thieves? Possibly. It was a one-ton truck, and it had orange clearance lights across the top of the cab. He did remember those cab lights shining through the rain. "This is a little embarrassing," he said to Riebesell.

"I know how you feel," Riebesell said. "If I'd picked up my company car here last night, I'd have walked right in on them."

"If that doesn't beat all." Hayzlett shook his head. He cranked the roll of film forward in his camera and removed it while Riebesell went to get the list of stolen equipment.

"This is a fairly complete list," Riebesell told him. "Because of the inventory we kept, it was easy to find out what's missing. I'd say they got about twelve thousand dollars' worth of stuff."

"Boy, that's a haul," Hayzlett said, skimming the four-page, handwritten list. He tucked the list into his briefcase and snapped it shut. "I think that'll be all I need for now, Wally. We'll be in touch," Hayzlett said, heading for the door.

"Thanks."

Hayzlett tossed the briefcase into the front seat of his car and drove back to his office, racking his brain to remember anything else related to the theft he might have noticed last night.

From behind his desk, he stared out the window, his gaze locking on the latticework of the gazebo on the courthouse lawn, as he alternately jogged his memory and jotted down notes for his report on the Cargill case. I'll get to the bottom of this one, he thought as he placed a plug of chewing tobacco behind his bottom lip.

Three days later, the thieves struck again, this time at a farm only a few miles from the Cargill plant. They'd cut through a window screen in an implement shed sometime after eleven o'clock at night. They'd made off with a Suzuki dirt bike, expensive Snap-On brand hand tools, three rolls of new barbed wire, and a case of 10W30 Skelly motor oil. Hayzlett got photos of the tire treads and shoe prints. They were the same as from the Cargill break-in.

Hayzlett had a feeling that these guys would strike again. He wanted to alert surrounding law enforcement agencies. Normally, to get the word out, he'd use the teletype or pass the word along by phone. But this time he'd be more thorough and circulate a memo to law enforcement agencies in surrounding counties.

Hayzlett composed a description—all he could remember—of the suspect vehicle. "Dual-wheel truck, possibly with a utility bed, about one ton in size, dark in color, with three clearance lights across the top of the cab." He noted that he had pictures of tire tracks and shoe prints.

On the third floor of the courthouse in Falls City, Richardson County Sheriff Cory McNabb skimmed Hayzlett's memorandum. McNabb thought for a moment, but he couldn't come up with any cases in Richardson County that might be linked. He tucked the memo away in his file cabinet.

CHAPTER 62

JUNE 25

Jimmy and David were exhausted. It seemed like they'd been doing night work around the clock all spring. Since James's death, they'd knocked off at least a dozen missions. Their inventory now included a boat and boat motor from western Kansas, lawn mowers, motorcycles, a hay rake, and other farm tools and machinery.

Tonight, they were off to Seneca, Kansas, some forty miles from Rulo, to pick up a crop sprayer. They'd seen it on the lot of Koehler Implements, on Highway 36, about a mile west of Seneca.

Ryan advised the two against taking the sprayer. "I saw some turkey vultures today, out in one of the fields. It's a bad omen. I don't think you should go out tonight."

"Let's ask Yahweh, then, to find out for sure," Jimmy suggested.

He and Ryan asked Yahweh's permission, and in the end, it was granted to go after the sprayer. About midnight, Jimmy and David left for Seneca in Jimmy's Ford truck.

They pulled quietly onto the implement lot at Koehler's, hitched the sprayer to their flatbed truck, and headed back to Rulo. A piece of cake.

*   *   *

Richardson County Sheriff Cory McNabb was an avid reader. He liked to read in bed, late at night. He'd just placed his book on the nightstand and had dropped off to sleep when the phone rang.

The police department in Sabetha, Kansas, fifteen miles south of the Nebraska border, had received a report of a possible cattle theft operation at a rest stop four miles south of town, at the junction of highways 36 and 75. According to the report, cattle were being unloaded from a blue pickup, pulling an aluminum trailer, into a brown truck with a goose-neck trailer. The suspects were possibly heading up Highway 75 into Nebraska. "Request stop and check to your satisfaction. And get ID if possible," the teletype read from Sabetha police.

Such late-night calls were not uncommon for McNabb, who was becoming accustomed to a sheriff's eighty-hour weeks. Originally hired as a deputy, McNabb had just become sheriff in April when Gene Ramer, who was losing his battle with cancer, had stepped down from the job.

McNabb, a nonstop talker and chain-smoker, was a colorful character by anyone's standards. Stocky in build, the thirty-five-year-old McNabb had dark, wavy hair and a thick, bushy mustache that covered his entire upper lip. He would have been a great endorsement for an old-fashioned shaving mug.

McNabb threw on his tan uniform, holstered his .38 on his hip, and jumped into a patrol car. It was a few minutes before one in the morning when he pulled out of the gravel lane to his two-story, stucco country house. The night was still. A reddish moon—a blood moon—ascended in the southeastern sky.

McNabb turned west onto Highway 159, followed it about nine miles, and then picked up Highway 8. As usual, there was no traffic on the back roads this late. He called his deputy and sent him up Highway 75. McNabb figured one of them would come across the thieves, if that's what they were.

Then, just as McNabb rounded a curve on the edge of tiny Salem, Nebraska, he saw the oncoming headlights of a vehicle. As it passed, he could see that it was not a truck pulling a load of cattle. "Nope, that's not it," he said, clicking his tongue.

The passing vehicle was an older model truck, pulling what he thought looked like a crop sprayer. Nothing really out of the ordinary, it seemed . . . at first.

As McNabb glanced in his rearview mirror, he noticed that the sprayer had no taillights. He debated whether to turn around and pull the vehicle over.

"Hell, I better check this out," McNabb muttered. As far as the other call was concerned, he figured his deputy had the highway covered north of Sabetha, and McNabb could still keep an eye out for the cattle truck here along Highway 8.

As he pulled over onto the shoulder to make a U-turn, he looked back in his mirror again. He thought he noticed the truck speeding up. Years of experience in stopping cars had taught McNabb he could often read something in a driver's subtle behavior once the driver saw him making a U-turn.

Now, instinct told him something might be amiss. It was unusual for anybody to be pulling a sprayer at this hour of the morning. He turned on his red light. Still, he figured the stop so routine that he didn't even notify his dispatcher.

The truck ahead slowed and pulled over to the shoulder. They were just inside the small town of Salem, under a streetlight. As McNabb rolled up behind the truck, he got a clear view of the license plate mounted on the upper left side of the truck's stock rack. Out-of-state tag—Kansas. BR 4303. Expired, too.

Inside the cab, Jimmy saw the look of disbelief on David's face; never, in all their months of night work, had they even come close to getting caught. Yahweh had protected them. But now a cop was on his way up to the truck.

"Shit! We should've put clamp-on lights on the sprayer!" Jimmy whispered. "We're going to get a ticket for no lights."

"We might be able to talk our way out of it," David said. "We'll just say we're not far from home."

Having only seconds to discuss it, neither was sure what to do. Should they resist?

McNabb, leaving his headlights on, walked up to the driver's side of the Ford truck and peered into the cab. Up close now, he thought he recognized the driver as being from around Rulo, but he couldn't attach a name to the face. The passenger looked familiar, too. "You know you boys are pulling this sprayer without any taillights?"

"Uh, yeah," Jimmy said.

"Where are you going with this sprayer at this hour?"

"We're going home to Rulo," Jimmy answered.

"You both live in Rulo?" McNabb asked.

"Yeah."

"I'll need to see your driver's license," he said to Jimmy.

Jimmy pulled out his wallet.

McNabb held his flashlight to the driver's license. He handed it back to Jimmy.

"What's your name?" McNabb asked David.

"Kenny Adams." Ryan had told David to have an alias ready ever since he'd left Beatrice and they'd taken the neighbor's cattle. This, however, was the first time he'd used it.

"Is this your sprayer?"

"It's our uncle's," Jimmy answered.

Something didn't seem right. These guys were nervous— too nervous. They aren't telling the truth, McNabb thought.

McNabb decided to push it. "You know, I'm going to ask both of you to step outside here for just a minute." He shoved his flashlight in his rear pocket.

Jimmy and David moved slowly from the cab of the truck. David, his heart pounding, joined Jimmy on the other side of the cab. Now they stood in the beam of McNabb's headlights, both men with their right hands buried deep in their jean pockets.

"I'll need you guys to take your hands out of your pockets," McNabb instructed routinely.

Neither man moved.

McNabb felt the adrenaline rush as he went for his gun. "I said, hands out of your pockets. I want to see both hands now!" he said, pointing his .38 at them.

Slowly, both Haverkamp and Andreas pulled their hands out of their pockets.

"Okay, both of you . . . across the hood of the car. Come on! I want you both across the hood." A trace of nervous tension registered in McNabb's voice. He patted them down, finding .25 caliber pistols—full clips, hammers back—in each man's pocket. "I don't know what you guys are up to, but I intend to find out."

McNabb pulled Jimmy's arms behind him and hand-cuffed him, and then cuffed David. He pushed them around in front of the headlights of his car. "Now, stand there."

McNabb looked inside the truck, where he found more guns—two HK 99 pistols, both loaded—and two twelve-inch hunting knives. Holy Christ! he thought. These aren't your everyday thieves.

McNabb read both Haverkamp and Andreas the Miranda warning. "Did you guys steal that sprayer?"

"Well . . . uh, yeah," Jimmy said, hanging his head.

McNabb, still thinking that Haverkamp and Andreas might be involved with the possible cattle theft near Sabetha, first radioed in to his deputy that he'd stopped two armed suspects. He wanted to warn the deputy of possible armed accomplices.

Then, McNabb radioed his dispatcher. "I need some help out here, and get hold of Terry Becker from the state patrol. We need to take a couple guys in."

When Becker arrived it was nearly three in the morning. McNabb's deputy drove over, too. He'd seen no signs of cattle rustling. It must have been a false alarm.

"Terry, if you guys can take these two in, I'll drive this truck and sprayer in," McNabb said.

"That'll be fine," Becker said.

Still shocked at being arrested, and fearing Yahweh's wrath, Jimmy and David were hauled off to jail.

McNabb got behind the wheel of the Ford truck and turned onto the highway, pulling the sprayer behind him. As he drove he noticed the clearance lights across the cab, reflecting down on the hood of the truck. Cab lights. This truck matched the description of the truck the Missouri deputy had circulated two or three weeks ago.

*   *   *

Back in Falls City, Jimmy and David were led to cells at the Richardson County jail, on the third floor of the courthouse. Their clothes and shoes were taken from them; they were issued standard jail clothes—orange coveralls. Although confused and frightened about what lay ahead, David felt a sense of relief wash over him as the cell door slammed shut behind him. For the first time in months, he acknowledged the silent part of himself that had always doubted the stealing. Maybe now he could escape the weariness of it all. Finally, it was over. He fell fast asleep.

Jimmy sat on the edge of his bunk. He still couldn't believe they'd been arrested. Mike had assured them they'd never be caught. Yahweh was guiding them, protecting them. Mike was wrong. Now Jimmy couldn't help considering the verses in the Bible that spoke of false prophets. If what a man said didn't come to pass, he was a false prophet. But he still feared Ryan's wrath, so Jimmy kept his doubts to himself.

At dawn, McNabb was on the phone to Deputy Sheriff Melvin Hayzlett, in Holt County, Missouri, inquiring about the tire prints he'd photographed earlier in the Cargill theft case.

"Sounds like you got something there," Hayzlett said. "I'm on my way over now." By ten o'clock, Hayzlett was in Becker's office with the envelope of photos under his arm.

Becker and McNabb were meeting with the Nemaha County sheriff, who confirmed that the crop sprayer had been stolen from Koehler Implements in Seneca.

McNabb drove Hayzlett and Becker to an empty building on the edge of Falls City that had once housed a farm implement dealership. It was where he'd parked the Haverkamp truck. He'd wanted it out of sight in case there had been an ongoing search for an accomplice in the original report of a cattle theft.

"It looks familiar," Hayzlett said as they walked into the building. Hayzlett let his eyes run over the truck as he walked around to the rear of the utility bed. "Hey, look at this," he said, pointing to an eighteen-inch toolbox.

Becker and McNabb walked around from the other side of the truck to examine the toolbox.

It had the word *Cargill* stamped across it.

"Well, I guess that tells us something, doesn't it?" Hayzlett asked.

"Yeah, I'd say it does," Becker agreed.

Hayzlett opened an envelope and pulled out his stack of black-and-white, five-by-seven photos of the tire treads and shoe prints from the Cargill case. He shuffled through the stack, looking for the shot of the front tires. When he found it, the three of them squatted in front of the right front tire and compared the tread with that in the photo.

"Looks like a match to me," McNabb said.

"Yep," Hayzlett said. "For sure they're the same kind of tread that I've got pictures of. We'll want to send the tires to the crime lab in Kansas City for a positive ID." The Regional Criminalistics Lab could take the tires and Hayzlett's photos and determine, without a doubt, if they were the tires that made the tracks at the Cargill plant.

Once back at Becker's office, McNabb went up to the third floor and pulled the shoes they'd confiscated from Jimmy and David from the jail locker. He returned with a pair of Nikes and a pair of Keds and laid them on Becker's desk.

Becker turned the shoes over to examine the soles as Hayzlett laid out the photos of the shoe prints. They matched the photos with both pairs of shoes.

"We got 'em," Hayzlett said.

PART THREE

The Investigation

CHAPTER **63**

For Terry Becker, the Rulo farm was an unwelcome example of Murphy's Law—anything that can go wrong, will. Becker remembered his visit to the farm ten months earlier to check out the rumors of gunfire. Indeed, he'd considered the paramilitary business going on there a bit unusual, but he'd driven off, believing that no criminal wrongdoing was under way. Certainly he had no reason to believe the farm served as a base for a theft operation.

And now, Becker was giving no one at the farm the benefit of the doubt. His office was a hotbed of activity. Within hours, plans were laid to raid the Rulo farm. Based on Deputy Sheriff Hayzlett's evidence; Becker and McNabb got a search warrant.

Unsure of what they'd find at the farm, McNabb quizzed Haverkamp and Andreas. "Who all is out there?" he asked.

"Tim Haverkamp—he's twenty-three; he's out there. And some women and children," Jimmy said. "The women won't resist. I don't know about Tim." Mike Ryan's name was never mentioned; Jimmy was afraid to implicate him.

"Are there weapons out there?" McNabb asked.

"There are some Mini-14s out there," Jimmy said. "That's all I know."

Becker and McNabb knew they shouldn't go in alone; they weren't sure what they'd find. They called in help from sheriffs' departments in surrounding counties, as well as from the state patrol in Lincoln. About a dozen officers were now converging on Becker's office, and the state patrol helicopter was being brought in for air surveillance while the farm was secured.

"There's only one road in there to the farm," McNabb told the other officers. "I've been there. It's a dead end leading up to the house."

Becker nodded. He remembered the layout. "We'll go in two waves. McNabb and his deputy will be in the lead car," Becker said. "Heiden and I will go in the second car." Dean Heiden was a state patrol investigator from Lincoln. "Once we're on the property, we'll fan out to both houses and secure the entire area."

At 12:45, the lawmen loaded up and began the nine-mile drive to Rulo.

At one o'clock the line of official cars pulled into the driveway of the Rulo farm. The state patrol helicopter hovered directly overhead.

The four lawmen walked up to the locked gate.

Tim Haverkamp came out of the house and cautiously approached the gate.

"We have a search warrant here. We are authorized to search the premises," Becker said, showing Tim the warrant.

Tim froze, saying nothing.

"Do you want to let us in?" McNabb asked.

Tim backed away, still silent.

"Okay, fellas. Let's go," Becker said.

McNabb's deputy cut the lock and onto the property they went.

Mike Ryan panicked now. He watched from inside the north house. He grabbed Cheryl's arm and began asking questions of Yahweh.

"Yahweh, Heavenly Father, do you want us to fire on these guys?"

Yes.

"Should I open fire?"

No.

Then Ryan heard the voice of Yahweh telling him, "Protect yourself. Fire only if you need to."

Cheryl was breathless, afraid she'd be arrested—taken away from her kids. "Ask him if any of us will have to leave the farm today."

Mike asked. The answer was no.

There was a loud banging at the east door—Satan's door. The officers were attempting to break it down.

The children began crying; they clung to their mothers. Two of the boys ran into the next room to hide.

The banging at the east door stopped and Ryan heard commotion at the south door. Two officers were kicking it in.

Becker and Heiden got through the south door, only to find themselves on a large porch. The house frame had been built around a mobile home. They saw boxes of rifle ammunition stacked in the corner.

"Who are you? What do you want?" the excited voice of a man yelled from inside.

It was hard for Becker to hear over the roar of the whirling blades of the helicopter directly above them and the screaming of women and children inside.

"I'm Terry Becker with the state patrol. We want to talk to you."

"What's going on? We've got women and children in here. I don't want them hurt!" Ryan yelled back.

"I don't think anyone should get hurt, either. We just want to talk to you. We have a search warrant and are here to search the property. Will you come out and talk to us?"

"No! I'm not talking to you. I can see you from where I am and I'm going to count to ten. If you're not the hell off this property, I'm going to cut you in two. I've got thirty rounds that can come out of this damn thing real quick!" Ryan was armed with a Colt AR-15 assault rifle.

"I can assure you we don't want to harm anyone. You can come on out."

"Yeah, so you can shoot me . . . just like you did to

Arthur Kirk. I know you kill people. You're waiting for me to come out so you can assassinate me. You might get me, but I'm going to kill a hell of a bunch of you first. And you're going to kill women and children in the process. I'm not coming out. I'm going to defend myself!''

"I'm telling you no one will get shot," Becker tried again. "We just need to talk to you."

"You'll be the first to fire the shots. So, if you want to handle this with any sense, you better get the hell out."

Becker motioned to Heiden. They backed out of the enclosed porch. "Look," Becker yelled into the house, "I'll even take my gun off." He slipped off his shoulder holster and handed it to Heiden. "See. I'm unarmed." Becker held up his hands to show he was holding no weapon. "I want to work with you, not against you!"

The voice yelling from inside fell silent.

Finally, Ryan yelled, "If you leave your arms outside, you can come back on the porch. I'll come out there unarmed, too."

"No one needs to get hurt here. We have a warrant to search this property. Jim Haverkamp and David Andreas are in jail on theft charges." With that, Becker and Heiden removed their weapons, comfortable in knowing they were being backed up by some excellent marksmen.

Ryan calmed down. "Okay, come on in." He motioned Becker and Heiden inside and led them from the kitchen into the living room.

As he walked through the kitchen, Becker noticed a Xerox copying machine to the side of the room. Odd, he thought. From the corner of his eye, he caught a glimpse of a wooden cup rack on the wall; the bottom of the rack carried the legend in crude red paint, "To Ruth with Love, YHVH's Family." On a wall, "YHVH #1" was scrawled in red paint.

Heading into the living room, Becker saw a small arsenal. A Mini-14 stood in the corner. A .45 pistol lay on the table next to the couch. A wooden rack bolted to a desk held a KG 99 pistol. Would Ryan grab one of them? Instinct told Becker he wouldn't. They moved on through the house.

In a room down the hall, Becker thought he recognized

the woman huddled in the corner with children. It was Cheryl Gibson from Hiawatha, just across the border. She had been missing for over a year!

"Hey, this is more than we bargained for," he said to Ryan. "What's she doing here?"

"She's staying here with us, trying to stay away from her husband," Ryan said.

"We're going to have to talk about this," Becker said. He knew warrants were out for Cheryl and pickup orders had been issued on the kids.

The children were whimpering.

"You don't need to be afraid," Becker said to the women and children. "We just need to look around." His words seemed to calm them.

He turned his attention to the weapons throughout the house. "Any of these guns automatic?" Becker glanced around.

"Nope," Ryan said.

Becker picked up the Ar-15. "This gun looks like it is," Becker said, looking at Ryan.

"It's news to me," Ryan said. "That's the first I knew of it."

"We need to look around," Becker said as he and another investigator kept moving through the house.

The investigator went over to open the east door to let the other officers in.

"Don't open that door!" Ryan exclaimed.

"Why not? Is this door booby-trapped?" the investigator asked.

"No. That's Satan's door. If you open it, Satan will enter."

The investigator looked at Becker from the corner of his eye. He accommodated Ryan by backing away from the east door.

Now, other investigators joined Becker in a search of the house. Becker couldn't believe the number of guns lying around. There were guns and ammunition everywhere. Wooden crates of ammunition were stacked to the ceiling in one bedroom—and guns were mounted above doorways throughout the house. Upon close inspection, Becker found that all the guns were loaded and ready to fire. He shook his head.

McNabb, now joining Becker, walked into the adjoining bedroom, which had been turned into a barracks. At the end of the bunks stood footlockers. McNabb opened them. Each was filled with combat clothing and survival gear, cooking utensils and silverware. The floor was a mishmash of abandoned clothing and children's toys. There was a jumble of toy tractors, cars, and dolls in one corner, guns and ammo in another.

A narrow wooden stairway led down to a musty, dark room where preparation for the ultimate catastrophe seemed to have been the order of the day. Food had been stacked to the ceiling—gallon cans of every fruit and vegetable imaginable. The place was crammed, literally crammed, with food. Neither Becker nor McNabb had ever seen so much food in one room outside a grocery store. For one of the few times in his life, McNabb was speechless. Disbelieving, they trudged back up the steps.

As they searched each room, a technician snapped photos.

Becker came across a car title lying on a table at one end of the living room. It was for a Datsun, registered to a James Thimm.

"Who's this James Thimm? Does he live here, too?" Becker asked.

"He was here, but he moved to Texas."

"Why's his car title here?"

"He sold his car to Tim Haverkamp before he left," Ryan said.

Becker accepted the explanation and moved on through the house.

By the time the search of both houses was complete, officers had found some fifty or sixty weapons. Outside, they test-fired them; altogether, they found fourteen fully automatic weapons.

"These guns are illegal, Mike," Becker said.

Ryan nodded that he understood, but said nothing.

With the illegal weapons seized and the premises secured,

Becker turned to Ryan. "Mike, what we came out here to check for was stolen property. We have reason to believe that Jimmy Haverkamp and David Andreas have taken some equipment that's being stored here at the farm."

Again, Ryan nodded. "They told me they was buying that stuff, but I had a feeling they was up to something like that," he said, shaking his head.

"What do you mean?" Becker asked.

"Well, I was just staying here. This ain't my place. I didn't figure it was any of my business, but I had an idea something was going on. I told them they'd get caught."

"Will you show us where this equipment is?"

He led them out to the shed were the equipment was stored.

Becker kept an eye on Ryan. This guy may act like he doesn't know what's going on, but he's obviously a ring-leader here, Becker thought.

The officers were astonished. The shed looked like a combination implement lot and flea market—tools and equipment were stacked to the rafters.

"Can you point out which of this stuff is stolen," Becker asked Ryan.

"I can try," Ryan said.

Officers marked the equipment with yellow chalk, indicating that it was stolen property. Very little of the equipment belonged to the farm; they marked virtually everything.

The second group of officers entered the south trailer. They found an angry Dennis Ryan in one of the bedrooms. On the bed next to Dennis lay a 9-mm pistol, a .45-caliber pistol, a .22 rifle and a KG 99 pistol.

"The pigs are here. The fucking pigs are here," Dennis yelled. "We ought to shoot the motherfuckers!"

Officers found three young boys huddled together in the next bedroom. They found another child hiding in the closet.

The officers assured the little boys that they were safe and led them all, including Dennis, outside.

McNabb moved through the south trailer; he had noticed the outside of the trailer was marked by bullet holes. Now he was seeing bullet holes in the walls inside. "My God, it looks like this whole dern place was used as a target range," he said to one of the deputies from Kansas.

South of the two dwellings, officers searched through a toolshed and moved on down to the hog confinement shed. There, they found several hundred ten-pound bags of charcoal stacked at one end of the building; nearby they discovered fifty-gallon drums of potassium chlorate, a crystalline salt used as an oxidizing agent in explosives.

The officers worked in the implement shed, going over the equipment, until late in the evening. Ryan had been a model of cooperation all afternoon.

As they wrapped up the day, Becker gathered the lawmen outside the north house. "We've got to take Cheryl Gibson in—Brown County has a warrant."

"I'll take custody of her and the kids," McNabb said. "Why don't we leave them here at the house overnight? I'll stay out here, make sure no one leaves."

McNabb waved the officers on as they left for the day. He settled in for the night, watching the house from the front seat of his car.

Inside the house, Ryan spoke with Yahweh in his white room. He came out and told the others that Yahweh was very mad. "Yahweh always told me others out here would cross Yahweh or lose faith. The raid was Norbert's fault," he told the women.

CHAPTER **64**

"Confrontation Avoided in Camp Arrests—
Weapons Seized from 'Survivalists'" was the headline in
the *Omaha World Herald*. The raid was headline news
across the region.

According to the press accounts, lawmen had confiscated
dozens of weapons, many of them illegal, and had inven-
toried nearly one hundred fifty thousand dollars' worth of
stolen equipment. Jimmy Haverkamp and David Andreas
were charged with the thefts and were being held in the
Richardson County jail, each on an eight thousand dollar
bond. Ryan was charged with possession of a machine gun;
he posted a seven hundred fifty dollar cash bond.

Becker scanned the morning headlines from his desk. For
him and McNabb, the job was just beginning. Their phones
were ringing nonstop with inquires about the stolen property. Farmers and law enforcement agencies in three states
were hoping to locate equipment stolen over the past year.
But Becker needed to find out the names of everyone who
had lived at the farm over the past year. Others might have
been involved in the thefts.

Becker dropped his newspaper and grabbed the ringing
phone. "Terry Becker here."

"Terry, this is Rick Stice. I'm calling from down in southern Missouri. I just wondered what was going on up at the farm." Stice had heard about the raid when his sister in Falls City had called him.

"What are you doing in Missouri, Rick?"

"I've been staying here at my brother's, working for him here."

"Well, Rick, we had quite a day out at your farm. We arrested Jimmy Haverkamp and David Andreas on the road with a stolen sprayer. Then we got a search warrant and found all kinds of stuff at the farm."

"Say, was James Thimm out there?" Rick asked.

Becker thought for a moment. He didn't immediately recognize the name, but it sounded familiar. Then he remembered—it was the name on the car title. "No," Becker said. "Thimm wasn't out there, but his car was."

"Oh," Rick said. "Who else was out there?"

Rick was pumping him for information, Becker knew. He decided to play along. Becker explained that they'd found Cheryl Gibson and her children. "Your two kids were there. By the way, Rick, where's your other son?"

"Oh, he's with me," Rick answered. "Are my two kids okay?"

"Yeah, they're fine. Listen, Rick, why don't we get together? We'd like to talk to you."

"Tell you what, I'll call you back," Rick said.

"Okay, Rick, please do." Becker jotted the name *Thimm* down on his notepad. As soon as he could wade through all these phone calls, he needed to check on the whereabouts of this guy James Thimm.

CHAPTER 65

On the night of the raid, Lester Gibson had received a call from his attorney at ten o'clock, informing him that Cheryl and the kids had been found.

"I'd suggest you go up there and watch the farm overnight," the attorney told him. "There may be some law enforcement there, too, but I think your being up there would be a good idea."

"I'll be there!" Lester replied, wild with excitement. He made two phone calls before dashing out the door. One call was to a *Kansas City Times* reporter, who was staying overnight in Hiawatha; he had been in town doing a story on Lester and his missing family. The second call was to Dennis Whalen, to let him know they'd found Cheryl.

"I'll meet you at the farm," Dennis told him.

The three of them sat in Whalen's van all night, sipping coffee from a thermos and smoking cigarettes. The reporter put his story together as Dennis and Lester waited for daylight.

Lester was as nervous as Dennis had ever seen him. Lester hadn't seen Cheryl or his children for fourteen months, and now, they were just a few yards away. Lester was angry at Sheriff McNabb for holding Cheryl and the kids overnight. "He should have honored the Kansas warrant and turned them over to Brown County authorities," Lester told Dennis. "Damn, that pisses me off."

"Yeah, I know," Dennis said, "but just hold on. You'll see Cheryl at the courthouse and I'm sure visitation will be arranged real soon for you and the kids." At daybreak, they drove into town.

Later in the morning, at the Richardson County courthouse, Lester and Dennis were joined by Lester's attorney and Dave Cazlett, a friend and editor of the Hiawatha newspaper. Seated on a bench on the courthouse lawn, they waited for McNabb to arrive with Cheryl.

Lester was wired—trembling nervous. He didn't know what to expect at seeing Cheryl.

Just then, McNabb pulled up across the street in his squad car. Cheryl was in the front seat with him.

Dennis grabbed Lester as he started to get up from the bench. "Don't move. Don't even go near her. Stay here. Don't approach her right now."

"Jesus, it's hard," Lester said, straining to see Cheryl as she walked around from the other side of the car.

Then he saw her. His reaction was one of joy and shock. She looked so pale, so white. She wore no makeup and her hair was straight. She was thinner. She just looked so different, he thought.

As Cheryl and McNabb walked up the sidewalk to the courthouse, they passed within a few yards of Lester.

Her eyes looked so blank, Lester thought.

She glanced his way, but seemed to look right through him. She acted as if he was a stranger she'd met on the street.

Cazlett walked up to Cheryl. "How are you, Cheryl?" She ignored him.

Lester's heart was in his throat. His eyes filled with tears.

"Take it easy, Lester," Dennis said. "Just take it easy. You'll have to be patient with her; right now, she's not the same person you knew."

Outside the courtroom, before the proceedings began,

Lester got to McNabb. "When do I get to see my kids? Aren't you going to get them out of that farm?"

"They're in no danger. They're just fine," McNabb told him.

Lester contained his anger and walked off.

It was a long day in court. That morning, both Cheryl and Lester testified during a hearing on the Kansas civil order to take the children into protective custody. Cheryl began to cry when the children were ordered into the custody of Kansas Social Rehabilitation Services. In the afternoon, Cheryl was arraigned on the Class E felony charges for interfering with child custody and posted bond of $1,250. A date for an extradition hearing was set; Cheryl was fighting extradition to Kansas. She returned to the Rulo farm later in the day.

Lester knew that with the kids in Kansas, it would only be a matter of time before Cheryl came back. Just be patient, Dennis Whalen told him. Only time would tell what would become of their relationship.

Exhausted and frustrated, Lester tried to sound civil when he approached McNabb again. "When do I get to see my kids? You know I'm dying to see them."

McNabb, seemingly unsympathetic, informed him that he'd have to wait until the children were in the custody of Kansas Social Rehabilitation Services. They would be cared for in foster homes.

The children were assigned to the home of a social worker; it had been difficult to find a place where all five of them could stay together. Finally, a visitation was scheduled for Lester on the morning of the twenty-seventh.

Lester arrived at the social services office with gifts under each arm for the children. He was taken into a room and seated at a table.

"Lester, take this very slowly," the social worker told him. "Don't be hurt if the kids won't talk to you or if they act like they don't know you. You can almost expect that kind of reaction."

"Okay. I understand," Lester said. "I'm just so nervous over seeing them."

"That's normal, too," she told him. "We've talked to your kids, too, to try to prepare them. At first, Lester, I suggest you stay in your chair on your side of the table; let the kids warm up to you gradually."

Lester agreed.

"I think we're ready now," she said, walking across the room to open the door and motion the children in.

Lester's five children appeared in the doorway.

Emotions racing, Lester burst into a smile. He was thrilled to see them, yet astonished at how much they'd changed, how much they'd grown. And they were so pale—they appeared sickly. The social worker had told him that the children had rarely been allowed outside for over a year.

The two littlest boys, Eric and Josh, came into the room first—they looked curious. The next boy, Brian, followed along with Elizabeth, the oldest, who carried the youngest girl, Heather.

"Hi, kids. Gosh, I'm glad to see you," he said, trying to sound calm. He could barely control the quiver in his voice.

"Hi, Daddy," the three oldest said. They, too, were nervous. The two littlest ones were silent.

"I've missed you so much. You don't know how much I've missed you," he told the kids.

"Who's that man?" the little girl, Heather, asked. She was almost two and a half now. She hadn't seen her father since she was sixteen months old.

Lester was sad to hear that his daughter didn't know him.

"That's your daddy," her older sister told her.

"That's not my daddy," she said, looking up at Elizabeth.

"Yes, it is," Brian told her.

Heather looked at Lester and asked, "Do we get to go outside?"

"Sure you do. That's a promise."

Then, Brian slowly walked around the table to Lester and extended his arms. Lester grabbed him and held him to his chest.

Brian cried. "I'm sorry, Daddy. I'm sorry."

Lester tried to talk through his sobs. "It's okay, Son . . . it's okay."

The other kids huddled around Lester now. Tears streamed down his cheeks as he wrapped his arms around the children. Finally, his search was over.

CHAPTER **66**

Mike Ryan had lost control. Destroy the evidence, he thought. He ordered James's clothing burned. He asked Yahweh about moving the bodies from the field. Yahweh told him that they should be left alone. They would go undetected.

"Ruth, I want you and Lisa and the kids to leave the farm. You go to western Kansas until all this blows over." He wanted them to stay with Lynn and Deb Theile; Deb was Norbert and Maxine's eldest daughter.

"I don't want to leave," Ruth said to Mike, worried about the possibility of more trouble with the law. She wanted to be around to see what happened. Too, she resented moving out and leaving Mike alone with Cheryl.

"I've already asked Yahweh. You guys are supposed to go. You've got to go."

"I'm afraid if I leave, it'll be the last time I'll ever see you," Ruth said tearfully to her husband of seventeen years.

"No, no, no. They're not going to find out anything. It will all be okay. You've got to trust Yahweh," Mike insisted.

"I just have this feeling that more things are going to

blow up.'' She could tell that Mike was troubled, despite his assurances from Yahweh. She and Lisa prepared to leave for western Kansas with the children.

Cheryl was distraught over her kids being taken. ''What if I never get them back?'' she asked Ryan. ''I may have lost them! Whoever has them may brainwash them,'' she said, crying, knowing that only they on the farm knew life's truths.

''Now, you listen to me,'' Ryan said. ''Yahweh says point-blank that you'll get your kids. If worse comes to worst, we'll steal them and run for it. Yahweh is going to take care of all this.''

Three days had passed since the raid. Ryan began to relax. So far, so good, he figured. He'd cooperated with the lawmen during the search of the farm; they'd been convinced of his sincerity, he knew. Again today, he would be convincing. He was scheduled for a nine thirty interview in the Haverkamp-Andreas theft case with Terry Becker of the state patrol.

Ryan nervously took a last drag off his cigarette, then snuffed it in an ashtray in the hall of the courthouse. He threw back his shoulders and walked into Terry Becker's office on the first floor.

''Come on in, have a seat,'' Becker said as he looked up from his notepad. ''Be with you in a second.''

Ryan settled into the dark wooden chair in front of Becker's desk.

''Mike, I need to ask you some background questions, first of all,'' Becker said, leaning back in his chair and crossing his arms. ''Mostly about how you and your family came to live at the Rulo farm, who all has been living there—things like that. When did you first move to Rulo?''

Ryan spoke rapidly, explaining in detail, that he and Ruth and their family had moved to the Rulo farmhouse in June 1984. Ryan explained that Cheryl and her family had moved in, along with Cheryl's sister Lisa, who had a new baby. ''Rick Stice still has two kids out there. He left a while back and took his youngest son with him. He just didn't agree with our beliefs and he left. His other two kids wanted to stay on the farm with Lisa.''

This guy tends to ramble, Becker thought. ''And what about this James Thimm who was living on the farm for a while? Where did he go?''

''James stayed with us for four or five months. Then he decided he didn't believe like we did anymore. He just up and left.''

''So that's the last you saw of him? Do you know where he is now?''

''Nope. All I know is he went south . . . to Texas.''

''Did he leave all of a sudden, or did he plan to leave?''

''It was real quick, because right before he left, he bought a motorcycle at Coulter's Cycle Shop in Auburn. But then he left and didn't make the payments on it.''

Thimm—Texas, Becker jotted in his notebook. ''Let's go back to the beginning. Why did you want to move to Rulo?''

''Well, partially because I had a big blow-up with my brother-in-law, Steve Patterson, and we wanted to leave the Whiting area. Plus, we were training to survive in case of a nuclear holocaust or an attack where United States citizens will not have the help of the government. They'll be on their own. So we ended up at Rulo.''

''Did you have any large weapons out there . . . and did you ever have any grenades?'' Becker asked, indirectly asking about the rumors he'd heard months ago of explosions at the farm.

''Well, the biggest weapons we carried were the AR-15s and the Mini-14s. We did practice with dummy hand grenades and sometimes would use M-70 firecrackers for simulation.''

''Where did you get these AR-15s?''

''We bought most of the weapons at Randy Engelken's in Seneca. He owns the H & E Gun Shop. Randy also put the kits in to make the guns automatic,'' Ryan said, trying to shift the blame to Randy. ''But I was surprised to find the AR-15s were fully automatic. Randy was only supposed to put in the different bolts. But he must've put in the fully automatic kits. We got three Browning shotguns in St. Joseph, Missouri.''

In truth, Randy Engelken had not converted the weapons.

''I see,'' Becker said. ''Are you still a member of the Posse Comitatus?''

''Nope. I haven't attended a meeting in over a year. In fact, I haven't even left the Rulo farm, except to get supplies for the women and children.''

Becker looked up from his notepad. ''Do you still believe in what the Posse teaches?''

''I believe in a lot of their teachings, but not the violence part. I got into their religious beliefs, but not all that stuff on the Constitution.''

''Mike, about the other people at the farm. I take it you met all of them through the Posse originally?''

''Yeah, that's how I met all the guys. Now, Cheryl Gibson became interested in the religious survival group when everyone got together at her brother's house to listen to tapes and read the Bible. One day Cheryl and the kids came to Rulo and she said she didn't want to go back to Lester. She had filed for divorce and her attorney told her that she would lose her kids—they'd be split up and put in separate homes. She apparently was told by her attorney she should leave town.''

''With all of you living in a commune-style arrangement, were you involved with any other women at the farm? Sexually involved?''

''I had no sexual conduct with anyone at the farm with the exception of my wife, Ruth.''

''Mike, in the past couple of days I've heard something about people at the farm being archangels. Have you ever called yourself or referred to yourself as an archangel?''

''No, I have never considered myself an archangel, but I do believe there are angels in certain persons and these people are in the United States.''

''Now, Mike, about the stealing that was going on with Haverkamp and Andreas. Did you have any involvement in that?''

''No. They did all the stealing that was going on and I

figured I didn't own the farm, I was just staying there, and I could not control what they did.''

"Was there a lot of planning or thought put into how all this stealing was done—what would be taken, where it would be taken from?'' Becker asked.

"To my knowledge, there was no planning of the stealing. I did not agree with it, pure and simple. I did ask Jimmy about some of the tools I saw out there because they were marked 'Cargill.' Jimmy just told me the less I knew the better. I will say none of the stuff that was stolen was ever sold; it was all kept at the farm.''

Becker concluded the interview by asking Ryan about how the group was financed at the Rulo farm.

Ryan said that the men did odd jobs and received help from Norbert Haverkamp. "Most of the money went for clothing and food supplies that we stored.''

Having seen the basement of the Rulo farm, Becker had no trouble believing that. "I think that'll be all for now, Mike. Thanks for coming in.''

"You bet,'' Ryan said, standing up, shaking Becker's hand. "You bet.''

Ryan strolled out of the Richardson County Courthouse, confident that he had Terry Becker in the palm of his hand.

Later, in his office, Becker finished up his notes on the interview and turned them over to his secretary for typing.

When the phone rang, he was glad to hear again from Rick Stice. "Rick, we really need to get together and talk.''

An FBI agent in Omaha had been in touch with Becker. The feds had gotten involved after the illegal firearms were seized. The FBI agent wanted to recruit Rick as an informant to develop intelligence information about paramilitary activities in the area.

Becker scheduled a July 11 meeting with Stice in Sedalia, Missouri.

The FBI agent wasn't the only one who wanted more information about paramilitary activities at the Rulo encampment. The media was hungry for behind-the-scene looks at the activities on the secluded farm. The stories of weapons and stealing in the name of God made great copy.

CHAPTER 67

"What do you want?" Ryan yelled to the reporters who had just pulled up at the farm's gate. "You're trespassing!"

The journalists were surprised to hear the voice coming from the house. They had no idea anyone was still living there; they'd been in the area interviewing Rulo residents for reaction pieces and had come by to get some shots of the farm.

Free-lance photographer Charlie Arnot sensed an interview might be had if they played it right. "We just want to talk to you for a few minutes," he said.

"Get out of here or I'll call the law," Ryan hollered back.

"We don't want to interfere with your privacy. We'd just like to hear your side of the story—from someone who lives out here," Arnot yelled, trying to sound polite.

There was no response. Arnot looked at his colleagues, not sure what to expect next. Two other video photographers and a retired judge, Samuel Van Pelt, had accompanied Arnot. The judge was researching paramilitary groups. He was doing an independent investigation for the governor on the state patrol SWAT team's shootout with Cairo farmer Arthur Kirk.

Then Ryan responded, "You can come up to the door here, without a camera or microphone, and I'll talk to one of you."

"I'll be right back," Arnot said. "Maybe there's an interview here." He climbed over the gate and hustled up to the door of the north house.

Ryan had on blue jeans and a blue, long-sleeved shirt with a sunset embroidered on the back. He stepped outside.

"I'm Charlie Arnot from Lincoln," he said, extending his hand.

"Mike Ryan." Ryan shook hands.

"I saw the big story in the newspaper about the raid and thought some of you here might want to fill us in on your version of things," Arnot said.

Now Ryan considered the proposition in a new light—telling his side of the story. He liked the sound of that. He launched into a nonstop account. "Well, they arrested Jimmy and David when they had no right to stop them in the first place, and then they come out here and Tim stops 'em at the gate. They came on in with their guns, and it's a good thing someone didn't get hurt. I'll tell you, though, the way Becker and McNabb handled that situation, it was okay!"

"Wait a minute, Mike," Arnot interrupted. "If you have this stuff to say, why don't you do an interview with us and tell what you want to be told."

Ryan thought for a minute. "Okay, I'll come down to the gate and talk with your guys. But you're the only one that can ask questions."

"It's a deal," Arnot said, smiling.

Almost eager now, Ryan stepped up to the microphones.

The cameras rolled, and Arnot fired the questions. "We understand that you've been preparing for some kind of invasion . . ."

"We believe that an attack will come from what we feel is a nuclear strike from Russia . . . just like in the show *Red Dawn*. If something like that was to happen, what kind of chaos would it cause?

"We have a lot of food stored—I mean a lot of food—and it's all natural food, such as wheat and corn, beans, peas, you name it. If something like this would happen . . . you've got to have something to exist with. We wouldn't keep it all here . . . it's for everybody. Because this is everybody's country, isn't it?''

"You bet," Arnot answered. "Now, what about the arms . . . why were the weapons and shells stockpiled?''

"For our safety, when this happens, if it happens. But the law confiscated a lot of the weapons . . . and I'm going to contact two or three people next week about buying the rest of the guns. But we're going to keep a couple of them. We've already got somebody working on selling most of the ammunition.''

"You have been associated with every right-wing group there is, including the Posse, but you've said you have problems with the Posse . . .''

"Okay, the Posse . . . I don't believe in," Ryan said. "I've been accused of being with the Posse. I have nothing to do with them. Those Posse guys got mad at me . . . I told 'em, you sit around griping about things and advocate getting rid of this person or that person. I said your brains don't work. And I left.

"I've been accused of all kinds of things. I do know James Wickstrom . . . I like the man. I don't go along with all his ideas and he knows it. We've sat and talked about it. I don't knock him because that's his business. He done a talk show for Phil Donahue and Larry King. They met and talked to him. Well, then, should we list them as radical? As being Posse?''

"Do you feel like you've gotten a fair shake in the media?'' Arnot asked.

"No, no way at all," Ryan said, now zeroing in on his chance for propaganda points. "The fair shake I feel we've got is from Sheriff Cory McNabb and State Investigator Terry Becker. I don't care if they see this; you can shut it off if you want to, but I think Richardson County has elected themselves a fine sheriff and they ought to keep him. I think the state of Nebraska has gotten themselves one hell of a fine investigator there in Terry Becker.

"Those two guys, as long as you tell them the truth . . . you shoot straight with them, they do it, too.

That's all I can ask for and that's why, you know, we have been so willing . . ."

Arnot, keeping his tone polite, probed into the thefts. "You were here at the farm while all this stealing was going on. Do you want to straighten that out?"

Ryan liked this interview. He had total freedom to make his points. "We've been staying out here . . . I guess you could call it hiding, in seclusion. I don't have my name on the title to the farm . . . so I didn't have much say. . . ."

Clarifying, Arnot asked, "It wasn't your property, so you didn't feel like you were in a position to say anything?"

"No, I didn't. We tried talking about it, but the thing I did put my foot down about was that they were not going to sell the stuff. I said they're not going to drag Cheryl or my wife into anything like that. They done it all by themselves. I mean, they were busy, I think. I feel sorry for Jimmy and David. This is the first time they ever messed up. If they've got time to serve, they just want to serve it and get it over with."

"Is there any one statement you'd like to make?" Arnot asked, drawing the interview to a close.

"Well," Ryan said, reflecting. "Other people have their religious beliefs. I have mine. People want peace, peace, peace. But people don't seem to understand that Yeshua said 'I came not to this earth to bring peace, but with a sword.'

"Look at their world . . . their wars . . . people being killed needlessly. Look at the boys that died needlessly in Vietnam . . . in Beirut. I sympathize with these families that have lost sons, dads, brothers. There's no sense in it."

"Sounds fair to me," Arnot said, ready to end the interview.

"I'm not going to run out here and bother anybody," Ryan said. He hadn't made all his points yet. He steered his conversation back to Becker and McNabb. "When they showed up the other day, there could have been bloodshed. But Terry Becker and I stopped and talked, and the weapons was put up. That's why nothing happened here, because we didn't want to hurt nobody."

"Makes sense to me," Arnot said.

"You darn right . . . Terry Becker and Sheriff McNabb proved that they got something on the ball because they stopped and listened. They put their guns down and that was the end of it. If you can't talk, it's all lost and some people will get hurt." Now, Ryan's voice quivered. "Our children mean too much to us. I was scared to death, I'm not kiddin'." Ryan began to weep. "Just . . . shut it off, man," he said, pointing to the camera.

"Sure, no problem," Arnot said.

Ryan leaned up against the gate, resting his head on his forearm.

At this point, Van Pelt felt it safe to enter the conversation. "Yeah, I can understand that. I felt it was really too bad that someone got hurt in that Kirk thing. I'm glad no one got hurt out here."

Ryan nodded.

Van Pelt, sensing they'd struck a chord in Ryan, wanted to draw him out further. Maybe they'd learn some more if they could keep him talking. Van Pelt knew that in these parts, bringing up the weather and crops was one sure way to get people to talk. He'd try it with Ryan. "I noticed you've got your fields plowed down there. Getting ready to plant winter wheat?" Van Pelt asked.

"Uh, no. That's for sweet corn," Ryan said, sounding unsure. He sure as hell wanted to lead the conversation away from the field where the bodies were buried.

"Sweet corn?" Van Pelt asked, genuinely puzzled. "It's too late for sweet corn, isn't it?"

"Ah, hell, I don't know. It's not my farm. I'm not runnin' the place," Ryan said. "Listen, guys, I think that'll about do it. Glad I could help you out. I gotta go back inside now."

"Thanks for the interview."

"You bet," Ryan said.

As the days passed, Ryan grew increasingly confident that he would come out of this unscathed. He made only one trip to the jail to visit Jimmy and David. His expression was deadpan when he gave them the order, "Yahweh wants you to take the blame. Leave me out of it. Tell 'em you did it and tell 'em where you got the equipment. Yahweh says it will be better for you that way."

That behind him, Ryan had new designs on getting the farm. With Jimmy in jail—and likely heading for prison—now Ryan had only Lynn Theile to deal with. ''I could easily get the farm,'' he told Maxine. ''I could make something happen to Lynn, like falling into a power takeoff.'' The power takeoff Ryan referred to was a six-inch, grooved shaft extending from the rear of a tractor; it powered other equipment—balers, augers, or mowers—coupled to it. Spinning at a speed of 1,000 RPMs, a power takeoff could mean instant death or serious injury if one became entangled in it. ''Or, I could have Dennis do something to Lynn. Dennis will do anything I tell him.'' Dennis had left with his mother, Lisa, and the children, and was staying at the Theiles' farm.

''Besides that,'' Ryan added, ''we need cash up here, now. Yahweh doesn't expect us to live on nothing!''

Maxine had never been more frightened. She offered absolutely no resistance to Ryan's demands.

The raid confirmed Garneta Butrick's worst fears. They were up to no good out there. What had happened to the children? Were they okay? When she called the farm, Ryan told her that her grandchildren were at the Theile farm in Norton, Kansas.

Garneta contacted the sheriff in Norton and asked him to check on the well-being of her grandchildren. She gave him their names and ages.

When the sheriff called her back, he confirmed that an Ora and Barry Stice were at the farm outside Norton, but no Luke.

Garneta prayed that Luke was okay and that he was with Rick somewhere.

CHAPTER 68

Hilda Schmidt smoothed her dress as a deputy led her and Carl into the visitation room at the Richardson County jail at the courthouse in Falls City. The newspaper account of David's arrest on theft charges had immediately drawn them to the jail. Perhaps this time David would tell them something of James's whereabouts.

The Schmidts took seats at one end of the long table in the visitation room. They noticed another couple seated at the other end of the table. The woman appeared to have been crying; she looked distressed. It was Norbert and Maxine Haverkamp.

Then, a deputy opened a door and ushered in David and Jimmy, both wearing orange coveralls.

David, his expression tense, managed a smile as he acknowledged the Schmidts. "Hi," he said, at a loss for words.

Hilda could see confusion in David's eyes. She'd come here in hopes of learning something about James, but she was worried about David, too. He'd been James's best friend, and Hilda and Carl both were shocked to hear of his arrest. The David they knew was not a thief. They were genuinely concerned.

"Hello, David," Hilda said softly.

Carl nodded.

David seated himself across the table from them and knotted his hands in front of his mouth.

"David, we're still looking for James. We haven't seen him in months. Can you tell us anything about him? Where he is? If he's okay?"

David saw the strain in Hilda's face. "No. I . . . I . . . I really don't know where he is," he stammered. "I . . . I haven't seen him for six months myself. Last I knew, he went south—to Texas."

David was more jittery than normal, Hilda thought. His face told her he wasn't telling the truth. Still, she tried again. "Do you know where in Texas?"

"No, I sure don't."

More stonewalling from David, Carl thought. He'd acted this way when they'd inquired about James's well-being out at the farm. "David, we're really worried. Isn't there anything you can tell us?"

David dropped his gaze and then looked up at Carl. "No, Carl, I can't. I just know that about six months ago he got tired of things and said he was going south to Texas."

"What was James doing there at the farm with the rest of you?" Hilda asked.

"He was just doing God's will, like the rest of us. And we were staying healthy, eating good, natural foods. Even the kids got healthier once they got to the farm."

Disappointed, Hilda and Carl didn't care to listen beyond this point. Both knew that David was lying to them. They bid him well and left.

At the other end of the table, Maxine took a Kleenex from her purse and dabbed her bloodshot eyes. "I'm scared for everybody," she told Jimmy and Norbert. "I just don't know how we got into all this mess," she said, sniffing.

"We can't even get you out on bond," Norbert said apologetically. "We're flat broke."

Jimmy was being held in lieu of the eight thousand dollar cash bond or 10 percent of a seventy-five-thousand-dollar appearance bond.

"It's okay. It's okay . . . don't worry about it," Jimmy said, trying to console his distraught parents. "Yahweh will take care of us, I know," he said, trying not to let on that his arrest had begun to chip away at the foundation of his religious convictions.

"Why were you taking all that equipment?" Norbert asked.

"It was Yahweh's plan. We were getting ready for a war," Jimmy said.

Norbert was stunned. He had learned of Jimmy's arrest from Maxine several nights before. He had been on the road with business. Maxine had reached him about two thirty in the morning; she was crying hysterically when she told him that Jimmy had been arrested. She also broke down and told Norbert that Lisa had had a baby. Norbert had not even known she was pregnant. There was a lot that Norbert didn't know.

"Mike's mad at us," Maxine said to Jimmy. "He says your arrest was Norbert's fault. He's threatening to kill Lynn and get the Rulo farm and he's mad because we're out of money. We just don't have it. We just gave him seven hundred dollars from the wheat and three thousand from the cattle sale, plus twelve hundred in cash." Maxine felt used, humiliated.

"Just stay away from there and don't cross him," Jimmy said. "Mike's lost it. Whatever you do, don't cross him." Jimmy knew that his folks didn't fully know what the man was capable of doing; they still didn't know of the two murders.

A tearful Maxine nodded that she understood and hugged Jimmy as she and Norbert got up to leave.

"I'll be okay," Jimmy said. "Mom, when you get home, would you call Randy, the guy over at the gun shop in Seneca where we bought most of our guns, and ask him if he has the records of our purchases. I'd just like to know." Jimmy wondered if Ryan had told him the truth about the law not being able to trace the guns back to them; Ryan had told Jimmy that he had stolen the yellow sheets—the records gun sellers keep for the Bureau of Alcohol, Tobacco & Firearms.

"Sure, Jimmy," she said.

Jimmy watched them go out the door. He was worried. Mike Ryan had killed before and liked it. Would he go after someone in Jimmy's family next?

Outside the courthouse, Carl and Hilda Schmidt were pulling away from the curb.

"I wonder why David won't tell us. He knows where James is," Hilda said with a deep sigh.

"Yep. He sure does."

"I just keep hoping," she said. The reading Hilda had done showed that most cult members eventually severed cult ties and returned home. "I just keep hoping that James will come back on his own eventually."

CHAPTER 69

OSAGE BEACH, MISSOURI JULY 11

Terry Becker and FBI Intelligence Agent Weysan Dun took a table at the RAX Restaurant and waited for Rick Stice. Rick was living in nearby Plato, Missouri, working as a mechanic at his brother's auto repair shop.

"Whenever Stice has called me, it's been to see what he could find out from me," Becker told Dun. "It'll be interesting to see if he's willing to tell us anything."

Becker looked up and saw Rick coming in the door. "Here he is."

As Rick approached the table, both men stood up. Becker shook hands with Rick and introduced him to Dun.

Rick extended his hand.

Becker noted the surprise registering on Rick's face when he saw that Dun was Oriental. He was tall, too—about five ten. So much for the Posse stuff about white supremacy, Becker thought.

The men ordered sandwiches and Dun led most of the interview. It was the FBI that wanted to develop Rick as an informant to learn more about possible domestic terrorists in the Midwest.

For an hour, they covered a lot of things the two lawmen

already knew—where the men on the farm got the weapons, how many guns they had, who was living at the farm. Becker found Rick helpful in mentioning names of other Posse Comitatus members in Nebraska and Kansas he had met before the Rulo group split off.

Dun took meticulous notes, causing the interview to drag.

Becker sensed that Rick was withholding information, but it was a start. At least they could establish a working relationship with him. These things took time, he knew.

Then, Rick started asking questions. "You saw my two kids when you were at the farm . . . and they were okay?"

"Yes, they seemed fine," Becker said.

"Where are Jimmy and David?"

"They're in jail in Falls City," Becker said.

"What about Ryan?"

"Well, he's still at the farm. We've talked to him."

Rick took a bite of his sandwich and said nothing. Then he asked, "Have you talked to James Thimm?"

"No. We want to talk to him. Ryan says he went south to Texas. We haven't got that far yet," Becker said.

"Do you know where in Texas?" Rick asked.

"No, but we'll be checking that out. Why do you ask?"

"Just curious."

Finally, Becker knew they'd learned all they were going to. Perhaps with time, Rick would be more forthcoming.

They set another meeting for four weeks later, August 9, in Sedalia, Missouri.

In Sedalia, they met in Dun's motel room. Becker could see the strain on Rick's face when he came into the room. He was troubled about something. Maybe he needed to get something off his chest.

Becker and Dun sat in two armchairs at a small table by the wall. Rick sat in a chair opposite them. "Heard anything more about James Thimm?" Rick asked.

"No, we haven't," Becker said.

"It's just that he was in bad shape when I last saw him in April. Really malnourished, emaciated like, very weak. He looked like an old man and he was only twenty-six," Rick said.

This was news—the first they'd heard anything about James Thimm. "How's that, Rick? What happened to him?"

"Mike Ryan would beat him up a lot. James went through a lot of abuse. Ryan constantly bullied him, really wore him down physically, and mentally, too. He was so beaten down when I left that he was totally subservient."

Expressionless, Dun asked, "Why was Ryan doing this?"

"Ryan was in charge out there. He was the leader. He was very perverted and very smart, very clever. Everyone was afraid of Yahweh and Ryan. If you crossed him, he'd beat the pulp out of you. We were all afraid of him."

"You're saying Ryan had the blind obedience of everyone at the farm?"

"Yep. Whatever Ryan told us to do, we did. I also got beaten up a lot—from January of this year through March, then until I left. After I left the first time, when I came back, I was beaten up and chained to the porch. At night he made me take my clothes off and chained me to the porch."

"Why?" Becker asked.

"Ryan said we had fallen from favor with Yahweh. That we had become slaves. We had to stay over in the south trailer. I couldn't even go in the north house and see my kids." Rick paused and pulled at his upper lip. His eyes filled with tears. "When I escaped, I couldn't go in to get my kids or they would have known I was leaving."

"Take your time, Rick, it's okay," Dun said.

Rick took a deep breath. "It's hard to talk about a lot of this. I've been trying to put it out of my mind . . . the things that went on out there."

"Rick, a moment ago you said when *we* fell from favor. Who was *we*?"

"That was me, James Thimm, and my son Luke. See, Ryan began abusing my son Luke, too."

"Now, how old is Luke?"

"Five."

"What was happening to Luke?" Dun asked.

"Mike would beat him with belts and boards. One time he made him stand naked outside in the snow." Rick stopped. He swallowed hard. "Mike made me hit Luke," Rick said, his voice quivering. "He made me do a lot of shit to Luke, too!" Rick covered his face and sobbed.

Becker and Dun waited.

Rick pulled a handkerchief from his hip pocket and wiped his nose.

"Rick, where is Luke now?"

"Where Luke is, he's okay. Nobody is going to bother him. He's safe."

Becker was sure Rick wasn't telling the whole story. But he knew better than to press hard if they wanted to develop Rick as an informant. Take it easy, Becker told himself.

"Did you know about the thefts?"

"Yes."

"Did you help?"

"Yeah. We all did."

So Ryan was a part of the theft, Becker thought. "Tell us more, Rick."

Rick told them how the thefts had gone on for over a year and how Mike Ryan had directed them. "Mike said it was Yahweh's will." Rick detailed specific thefts—how they took the backhoe from Brown County, Kansas, in October 1983, and the various livestock thefts, including the cattle they took from David Andreas's neighbor in August 1984. The cattle had been sold in St. Joseph, Missouri, he said. He told them about some of the stolen equipment. Rick even told them that he'd written a rubber check for four hundred dollars to the James Oil Company in Falls City the last time he had run off.

Both Becker and Dun took notes now.

Rick brought the conversation back to James Thimm. "I'm worried about James Thimm. If he wasn't at the farm, I'm afraid he's dead."

CHAPTER 70

"We've got to locate James Thimm," Becker told McNabb as they slid into a booth at the local coffee shop. They gobbled down hamburgers, a quick lunch—a chance to keep in touch on the investigation. "Dun and I talked to Rick Stice again. He seems to think that Thimm may be dead, so I'm working on locating him."

"Any evidence?" McNabb asked.

"No. Rick just told us about a lot of beatings and other physical abuse out there. And he says this Thimm was in bad shape the last time he saw him."

Becker let McNabb know, too, that from the information they were getting from Stice, Ryan was much more involved in the illegal activity at the farm than he was letting on. "Rick says Ryan helped organize the thefts out there."

"Well, I'm keeping a close eye on our buddy Mike Ryan," McNabb said, sipping black coffee from a thick mug. McNabb had dropped in on Mike Ryan several times after the raid. As long as McNabb had access to the farm, he wanted to maintain a rapport with Ryan as the investigation unfolded. They had developed a seemingly amiable relationship.

"It's okay with me if he thinks I'm a good guy," McNabb told Becker. "Because when I have a question about something, I can go ask him. He may not always tell me the truth, but at least he tells me something."

Becker agreed. "Yep. We need to keep a close eye on him while we're getting this put together."

Both Becker and McNabb wanted to keep the rumor mill under control. After all the media attention, Rulo, Falls City, and other little towns in the three-state region were rife with rumors.

"I can't go into a restaurant or coffee shop without hearing all kinds of crazy stories that are being cranked out of the dern rumor mill," McNabb said.

So far, he'd heard that a new group at the farm was rebuilding their arsenal, that a bunch more weapons had been shipped in—they were restocking; that survivalists now had fifty more men—a small army—out at the farm, and that this army was going to burn the courthouse and bust their buddies out of jail.

"What's. Ryan say when you stop out there?" Becker asked.

"Oh, I just sit and listen, let him ramble on and on about the crooked government. He gets real wound up and emotional. It takes him about ten minutes to get himself worked up as he preaches. Then he calms down. He talks about how the monetary system is screwed up in one breath and then he'll be talking about the Antichrist or the Battle of Armageddon in the next."

Becker just shook his head.

"Sometimes when he comes out to the gate to meet me, he'll be carrying a big corn knife or machete. We'll talk over the gate," McNabb said.

"Anything more out of Haverkamp or Andreas?"

"Nope."

Becker and McNabb had had little contact with Jimmy and David after their initial interrogation. Both lawmen were sensitive about treading on rights that might harm the case.

The only information Jimmy and David had disclosed were sketchy details on a few of the thefts they'd committed. After that, they'd shut down. They'd been zombielike, and provided only vague, calculated answers. If asked a specific question about a theft, they'd admit to it, but not provide any details.

McNabb's efforts to build a rapport with Ryan included letting Tim visit Jimmy and David in jail. They were being held in cells on the third floor of the courthouse. Occasionally, McNabb made it a point to accommodate Tim's visits outside regular hours.

Tim was bringing the same message every visit: "Tell them you stole the stuff. Don't get us involved. Take the fall. Take your punishment. That's what Yahweh wants!"

Take the fall . . . that was easy for Tim to say, Jimmy thought. Tim was a free man. Jimmy had been locked up for over a month now and he grew wearier, more afraid. Yahweh wasn't answering his prayers to get him out of this mess.

Jimmy pored over his Bible. He kept returning to the verse that talked about false prophets. "When a prophet speaketh in the name of the Lord, if the thing follow not, nor come to pass, that is the thing which the Lord hath not spoken . . ." Jimmy reflected on all the things Ryan had said and predicted—all the things Ryan had been wrong about. Lies. Especially the lie Jimmy could prove in black and white. Ryan had told him that he'd registered several guns in Jimmy's name, but when Jimmy had Maxine check it, she found the guns were in Ryan's name. Gradually, the truth had dawned on Jimmy, and now he knew. Mike Ryan was a false prophet.

Jimmy would have to cope with all that later. Right now, he was afraid for his parents and his brother-in-law, Lynn, in western Kansas. What might Mike Ryan do to them, he wondered. He knew Ryan was mad at them. Finally, Jimmy could no longer contain his doubts, his fear. He opened up to David. "David, did you ever think that things weren't quite right out at the farm?"

David sat straight up on his cell bunk and looked at Jimmy. "Yeah. I sure have. You mean you have, too?" David's expression prompted Jimmy to continue.

"Dammit!" Jimmy said, hitting the side of his bunk with his fist. "Ryan lied to us. He used us. The whole damn thing was a bunch of lies!"

"You're right," David said, letting out a deep breath. "I've been realizing that now, too."

"All the stealing going on out there . . . what was going on in our minds? Why did we do all that shit?" Jimmy asked, exasperated.

"I guess he suckered us," David said. "Makes me feel pretty stupid."

"Nothing ever got done out there. We were supposed to be getting ready for things, building a shelter. That never got done. Why'd we even take the backhoe? What were we thinking?"

"I don't know," David answered. "We'd have been better off just keeping our jobs and building a shelter in our spare time. Ryan didn't help us do anything."

"And Ryan was always blaming everybody else. First things were my fault, then Dad's fault, then Mom's. Now he's written them off because they're out of money. Ryan just uses people and throws them away."

"It was just one lie after another," David interrupted. "He just made a mockery out of God and we bought it," he said sadly. "Did Ryan ever ask you to spy on anyone out there?"

"No, but I figured he was doing stuff like that. I never trusted anyone out there. I didn't know who was reporting back to Mike," Jimmy said.

"He wanted me to spy on you and Maxine—to see what you were saying and then report back to him. I never did it, but that's how he acted like he could read minds . . . he'd repeat what others told him. Just worked us all against each other."

"God, I hate being in this jail, but I'd rather be here than out there with Ryan," Jimmy said through clenched teeth.

David nodded silently.

"And, you know," Jimmy paused, "two innocent people were killed out there."

David looked down, shaking his head. "I know. I can't believe that part of it."

Jimmy sat on his bunk and rubbed his face with both hands. Then he looked up at David. "I know Ryan's mad at Mom and Dad and Lynn, and I have no doubt that Ryan will kill again. I'm afraid he'll go after one of them next. Ryan hasn't got you, me, or Rick to pick on now. He'll go after somebody. We better speak up and tell the authorities what we know. I don't want anything to happen to Mom and Dad."

"I think you're right," David said. "As long as Ryan's out at that farm, they're not safe."

Jimmy and David decided to summon their attorneys. "We should tell the sheriff what we know," Jimmy said.

CHAPTER 71

HIAWATHA, KANSAS AUGUST 12

Rick Stice waited in the lobby of the Best Western Inn, in Hiawatha. Terry Becker and Weysan Dun arrived within minutes. Since they'd last met in Sedalia, Missouri, Rick had called Becker, telling him he had more information. They'd scheduled a meeting over lunch at the restaurant of the Hiawatha motel.

They made small talk while they made selections from the menu, then Becker and Dun opened notebooks, ready to get down to business.

Rick seemed emotionally more stable than he had been a month earlier, Becker observed. Apparently he'd regained strength as he'd distanced himself from the events at the farm.

"Rick, you told Terry on the phone that you had some more information to tell us about your son, Luke," Dun said.

"He's dead." Rick blurted it out.

Becker and Dun sat motionless for several seconds. They could hardly believe what Rick had told them. Dead?

"He's what?" asked Becker.

"He's dead. Mike killed him."

Dun, recovering, asked, "Rick, when did this happen?"

"It happened toward the end of March. It was when I came back after I left the first time—about ten days later."

"What happened?"

"Well, Mike was over at the south trailer giving James Thimm a bunch of grief, accusing him of having bad thoughts with Yahweh and stuff and he was just in this rage. Then he stormed out of the trailer, and when he did, he shoved Luke out of his way. Luke hit his head on the corner of a metal book rack along the north wall of the trailer."

"Then what happened?" Dun asked.

"Luke stood up, then started shaking and fell on the floor. His breathing was funny . . . he was making raspy sounds. I tried to massage his chest; for a while, he seemed to breathe normal again."

"Then what?"

"Mike said put him in the bedroom and we'd have to wait and see what happened."

"Do you know when he died, Rick, what time it was?"

"No. It was sometime during the night, but I was chained up to the porch when it happened."

"Let's back up a minute. Where was this book rack?" Dun asked.

"It was between the hallway and the living room windows of the trailer."

"Who was there when it happened?" Dun asked.

"James and Tim were at the south trailer, but I don't know if they actually saw it."

"When did you realize Luke was dead?"

"The next morning. Ryan announced that Luke was dead . . . just to the men. The women found out about it, but none of the kids knew."

"What did you do with the body?" Becker asked.

"Mike said Yahweh wanted James and me to dig a grave. It was about a quarter mile south of the trailer, just beyond the main ditch that divides the farm in half. It's located directly in front of a clump of trees past that ditch."

Rick went on to describe more of the beating and abuse that Luke had suffered. He explained more, too, about the abuse of James. He told them of James being shot in the face by Dennis. "James lost a lot of blood. Ryan gave him medical treatment and I tried to tend to him. He didn't die from the gunshot wound, but it really weakened him. That's why I think James just didn't have the strength to get away toward the end."

"What did Ryan say about the shooting?" Becker asked.

"He said, 'Yahweh was the one who shot James.' He also said to me, 'Two of you have been shot now, you could be third.'"

"Did Mike Ryan sexually abuse or generally abuse any other children at the farm?" Becker asked.

"I don't have any knowledge of it, but I think he spanked and yelled at some of the other kids."

Becker and Dun closed their notebooks. It was a short meeting. The pace of the investigation was about to go into high gear. Dun, still wanting more information about the farm and Ryan, made arrangements to talk with Rick again the following day. Becker raced to a pay phone in the lobby to call his boss in Lincoln. "It looks like we'll be going back to Rulo," Becker told the lieutenant.

Becker and Dun and their agencies went into action; however, they weren't going after Ryan that same afternoon. Becker would submit the affidavit for the arrest warrant—that could take a day—but mainly, they wanted to nail down the James Thimm angle. Maybe they were dealing with two homicides.

The next day, Becker was off for Beatrice, Nebraska. He would call on James's family and friends; maybe somebody would know where he was. Maybe the guy wasn't dead. So far, there was no evidence that he was, just Rick's guess. But now, with one death at the farm, anything was possible, Becker thought.

Once in Beatrice, Becker's first stop was at the parsonage of the Mennonite Church where James had once been a member. The reverend greeted Becker warmly at the door and welcomed him.

"I'm trying to locate a James Thimm. I believe he used to belong to your church. Have you seen anything of him recently?"

"No. I haven't seen James in about a year and a half. I'd say that's when he quit coming to church," he told Becker.

Becker thanked him and was on his way. In the process of talking to friends and family, Becker also wanted to corroborate information Rick had given them. Becker stopped at the sale barn in Beatrice—he wanted to verify Rick's account of stealing cattle from David Andreas's neighbor in 1984, and then selling it at the sale barn.

"Sorry," a polite clerk told him at the counter in the office. "Most all our files were destroyed in a flood here. We would have no documents of that sale."

Next, Becker proceeded to the Gage County sheriff's office. There, he did find a theft report. A clerk pulled a two-page report from the file that outlined the theft of six head of cattle on August 14, 1984. The report contained a lengthy, typewritten account of the theft, along with notes from an interview with David Andreas's father immediately after the incident. Mr. Andreas explained that his son David had been taking care of the cattle for their neighbor; he also said that his son had moved away suddenly, leaving a note on the kitchen table. The report quoted Mr. Andreas as saying "this is definitely out of character for David . . . I know that things have started to wear on my son due to the fact that he had some outstanding debts on farm equipment."

Becker drove on to the house of Carl and Hilda Schmidt. Carl was in the driveway, changing the oil in his car, when Becker pulled in. Becker got out of the car and introduced himself.

"Are you Carl Schmidt?"

"Yes, I am," Carl said, turning up his greasy palms as a sign that he couldn't shake hands.

"Mr. Schmidt, I'm involved in an investigation down in Rulo; we're interested in talking to your son. Have you seen him lately?"

Carl thought before he spoke. "No. No, we haven't seen James for a while now."

"Do you know where he is?"

"No, I'm sorry to say we don't. Is there a problem?"
Becker could see the worry in his eyes.

"Well, I can't really say; we just wanted to locate him to talk to him. Can you tell me when you last saw your son?"

"That would have been late July of last year; actually, it's been a year now," Carl said.

"Would you have a picture of your son I could have?" Becker asked.

Carl paused again. He and Hilda, in their wait for James to come around, had decided they'd never do anything that would cause James trouble. Has James done something? he wondered. Why does this officer want a photo? Finally, he answered. "You know, my hands are all greasy. I don't think I can get you a picture right now."

Becker found James's real father, Frank Thimm, who managed another sale barn on the north edge of Beatrice. Frank Thimm introduced himself and invited Becker into his office. "We used to be very close, James and I, but I haven't seen him for over a year now. I don't know what happened. It's his religion, you know. I even went with him to one of those meetings and listened to some colonel speak. But I was convinced they were just a bunch of radicals. I still can't understand why James was so involved."

Becker pressed on. His next stop was the Andreas house, where he spoke with David's mother, Viola.

"I recently visited David, at the jail in Falls City, and he said he had not seen James in six months."

"That's all he said—that he hadn't seen him in six months?"

"Yes, and you know it's really unusual, since Dave and James were very close friends."

"Thank you, Mrs. Andreas." Becker headed to his last stop—the home of James's sister Miriam, from the Thimm family.

Miriam had not seen her brother since June 1984. They were close, she explained, having been in high school together. "But James would never tell us where he was going. He was into this strange religion thing. We used to sit up late at night and talk about it, but I never understood it and could never seem to make him change his mind about any of it.

"I went up to see David at the jail, and he said he hadn't seen him in six months."

Becker was confident about nailing Ryan on charges of theft, but he had several more pieces of information from Rick Stice that needed corroborating. The next day, he and Weysan Dun drove to Hiawatha, where the Brown County sheriff verified the theft of the backhoe.

"Oh, yeah, that was back in October of 1983," Sheriff Jim Wolney told them as he rummaged through his files. He pulled a report from the file drawer. "Yep, the report was written on October 17, 1983. The backhoe belonged to the Reese Construction Company out of Scandia, Kansas, says here. Felony theft. Valued at thirty thousand dollars."

The sheriff made a copy of the file. Becker stuck it in his notebook, thanked the sheriff, and moved on.

Back in Falls City, they even verified Rick's four-hundred-dollar rubber check to the James Oil Company. The county attorney obtained a copy of the check from the bank.

After two days of intense investigation, Rick's story was hanging together from beginning to end. In addition to Becker's work, Dun had corroborated Rick Stice's story about selling the cattle stolen from David Andreas's neighbor in August 1984. Dun found that the John Clay Heady Fannen Livestock Commission Company did have records of several head of cattle sold through their company under the name Norbert Haverkamp in August 1984.

"We're getting close to an arrest for murder," Becker told Dun. First, they were going to arrest Ryan for theft. Then, once they'd recovered the body of Luke Stice, they'd file formal murder charges. Becker and the county attorney already had obtained a warrant to search for Luke's remains. They still didn't know what had happened to James Thimm, but if the worst was true, additional murder charges would follow.

Preparations for Mike Ryan's arrest were made rapidly. Rick Stice was taken to Omaha, where top FBI officials quizzed him about the layout of the farm, whether or not it was mined, and what kind of show of force he thought Ryan would make if officers went in. And, based on interviews with Rick, it appeared there were likely more unregistered, illegal weapons at the farm. Tim Haverkamp would be arrested for possession of an unregistered, automatic firearm.

The plan was for all the law enforcement officers to meet Saturday morning at the National Guard armory in Falls City to prepare for an invasion of the farm.

By six o'clock Saturday morning, the interior of the armory was a sea of blue and green uniforms as some eighty officers gathered, including the director of the Nebraska-Iowa FBI, Jim Ahearn, and his number-two man, John Evans. The top man of the Nebraska state patrol, Superintendent Robert Tagg, and his second in command, Major Don Nieman, were on hand as well.

Dozens of other FBI and patrol officers now milled around in the armory, along with sheriffs and their deputies from surrounding counties, and local police from area communities. SWAT teams from both the state patrol and FBI were on their way, too.

Becker and McNabb, both overwhelmed by the show of manpower, thought it excessive, and weren't convinced that they should go onto the farm with guns blazing.

In an armory office, Becker and McNabb met with Weysan Dun, the other FBI men, and the Nebraska state patrol officers.

"Terry, it's your show," Major Nieman said. "What do you think we should do?"

"Well, you can send all these men in if you want a shoot-out, but I think McNabb and I could go in and get Ryan to come to town with us. We only had a handful of guys when we went in the first time, and we handled it okay."

The others agreed that it would be best to lure Ryan into town. Then the teams of men could go onto the farm, secure it, and begin the search for the bodies.

"Gentlemen, here's what I propose we do," Becker continued. "Sheriff McNabb has built up an excellent rapport with Ryan. Let's send him in and have him tell Ryan we want to talk to him. Bring him in to the office and arrest him here. That will remove the initial threat.''

The plan adopted, McNabb was to go out to the farm around midmorning. It was now eight o'clock.

Meanwhile, McNabb had a message from a deputy that Jimmy Haverkamp and David Andreas wanted to talk to him over at the jail. It was important, they said.

''I'm too busy right now. They'll have to wait,'' he said.

CHAPTER 72

The main street in Falls City was already packed—the annual Cobblestone Festival was under way. Merchants stacked sale goods on tables up and down the sidewalk as craft enthusiasts, selling everything from Indian jewelry to custom T-shirts, lined the town square with their booths. Food vendors plopped funnel cake batter into vats of boiling oil and stuck hot dogs onto rotisseries.

One block over, the Lion's Club was wrapping up its pancake feed; parade organizers checked the line up of high school bands, floats, and Shriners on miniature motor scooters.

Around nine o'clock, Ryan and Tim drove through town. They'd come into Falls City to pick up a newspaper. Ryan had been keeping up with the news lately, watching for stories about the Rulo farm.

Ryan was taking in the hoopla when the state patrol van, carrying the SWAT team, passed them. Jolted at the sight of the van filled with men dressed in camouflage, Ryan eyed the vehicle suspiciously. What were they doing in town? Where were they going? He watched in his rearview mirror to see where the van was headed. He saw it turn west. That direction would take them toward the armory, he reasoned. He breathed a sigh of relief. "I guess the National Guard is out training this weekend," he said to Tim.

"Must be," Tim replied.

Ryan picked up a newspaper and returned home.

About nine-thirty, McNabb arrived at the farm. Muscles tightened in the back of his neck as he drove up the lane. He knew Ryan was clever, perceptive. One wrong word or inflection on McNabb's part could blow the whole game plan. McNabb slammed his car door and started toward the house.

Like always, Ryan came out of the house, meeting him at the gate.

"Mornin,' Mike," McNabb said, feeling his heart racing.

"Mornin,' Sheriff," Ryan said cautiously. "What's up?"

"Mike, the feds are in town. They want to talk to you and Tim. I figured you'd just as soon go in there and talk rather than have me bring them out here."

Ryan stared long and hard at McNabb. "What do they want?" he asked.

"I don't have any idea," McNabb said emphatically. "The feds don't tell me anything. They're in Becker's office and they want to talk to you. Like I said, I thought it best if you went in there and didn't have them wandering around out here."

Ryan, his eyes still locked with McNabb's, cocked his head as he considered the sheriff's order. Ryan knew he had McNabb in the palm of his hand. McNabb hadn't caused him any real grief so far. And now, apparently, he was trying to do him a favor. Yeah. Ryan guessed it made sense. "Well yeah, I guess I could do that."

"Come on, then. I'll drive you in," McNabb said.

"You'll bring us back, won't you?"

"Yeah, if they don't put you away for a couple hundred years." McNabb managed a grin.

Ryan started for the house to get Tim. Then he turned toward McNabb. "I thought I saw the National Guard out this morning," Ryan said, testing the connection between the SWAT team he saw and his being taken into town.

"Yeah, I suppose you did," McNabb said coolly, cautiously.

Ryan turned slowly and started toward the house.

McNabb lit a cigarette and inhaled deeply. Ryan had seen the SWAT team, he thought. What if we've spooked him? McNabb took another deep drag off his cigarette and waited.

Then, Ryan came out the door with Tim behind him.

McNabb opened the door to the backseat. "Hop in."

McNabb parked in front of the courthouse and ushered the men up the sidewalk to the north entrance; Ryan pitched his cigarette as McNabb opened the courthouse door for them. A few steps down the hall and they were in front of Becker's office. McNabb opened the office door and stood aside. As Ryan and Tim stepped inside, McNabb shut the door behind them.

At first, Ryan looked surprised at seeing the office so full of people—Becker and eight others, all federal agents. Then, he shot a cold stare at Becker. He knew he'd been set up.

Becker wasted no time in getting to the point. "Mike, we've got a problem here. You're under arrest."

Weysan Dun stepped forward and introduced himself as an agent with the FBI. "Mike you're under arrest for interstate transportation of stolen property."

Before Ryan could react, two FBI agents pulled his arms behind him and clamped handcuffs around his wrists. They informed Tim of the firearms charges against him, cuffed him, too, and whisked both of them off to squad cars waiting to transport them to Omaha, where they'd be held in separate jails in Douglas and Sarpy counties. It was all over in a matter of minutes.

Three FBI men and a sheriff's deputy clustered around Ryan as he was led outside to the squad car.

"You'd think we killed nine hundred thousand people!" Ryan grumbled as he slid into the backseat of the car.

Once inside the car, an agent showed Ryan a copy of the

warrant, and explained that he was charged with interstate transportation of stolen property, interstate transportation of stolen cattle and possession of unregistered firearms.

"I ain't never stole nothing," Ryan remarked.

Ryan, though angry, was silent during most of the hour and a half ride to Omaha. He kept looking down at the steel handcuffs around his wrists, pulling at them. He was powerless, totally powerless now. Who had made this happen? Who was to blame? His thoughts turned to Lester Gibson. Maybe it was Gibson's nosing around, searching for Cheryl that had something to do with his arrest, he thought. "A creep like Gibson running around there, I should have stomped him a hundred thousand times," Ryan muttered.

Once Mike Ryan was in custody, McNabb returned to the farm and brought Cheryl into the sheriff's office. No one was left on the farm now, as far as they knew. The search could begin.

Dozens of officers filed through the gate and fanned out across the farm. The first group of officers searched for mines and bobby traps, making sure the farm was secure for the rest of the searchers to come onto the property.

Once the area was secured, the rest of the law enforcement officers rushed in to begin the search for the grave of Luke Stice.

Upon delivering Cheryl to the courthouse, McNabb made a quick run up to the jail to see Jimmy and David. "What's up, guy?" McNabb asked, walking toward Jimmy's cell. "I'm real busy. We're looking for the body of Luke Stice out on the farm today."

"Yeah," Jimmy said, "but it sounds like you only know about one body."

McNabb literally stopped in his tracks. "What?"

"Yeah, James Thimm is dead. He's buried out there, too. I thought it was about time you knew."

"Hold on just a minute," McNabb said, shocked. "I want to get Becker and your attorneys over here before we start asking you anything about this. Hold on." McNabb raced down the stairs, summoned Becker, and called the attorneys representing each man and the county attorney.

The attorneys were aware of what Jimmy and David had to say. They had heard it all two days earlier and had been trying to get hold of McNabb themselves to set up a time to talk.

Now in cooperation with the law, Jimmy and David told their story of the death of James Thimm. They explained that given time to be away from Ryan, they had finally come to doubt him. Finally, they realized the cruel reality—he was a hoax.

"It just started to dawn on me that Mike had lied to me. I had my mom check on some gun registrations. Mike told me that he managed to destroy the gun seller's records of our purchases so that our guns couldn't be traced to us, but Mom found out that the guy who sold us the guns had all the records. Mike never took them. I finally realized Mike was lying about a lot of things," Jimmy said.

Cheryl now joined Jimmy in the visitation room.

He could see the confusion in her eyes. "Cheryl, something's wrong. Mike lied to us. I'm telling them about the bodies."

"Bodies?" Cheryl asked, her denial wearing thin. "That's not so. It just isn't!" Even if there were bodies at the farm, she knew it was Yahweh's will and Yahweh would take care of it.

"Cheryl, snap out of it!" Jimmy said. "There are two dead bodies at the farm—Luke and James. Ryan lied. It's over."

"No!" Cheryl said, flustered, her resolve crumbling.

"It's over, Cheryl. It's all over," Jimmy said softly.

Bodies, Cheryl thought. Dead bodies. Yahweh wouldn't let this happen. If there were bodies, Yahweh would let it go undetected. Dead bodies. Ryan killed them! Oh my God! She began to cry hysterically.

David and Jimmy agreed to return to the farm with the officers and show them where the bodies were buried. Clad in their jail-issued orange coveralls, Jimmy and David spent the afternoon leading investigators around the property. One patrol officer videotaped the walk-through.

Jimmy and David pinpointed the grave sites as best they could, then led the pack of officers over to the hog confinement shed and described in detail how James Thimm had been tortured by the group of men. David choked back tears at one point as they recounted the events of the previous spring. Jimmy became weak-kneed and had to sit down.

In the background, the sounds of the backhoe could be heard as it dug through the weed cover in the field below. Now investigators searched for two bodies. Becker had obtained a second warrant to recover the remains of James Thimm. Once they found his body, Ryan would face a second murder charge, and murder charges would also be filed against Tim Haverkamp and Dennis Ryan.

Soon it was dark, the search was called off until morning.

About one-thirty the next afternoon, diggers found the first body. It was that of Luke Stice. They lifted the dirt-encased form out of the grave, zipped it into a body bag, and placed it in a waiting ambulance.

Forty-five minutes later, James's body was recovered. It was placed in a body bag and slid into the ambulance.

"We'll have to get somebody over to notify the families of James Thimm and Luke Stice right away," Becker told McNabb. "I don't want word of this slipping out before they're notified."

McNabb looked down into the grave.

"You know," Becker said, "I can't understand how one man can convince a group of others that he is above mankind . . . how Ryan convinced everyone that he was beyond humanity. I just can't comprehend it," he said, shaking his head.

He and McNabb watched as the ambulance pulled away, heading for Lincoln General Hospital. There, autopsies would be performed.

Now that both bodies were recovered, Becker and McNabb headed to Omaha to serve murder warrants on

Ryan and Tim. First they stopped at the Sarpy County jail, on the edge of Omaha, to serve Tim. He was speechless as he was informed of the first-degree murder charge against him. Becker and McNabb moved on to the Douglas County Corrections Center, in Omaha, where Ryan was being held.

Ryan's expression was one of disgust as he shuffled into the visitation room of the corrections center. Wearing orange coveralls, he slouched in a chair across the table from Becker and McNabb.

Ryan acted like their visit was an imposition, Becker thought. Becker made the encounter a brief one. "Mike, I have warrants here for two counts of murder in the first degree," Becker said and began reading Ryan his Miranda rights.

Ryan interrupted him. "I'll talk to my attorney," he said coldly, looking right through Becker.

For Terry Becker the saga was nearing an end. He had one more arrest to make the next day. Exhausted, he flew to Norton, in western Kansas, where he interviewed Dennis Ryan and served him with a murder warrant.

Dennis sobbed as he was led to a cell in the Norton County jail.

"Son, we have to keep you. You're under arrest for murder," the sheriff told him.

Ruth began crying hysterically. She had willingly brought Dennis to the sheriff's office for questioning, but she had no idea he would be arrested. Ruth was shocked by the charges against her son. Mike had always promised he'd make sure Dennis didn't get messed up in any of the trouble at the farm. It was two weeks before Dennis's sixteenth birthday. "Dennis is just a boy," she pleaded. "He's a good kid. He didn't know any better. He was just doing what his dad told him."

Late that afternoon, back at the north house, Becker and his fellow investigators sorted through evidence. Virtually everything, Becker noticed, was intact—just the way Ryan had left it when he had been lured away. It was as if the lifestyle, the madness, had been frozen in time.

From the premises, investigators had confiscated a wealth of evidence—ninety-nine exhibits—which included: guns, gun parts, shells, shell casings, cannon fuses, blasting caps, bullet slugs embedded in sections of wall, sections of blood-stained tiles and carpets, over one hundred cassette tapes, marijuana paraphernalia, and survivalist literature— all of which were being collected as evidence for the upcoming murder trial. Investigators had pored over the premises for hours, carefully collecting and cataloging each exhibit.

By late evening, Becker was ready to call it a day. He closed his briefcase and arranged to meet investigators there early the next morning to wrap up things.

As he walked toward his car, he couldn't help noticing the sign posted on the gate to the farm. He stood motionless for a moment and studied it. POSITIVELY NO TRESPASSING— VIOLATORS WILL BE PROSECUTED—the same words he'd read a year ago. He shook his head and walked on through the gate.

EPILOGUE

Mike **Ryan's** murder trial for the death of James Thimm came to close on April 10, 1986, in Omaha. The hearing had been moved out of Richardson County after defense attorneys argued that pretrial publicity would make it impossible to seat an impartial jury. After six weeks of testimony and two days of jury deliberations, the jury found Ryan guilty of first degree murder. Ryan showed no emotion as the verdict was read.

Ryan alone was charged with the death of Luke Stice and he pleaded no contest to second degree murder, though he denied killing the child. Ryan always insisted that man's laws were of Satan and that he would answer only to his god Yahweh for his actions. Ryan claimed the deaths of James Thimm and Luke Stice were the will of Yahweh.

Richardson County Judge Robert Finn later sentenced Ryan to death in Nebraska's electric chair. Finn called the murders "the most heinous crimes in the state since the Starkweather mass murders of 1957." Ryan's has since appealed his death sentence.

Since 1986, Ryan has remained on Nebraska's death row. He spends his days in a single cell, measuring nine feet by twelve. The cell has one window—reinforced glass with horizontal bars. Ryan is permitted to have a radio, television, and reading materials. As a death row inmate he can have visitors only from 8:00A.M. to10:30A.M. on Sundays and Wednesdays. He's allowed two hours outdoors in the prison yard daily; he can sign up to make phone calls which are limited to fifteen minutes.

Dennis Ryan, tried as an adult along with his father, was found guilty of second-degree murder in the death of James Thimm. Dennis was sentenced to life in prison. During his testimony, Dennis had calmly described the slaying of James Thimm, insisting that it was Yahweh's wish. However, when the guilty verdict was read, Dennis sobbed into his hands and said, "I can't believe it. I can't believe it."

Dennis later denounced his father's teachings, explaining that his father had influenced him throughout the trial. "My dad would tell me things like 'Angels are going to knock down the doors of the Richardson County jail and we'll walk out of here.' I really believed it. It took be a while to break away from his beliefs because I feared him so. I worried that if he was right, I could burn in hell."

Dennis Ryan served his sentence in the Lincoln Correctional Center, Lincoln, Nebraska. During his time there, he completed his high school education and took college course in business administration; he also completed course work to be a paralegal.

During a 1993 interview for Nebraska public television, Dennis said, "I have a lot of shame, guilt, and sorrow over what happened. Looking back, it's hard to believe I was ever involved in something like that. I feel like a fool to have ever believed murder could be right. I don't expect forgiveness, because I can't really forgive myself, but I hope those I hurt can at least understand why I did what I did."

Despite his life sentence, Dennis Ryan became a free man eleven years after being sent to prison. His case was one of several dozen second-degree murder convictions the Nebraska Supreme Court reversed, saying that jury had not been given proper instructions. The case would have to be reheard. In order to avoid another trial, Dennis Ryan pleaded guilty to manslaughter. According to Nebraska law, he had already served enough years for a manslaughter conviction. Judge Robert Finn amended his sentenced. Dennis Ryan, then twenty-seven, walked out of prison on April 15, 1997. He moved to Kansas where he worked in a construction job before joining a telemarketing firm.

David Andreas and **James Haverkamp** were convicted of second-degree assault in the death of James Thimm. They were also convicted of carrying concealed weapons and possession of stolen property. Each was sentenced to twenty-six years in prison.

However, both served only half that time for doing "good time," having no infractions while incarcerated. While in prison, Andreas earned an associate degree in business and certificates in machine tool technology, air conditioning and auto body repair. Andreas was released from prison on November 22, 1998, after thirteen and a half years of incarceration. "It took a while to sink in that I was free. It was a culture shock in the beginning." How does Andreas look back on his experience at the Rulo farm? "I have a lot or regret. It was a real low point. I feel pretty stupid to think I got pulled into something like that. Since then, I've studied mind control techniques, and it helps me understand how things can happen when you allow yourself to be controlled by someone." Andreas currently works in the logging business in Illinois, where he moved immediately after his release.

Like Andreas, James Haverkamp was released from prison on November 22, 1998. He returned to Kansas to work with his family's business. During his incarceration, he received an associate's degree in business and a certificate for completion of a carpentry program.

Tim Haverkamp, initially charged with first-degree murder, pleaded guilty to second-degree murder in the death of James Thimm. He was sentenced to life in prison and sent to the Lincoln Correctional Center in Lincoln, Nebraska.

"I look back with a lot of regret," Haverkamp said. "At the time, I didn't have a lot of positive things going for me, and Mike Ryan claimed to have all the answers to my problems. In reality, he had none. I am very sorry for what happened. I had never been in trouble before Rulo and I've not been in trouble since.

While at the Lincoln correctional center, Haverkamp completed an associate degree in machine tool technology and later enrolled in college classes. He has participated in several life skills programs, including those on work attitudes and behavior, personal relationships and pre-release. He has been a member of the Christian Fellowship organization and the Seratoma Club of which he was president for two years. "During my time in prison I have strived to better myself and have received no misconduct reports. I have no intention of breaking any laws or ever being in trouble again."

Haverkamp was eligible for parole September 13, 1992. Since then he has had annual reviews by the parole board. During each review, the board discusses his case, assesses his record, and determines if a parole hearing should be scheduled. In May 1999, Haverkamp was transferred to the Hastings Correctional Center, a minimum security facility, in Hastings Nebraska.

Rick Stice received a six-month jail sentence, eighteen months house arrest, and five years probation on theft charges for stealing cattle. After completing his sentence, he moved to Missouri where he worked on a dairy farm. His children went into the custody of Nebraska Social Services. Since then, he has continued to work in the farming and trucking business.

Soon after the arrest of her son, **Ruth Ryan** realized that she, too, had been Mike's victim. "A lot of lives were ruined at that farm," she later said. "I knew Mike was capable of hurting an adult, but I never dreamed he would hurt a child." Ruth divorced Mike and later remarried. She and her husband live in a small, Midwestern town where Ruth went to work as a nurse's aide.

When her son Dennis was released from the Nebraska Correctional Center, Ruth was there. As reporters flocked around the van in which she waited, one reporter asked what they would do that evening on her son's first evening of freedom. Ruth replied, " Whatever he wants. If he wants to go out to dinner, that's what we'll do. If he wants to go to a movie, we'll go to a movie. I'm just glad to have my son back."

Lisa Haverkamp remained in the Midwest. She completed requirements for high school and then attended a community college in western Kansas. She later took a job in a bank, was married, and had another child.

Norbert and **Maxine Haverkamp** continue to make their home in the Midwest. During the investigation, Norbert told attorneys that Mike Ryan extorted nearly one-hundred thousand dollars from him over a two-year period. Fearing that Ryan would harm his family, Norbert had cashed in insurance policies to meet Ryan's financial demands.

Cheryl Gibson went through formal deprogramming and was reunited with her husband Lester about a month after she left the Rulo farm. Charges against her in Kansas for interfering with child custody were dropped. Several years later, in April 1999, Cheryl and Lester Gibson divorced. Both still live in the Midwest.

James Thimm's parents, **Carl** and **Hilda Schmidt**, were informed of their son's death on Sunday, August 18, 1985. Memorial services for James were held the following week. Carl, Hilda and Karen Schmidt, James' sister, attended everyday of the seven-week murder trial of Mike Ryan. After the guilty verdicts were handed down, the Schmidts issued a statement to reporters, saying, "We have been here for James. He is our beloved son and brother. This is the least we can do for him." Karen also told reporters, "We feel justice has been served well. However, it will never undo what they have done to our James. But we know he is fine now. He is whole again."

When Dennis Ryan was set free in 1997, the Schmidts told a reporter for the *Omaha World Herald* they were surprised by the judge's decision carried no conditions. "We were hoping that Ryan would get more counseling and some teaching," Hilda said. "He has never been in a normal society. He's had some counseling and group therapy. We hope that will help him to adjust to society and be a good citizen."

In January of 1998, Carl Schmidt died following a long

illness. The Schmidts had celebrated their 50th wedding anniversary in September of 1997.

Terry Becker left the Nebraska State Patrol in 1992 to become an investigator for a private law firm of two hundred fifty attorneys in Minneapolis. He is one of four investigators who investigate a variety of cases, ranging from personal injury to product liability. How does he look back on the Ryan case? "The thing that surprised me the most was how Ryan was able to manipulate people. He wasn't educated, but yet he could control everyone at the farm. In addition to that, I never could understand why he would mistreat a small child in order to get what he wanted. That was really sad."

Cory McNabb stepped down from his job as Richardson County sheriff in 1987. Today he lives in Missouri. Like other law enforcement officers, he most remembers the immense power Ryan had over his followers. "You'd think someone with that kind of control over other people would be rather sophisticated, but Ryan wasn't. Not at all. It's hard to believe he had the men involved in such evil acts especially when they had been good folks prior to meeting in Ryan. In fact, the night I arrested Haverkamp and Andreas, their plan was to kill me, but when it came right down to it, they couldn't do it. They just didn't have it their hearts."

John Evans retired from the FBI in 1989. He moved to Tennessee, where he began teaching law enforcement classes at Walters State Community College. He is now Dean of Public Safety at the college. Looking back, Evans considers the Rulo case one of the major cases in his FBI career. "The FBI first got involved in the case because the Rulo cult members were going into Kansas and stealing farm implements. Then, as we gained informants we found out about the murders. And once we raided the farm, we learned they had a lot of illegal weapons. The case developed quickly once we started investigating.

Evans recalls Mike Ryan's power dissipating quickly once the arrests were made. "Ryan had an overpowering personality and invoked fear in the followers, but he really had a 'house of cards.' When he started turning violent his followers turned against him. That's why the informants came forward. Once Ryan was in custody, the others realized he was not what he had pretended to be."

What strikes Evans most about the case as he looks back? "The murder of the child. It was just cold-blooded murder. I'm disappointed that any of the men sentenced to prison were ever released."

Richardson County Judge **Robert Finn** retired from the bench in October 1999 and moved to Arizona. "As I look back on the case, the thing that bothered me the most was sentencing Dennis Ryan to life in prison. He was sort of an innocent thirteen-year-old when his father started programming him, but I felt I had to sentence him since he was still showing no change in his beliefs during the trial. We have to protect society. I was glad I later had the opportunity to release him. He had been rehabilitated during his time in prison."

In 1984, just as the Rulo case was unfolding, the Reverend **James Wickstrom** was serving fifteen months in the Shawano County jail in Wisconsin on a conviction for impersonating a public official. Later, after Mike Ryan's sentencing, Wickstrom told the *Hutchinson News*, in Hutchinson, Kansas, that the killing of Luke Stice was a shocking violation of Yahweh's teachings. "What could this little boy have done to this man? When I heard that I cried. I knew it right from the instant that whoever had committed it was not doing the work of Yahweh. The teachings of Yahweh are that we are a race and are to be brothers to one another. You don't go out and kill your brothers. You kill the enemies of Yahweh. That is dictated."

Three years after the Rulo arrests, in October 1988, Wickstrom was prosecuted for plotting to distribute one hundred thousand dollars in counterfeit bills to white supremacists at the 1988 Aryan Nations World Congress in Idaho. Wickstrom was convicted on federal charges of conspiracy and counterfeiting; in 1990, he began serving a thirty-eight month prison sentence at the Federal Correctional Institution, Texarkana, Texas. He was released February 5, 1993.

Today, Wickstrom lives in Michigan. He continues to espouse his beliefs on a Posse Comitatus web site. However, it's believed that the Posse Comitatus' membership has dwindled significantly from what it was in the early 80s. Negative publicity on high-profile cases likely contributed to the movement's decline. Still, the number of hate groups in the U.S. is on the increase. According to the Southern Poverty Law Center, a watch dog/human rights organization, in Montgomery, Alabama, approximately one hundred thousand individuals belonged to some five hundred thirty-seven hate groups and chapters in the United States in 1998.

Little is left of the Rulo farm as it stood in 1984. The north house burned down in March of 1985, seven months after Ryan's arrest. Officials suspected arson. The other buildings were later torn down. The only building still standing is the hog confinement shed. In 1986, the farmland was taken out of crop production for conservation reasons; it was put in the USDA's conservation reserve program. According to conservation officials, continued farming of the highly erodible land, would have created silt problems and pollution, caused by rain washing away agricultural chemicals. For a decade, the land lay barren. In September of 1986, the eighty-acre farm was purchased and in recent years portions of the land has been planted in tall seed grass.

ABOUT THE AUTHOR

In addition to writing *Evil Harvest*, Rod Colvin is also the author of numerous magazine articles and two other nonfiction books—*First Heroes—The POWS Left Behind in Vietnam* (Irvington 1987) and *Prescription Drug Abuse—The Hidden Epidemic* (Addicus Books 1995). From 1979 to 1989, Colvin was a broadcast journalist in Omaha, Nebraska, where he covered the murder trial of two of the defendants in the Rulo cult case. He makes his home in the Midwest.

Addicus Books
True Crime
www.AddicusBooks.com

Evil Harvest—The True Story of Cult Murder in the American Heartland
Rod Colvin
1-886039-42-9 / $15.95

Battle at Alcatraz—A Desperate Attempt to Escape the Rock
Ernest Lageson
1-886039-37-2 / $16.95

Of Marriage and Murder: A Double Conspiracy (Spring 2000)
Lynn Willis
1-886039-41-0 / $16.95

Eye of the Beast—The True Story of Serial Killer James Wood
Terry Adams, Mary Brooks—Mueller, Scott Shaw
1-886039-32-1 / $16.95

Counterpoint—A Murder in Massachusetts Bay
Margaret Press and Joan Pinkham
1-886039-24-0 / $16.95

Suddenly Gone—The True Story of Serial Killer Richard Grissom
Dan Mitrione
1-886039-23-2 / $15.95
(Available only in mass market paperback)

Other Titles from
Addicus Books
www.AddicusBooks.com

The Family Compatibility Test $9.95
Susan Adams / 1-886039-27-5

First Impressions—Tips to Enhance Your Image $14.95
Joni Craighead / 1-886039-26-7

The Healing Touch—Keeping the Doctor/Patient $9.95
Relationship Alive Under Managed Care
David Cram, MD / 1-886039-31-3

Hello, Methuselah! Living to 100 and Beyond $14.95
George Webster, PhD / 1-886039-25-9

Overcoming Postpartum Depression and Anxiety $12.95
Linda Sebastian, RN / 1-886930-34-8

Prescription Drug Abuse—The Hidden Epidemic $14.95
Rod Colvin / 1-886039-22-4

Simple Changes: The Boomer's Guide to a $9.95
Healthier, Happier Life
L. Joe Porter, MD / 1-886039-35-6

Straight Talk About Breast Cancer $12.95
Suzanne Braddock, MD / 1-886039-21-6

The Stroke Recovery Book $14.95
Kip Burkman, MD / 1-886039-30-5

The Surgery Handbook $12.95
A Guide to Understanding Your Operation (Nov '99)
Paul Ruggieri, MD / 1-886039-38-0

Understanding Parkinson's Disease $14.95
A Self-Help Guide
David Cram, MD / 1-886039-40-2

Please send:

_____ copies of _____
(Title of book)

at $ _____ each　　　TOTAL $ _____
(Nebr. residents add 5% sales tax)

Shipping/Handling
$3.20 for first book.
$1.10 for each additional book.　　$ _____

TOTAL ENCLOSED　　　　　　$ _____

Name _____

Address _____

City _____ State _____ Zip _____

　　• Visa　　• Mastercard　　• Am. Express

Credit card number _____

Expiration Date _____

Order by credit card, personal check, or money order.

Send to:

Addicus Books
Mail Order Dept.
P.O. Box 45327
Omaha, NE 68145

Or, order TOLL FREE: 800-352-2873

or online at
www.AddicusBooks.com